PHL

D0421472

MEMOIRS OF GIAMBATTISTA SCALA
Consul of His Italian Majesty in Lagos in Guinea

Sampierdarena 1862

THE

**PAUL HAMLYN
LIBRARY**

DONATED BY

WITHDRAWN

THE PAUL HAMLYN

FOUNDATION

TO THE

BRITISH MUSEUM

opened December 2000

Giambattista Scala (from Brignardello)

FONTES HISTORIAE AFRICANAE, NEW SERIES
SOURCES OF AFRICAN HISTORY
2

MEMOIRS OF GIAMBATTISTA SCALA

Consul of his Italian Majesty
in Lagos in Guinea
(1862)

translated from the Italian by
BRENDA PACKMAN

edited by
ROBERT SMITH

Published for THE BRITISH ACADEMY
by OXFORD UNIVERSITY PRESS

Oxford University Press, Great Clarendon Street, Oxford OX2 6DP

Oxford New York
Athens Auckland Bangkok Bogota Bombay
Buenos Aires Calcutta Cape Town Dar es Salaam
Delhi Florence Hong Kong Istanbul Karachi
Kuala Lumpur Madras Madrid Melbourne
Mexico City Nairobi Paris Singapore
Taipei Tokyo Toronto Warsaw

and associated companies in
Berlin Ibadan

Published in the United States by
Oxford University Press Inc., New York

© *The British Academy, 2000*

All rights reserved. No part of this publication may be reproduced,
stored in a retrieval system, or transmitted, in any form or by any means,
without the prior permission in writing of the British Academy

British Library Cataloguing in Publication Data
Data available

ISBN 0–19–726204–X

Typeset by the Alden Group, Oxford
Printed in Great Britain
on acid-free paper by
The Cromwell Press Limited

THE
BRITISH
MUSEUM
THE PAUL HAMLYN LIBRARY
WITHDRAWN

966.901   SCA

This English edition is

DEDICATED TO THE MEMORY OF

JAMES PACKMAN (1905–1985)

who, discovering a copy of the original *Memorie*,
recommended that it should be translated.

Contents

List of Illustrations

Preface

This edition of Giambattista Scala's *Memoirs* of his years in Lagos and Abeokuta in the mid-nineteenth century is owed chiefly to James Packman who, when Deputy Librarian of the University of Ibadan, succeeded some thirty years ago in obtaining a copy of the *Memorie*, published in Sampierdarena in 1862, and to his wife Brenda Packman who made the English translation which is the basis of the one presented here. Thus it is to Brenda Packman and to her late husband that acknowledgement must first be made for their part in making this work available to English-speakers.

My thanks go next to Professor Robin Law of the University of Stirling who suggested that an edited translation of Scala's book would be of interest and value to Africanists and others and that, since I had made use of the *Memorie* when studying the 'consular period' in Lagos which preceded the annexation of the town as a British colony, I should prepare such an edition. Some ten years passed before I set about this task, and my further thanks are now owed to Robin Law for his comments on my preliminary editing and for useful suggestions. The delay was partly due to my lack of an Italian text until at the end of 1983 Professor Jacob Ajayi, my mentor and former colleague, procured for me a photocopy of a microfilm of Scala's book from the library of the University of Ibadan. I am greatly indebted to him. Similarly I thank Professor Sandra Barnes of the University of Pennsylvania for two important contributions: first, for making over to me (with Mrs Packman's permission) what was probably the last surviving typescript original of Mrs Packman's translation, and secondly, for sending to me photocopies which she had taken some years earlier of documents in the archives of Rome and Turin pertaining to Scala's consulship and life in Africa. I have also to thank Professor J. D. Y. Peel of the School of Oriental and African Studies, University of London, for his helpful comments on the typescript of this book and for making available to me references to Scala in the papers of the Church Missionary Society.

When compiling editorial material to accompany the text of the *Memorie* I was fortunately able to use the British Library, the London Library, and the library of the School of Oriental and African Studies in the University of London. To the librarians of these institutions I express my thanks for their services. Then I am especially grateful to Dr Elizabeth Dunstan of the International African Institute in London for generous help and encouragement and enabling me in various ways to profit from association with the Institute. I thank also Miss Janet M. Crabtree and Mr Richard Mills for converting into disc a much worked-over typescript. Finally, I thank the British Academy for a contribution to the cost of preparing this edition.

Mrs Packman took as her principle in translating Scala's text 'to let the author speak for himself in his own way', that is in his relatively simple and straightforward language, interspersed with occasional biblical, classical and literary references, flourishes which may be owed to Scala's sub-editor Federico Campanella. For my part I have concentrated on providing, first, an Introduction, and, secondly, notes to the text which are intended to explain and expand the background to Scala's account, giving information about the Yoruba people of West Africa, their history and politics, and the individuals who figure in his pages. In the case of place and personal names, I have usually retained Scala's spelling for their first mention in the book, with the present spelling (if known) placed in square brackets; in subsequent references I have usually substituted the more familiar, modern form. Occasional mistakes in Scala's text, such as those in dates where they can be checked, have been amended in square brackets after the original. I have treated the few Yoruba phrases cited in the text similarly. I have split up the longer paragraphs and have abbreviated Scala's title for the *Memorie* which was both over-long and slightly misleading; I have also amended some of the chapter headings. For details of books, articles, theses and other written sources cited in the notes, the reader should refer to the bibliography. Trade statistics, distances, latitudes and longitudes remain as in the original. A modern navigator is advised not to rely on Scala's sailing directions.

Editor's Introduction

The 'reduction' of Lagos by British forces in a combined naval and military operation at Christmas 1851, followed by the imposition of a treaty outlawing the slave trade, exposed this island kingdom of southern Yorubaland to the full influence of two groups of Europeans whose activities, sometimes antagonistic to each other but more often complementary, were already affecting other parts of the West African coast: the Christian missionaries and the palm oil traders. During the early 1840s the former, as agents of the Church Missionary Society (CMS) and of the Wesleyans, began their penetration of the interior. Bypassing the notorious slave port of Lagos they had settled first at Badagry. Then, two months after the bombardment of Lagos and the ensuing replacement of its king, Oba Kosoko, by his predecessor, Oba Akitoye (whom he had overthrown six years before), the Rev Charles Gollmer, a German-born priest of the CMS, paid a reconnaissance visit to the town. He found that he had been forestalled there by an advance guard of merchants, some of whom had already been prospecting the market in palm oil at Lagos before the reduction and who had concluded a commercial agreement with the reinstated Oba.

The export trade in slaves at Lagos seems to have begun in the 1760s, probably during the reign there of Oba Akinsemoyin, and to have been pioneered by the Portuguese, while British and French traders had become involved at an early stage. By the 1800s Lagos was the principal slave port on this part of the coast with, it has been estimated, some 7,000 to 10,000 slaves being sold there annually for export.[1] Meanwhile, the ideal of substituting 'legitimate' trade for the slave trade had originated with the Abolitionists of the late eighteenth and early nineteenth centuries. So far as West African imports were concerned, this trade proved to consist largely of palm products, the oil palm growing in providential profusion in the area. The encouragement and protection of legitimate trade were major objectives in the establishment of British Consulates in the Bights, the first being set up in the area of the Niger estuary and situated originally on the island of Fernando Po, and a few years later a second one at Lagos. The cultivation

---

[1] R. Smith, *Lagos Consulate*, 1978, 9–10; R. Law, 'Trade and Politics behind the Slave Coast', *JAH*, 1983, 347–48. See also R. Law (ed), *From Slave Trade to 'Legitimate' Commerce*, 1995, *passim*.

of cotton in West Africa was also coming to the attention of the European humanitarians in their quest to combat the slave trade through 'the Bible and the Plough'. Considerable efforts were made to stimulate local production but the trade in and export of cotton (together with some less important items) remained subordinate to those in oil.[2]

The 'palm oil ruffians', as these merchants have been called, somewhat unfairly, were in some ways the counterparts of the slavers whom they were replacing, a number of whom had accompanied Oba Kosoko to his exile at Epe down the eastern lagoon. In some cases, indeed, including possibly the author of these *Memoirs*, they were the same men in a different guise. Moreover, as the example of Domingo Martinez at Whydah and Porto Novo showed, the trade in oil could be combined with that in slaves as well as that in other merchandise. The structure of the oil trade was similar, at least in its early years, to that of its predecessor, being based on the extension of credit by European and American merchants trading from their ships with a host of African middlemen along the coast. On the other hand, the missionaries and humanitarians were not deceiving themselves when they looked to the oil trade as the legitimate activity which could replace the cruel and now outlawed export of human beings. The British, as two historians write, 'had not abolished the slave trade to make life easier for the slavers of other nations',[3] and the maintenance of their anti-slaving patrols at sea served both to reduce the continued smuggling of slaves across the Atlantic and to protect the new trade in palm oil for which the demand in industrialized Europe was growing fast. But despite the importance of Liverpool firms in the trade, there was no British monopoly. From the first a large, even predominant, share was taken by the Hanseatic merchants, while one of the first — he claimed, indeed, to have been the very first — of the legitimate traders to reach Lagos after the reduction with a cargo of merchandise for exchange against local products was the Sardinian national Giambattista Scala.[4]

Giambattista Scala was to spend a little over seven years in Yorubaland,[5] mainly in Lagos though passing his last sixteen months as a trader in

[2] K. O. Dike, *Trade and Politics in the Niger Delta*, 1956; S. O. Biobaku, *The Egba and their Neighbours*, 1957 (especially Chapter V, 'A "Buxton" State and Cotton'); M. Lynn, 'Consul and Kings', *JICH*, 1982.
[3] R. Robinson and J. Gallagher, *Africa and the Victorians*, 1961, 34.
[4] Scala seems to have been the first of the European merchants to reside in Lagos, as opposed to visitors trading or prospecting the role there.
[5] The people of South-Western Nigeria did not describe themselves, their language and their country as 'Yoruba' until the nineteenth century. The term 'Yoruba' was not, however, a neologism since it occurs in Moslem writing as early as the seventeenth century, having probably originated as a Hausa word for the kingdom of Oyo, the dominant state of Yorubaland. It

Abeokuta, the capital of the Egba people; he returned to Italy in 1859. He attained some importance in the developing commercial life of Lagos and its hinterland, and was evidently a man of energy and enterprise. From November 1855 he combined his business with the office of Consul (sometimes referring to himself as Consul-General) for Sardinia, the country to which as a Ligurian he belonged,[6] and he was presented in that capacity to Oba Dosunmu and his chiefs by Benjamin Campbell, the British Consul, in February 1856.[7] In association with Campbell, Scala also played a part in the political life of Lagos during the period of the British Consulate there, a decade in which the island came to be recognized in London (somewhat reluctantly), and accepted more widely, as a quasi-protectorate of Great Britain, and which was closed by its annexation as a British colony in 1861. The *Memoirs* which he published ten years after his return to Italy are a valuable, although not always reliable, source for the history of this period.

Little attention has been paid to Scala by historians of either Italy or Nigeria, although his *Memorie* were cited in the bibliography attached to Daryll Forde's volume on the Yoruba (1951) in the *Ethnographic Survey of Africa*.[8] He was, however, rescued from relative obscurity in the 1960s by James Packman, Deputy Librarian of the University of Ibadan (and later Librarian of the University of Ife) and his wife, Mrs Brenda Packman, who were encouraged in their researches by the late Professor Umberto Comi, formerly Cultural Attaché of the Italian Embassy in Lagos. In 1963 when on leave in Rome Mr and Mrs Packman located a number of letters from Scala, in his consular capacity, in the archives of the Ministry of Foreign Affairs, some of these being misfiled under 'Calcutta'. Mr Packman had already begun a search for *Memoirs* by Scala but for long could find no

came to be used in the wider sense in the 1840s by the liberated slaves in Sierra Leone and was then popularized by the Christian missionaries on the West African coast. Thus it now embraced an area comprising not only Oyo but also those smaller states whose peoples spoke differing dialects of what was recognizably a distinct language and whose rulers were called *Oba* (king). The word 'Yoruba' was known to and occasionally used by Scala in the forms 'Orobò', 'Orobù' and 'Yarriba' (pp. 26, 53, 55), although his meaning is not altogether clear since, for example, he seems to exclude Ijebu. Today six of the thirty-six constituent states of Nigeria are mainly populated by Yoruba and contain the once independent kingdoms of pre-colonial times. See Law, 'Ethnicity and the Slave Trade', *HA*, 1997; this also examines other names, mostly in disuse, applied to the Yoruba.

[6] In these years the unification of the Italian peninsula — the Risorgimento — was gathering pace. Liguria, as a part of the duchy of Genoa, had been incorporated into the kingdom of Sardinia under the House of Savoy in the Vienna settlement of 1815. In 1860, after the conquest of Sicily, the kingdom of Italy was formed under the Savoy rule, the capital moving from Turin to Florence in 1864 and to Rome in 1870–71.

[7] PRO, FO 84/1002, Campbell to Clarendon, 8 February 1856. The limits of the Sardinian consulate, as shown to Consul Campbell by Scala, were from Cape Formosa (in the east) to Cape Three Points (in the west, on the Gold Coast). Scala's appointment was apparently unsalaried.

[8] D. Forde, *The Yoruba-Speaking Peoples of South-Western Nigeria*, 1951.

trace of this in either Italy or England: no copies of the *Memorie* could be found in the libraries of Rome, Florence or Leghorn nor is there a copy in the British Library, the Bodleian or the London Library. Eventually, however, he came upon a copy in a bookseller's stock in London. This, published at Sampierdarena (near Genoa) in 1862, was presented by Mr and Mrs Packman to the library of the University of Ibadan. A photographic copy was later obtained for the library of the University of Lagos. Subsequently Mr Packman had the further good fortune to find from the same bookseller a useful, although uncritical, short study of Scala's life and work which had been presented as a paper to the First Italian Geographical Congress in 1892 by Professor G. B. Brignardello and printed as a pamphlet that same year in Florence. Mrs Packman meanwhile prepared the English translation of the *Memoirs* which follows this Introduction. There was not at that time sufficient interest either in the short but important period covered by the British Consulate at Lagos or in Scala himself to enable a publisher to be found for the translation, nor apparently has there been a reprint of the *Memorie* in the original Italian. In 1972, however, I gave a talk on Scala and his career in Nigeria to the Italian Institute in Lagos which was later published in the *Journal of the Historical Society of Nigeria*, and I also made use of the *Memorie* as a source for my book on *The Lagos Consulate, 1851–1861*, published in 1978. Subsequently, Professor Sandra Barnes of the University of Pennsylvania, while researching into the history of Lagos, collected copies of some of Scala's correspondence and related documents which she found in the archives of Turin and Rome. Meanwhile it appears that both the original edition of the *Memorie* at Ibadan and the photocopy at Lagos had disappeared from the respective libraries of the universities there. Finally, however, I was able to obtain from the University of Ibadan a photographic copy, taken from a microfilm, of the *Memorie* and also, as a gift from Mrs Packman, her late husband's copy of the short account of Scala by Brignardello.[9]

It is mainly from Brignardello's researches that the outline of Scala's life is known. He was born on 20 August 1817 at Chiavari, near Rapallo on the Ligurian coast, the youngest son of a seafaring family and a subject of the Sardinian kingdom as constituted by the Congress of Vienna in 1815. Both his father and one of his brothers were captains of merchant ships, while

---

[9] The microfilm at Ibadan, and therefore the editor's copy in London, has two missing pages, 180 and 181, while two pages, 236 and 237, are duplicated. One copy only of the transcript of Mrs Packman's translation of the *Memorie* survived intact except for two missing pages, 198 and 199 in the final chapter on Trade; these have been added here in the editor's translation. Finally, a copy of the *Memorie* has recently been located (through the good offices of Professor Bernardo Bernardi) in the library of the State University of Milan who have kindly supplied a photocopy to the International African Institute in London. *Note*: The page references in this note are from the Italian edition of the *Memorie*.

another brother became a trader in Australia. He had only a few years of formal education since at the age of 12 he ran away from home to join his father's ship at Genoa. At 18 he did a short spell of military service for the state, and shortly after this he obtained his Master's Certificate in seamanship at Genoa. He then engaged in trading voyages between Genoa and Brazil, visiting West Africa twice in or about 1846. It was during this period that he may have taken part in slaving activities. This was alleged, indirectly, by Consul Campbell who, after his first meeting with him (in Freetown) in 1853, told the British Foreign Secretary that he recognised Scala as 'one of those clever shrewd Genoese captains sailing under the Sardinian flag' who had often baffled the anti-slaving patrols of the Royal Navy.[10] Whether this was so or not, Scala professed to be so revolted by the slave trade which he had witnessed at Bahia that he decided to engage on his own account in the legitimate commerce of the African coast. To this end he had hired the Sardinian brig *Felicità*, under Captain Reggio, loaded her with tobacco, rum, foodstuffs, and various kinds of manufactured goods, and on 18 November 1851 set sail for Africa. After calling at Accra he arrived on 10 February 1852 at Lagos, 'the real centre of the slave trade' (as he calls it in his second chapter). He was thirty four years of age.

The story of Scala's subsequent career in Lagos and Abeokuta is told in his *Memoirs*, which can be supplemented (and corrected) by the British consular and missionary records. He gives little information in these *Memoirs* about the conduct or prosperity of his business (and no figures or other breakdown of his trade between, for example, that in palm products and cotton), but it seems to have afforded him a reasonable living while he took his part in the local commercial community which was growing rapidly as the legitimate trade extended. With the missionaries in Lagos and Abeokuta, dominated by the representatives of the powerful Anglican Church Missionary Society (CMS), Scala's relations were somewhat distant. Scala, as a 'Romanist', was initially treated rather suspiciously by the Protestants. However, as time went by, Townsend, the leading Anglican, came to accept Scala as a fellow-Christian and European, intelligent, an energetic trader and a 'moral man' — by which he probably meant that unlike other foreign traders Scala had not sought the companionship of a local woman. For his

---

[10] PRO, FO 84/920, Campbell to Clarendon, 29 July 1853. Campbell added that Scala had affirmed to him his intention of confining himself to legitimate trade in Lagos and that he thought Scala to be an enterprising man whom the African Steamship Company could suitably appoint as their agent. From this letter it appears that Scala visited Freetown from Lagos early in 1853 and then travelled back on the same ship as Campbell who was on his way to take up his consular post. Scala does not mention any of this in his *Memoirs*. Campbell's remarks, whatever the truth about Scala's background, are a reminder of the participation of Sardinians in the slave trade.

part Scala seems, as the *Memorie* show, to have found Gollmer, one of several German-born agents of the CMS, particularly obnoxious.[11]

Scala was present in Lagos during Kosoko's violent but unsuccessful attack in 1853 and he took some part in Consul Campbell's negotiations with the ex-Oba in 1854. His commercial standing was sufficient for him to take over for a time in 1856 the farming of the royal customs. The following year he began to contemplate removal to Abeokuta, a town which he terms 'the capital of the kingdom of Orubu [Yoruba], 140 miles to the north of Lagos... as yet unvisited by white men, except for an English missionary' (a somewhat inaccurate statement). His proposal reflects the natural and characteristic desire of many European merchants on the coast to establish closer touch with the producers of palm oil in the interior, a desire naturally resented and resisted by the African middlemen. In September 1857, according to the *Memorie*, Scala left Lagos for a reconnaissance visit to Abeokuta, where he was well received by the Alake (generally recognised as senior among the other Egba Oba) and by other chiefs. Scala thereupon set about building a house and store for himself on land which had been granted to him in the town, with a second store at Aro on the outskirts, and to collect quantities of cotton and palm oil. Early the following year he removed from Lagos to Abeokuta, leaving his countryman Signor Vincenzo Paggi in charge of both his business interests and of the consulate there (although Scala himself continued to hold the consular office).

In June 1859, his health by now undermined by his residence in the baneful Bight of Benin with its numerous fevers, and wearied, perhaps, by the long years of an apparently solitary and isolated life, Scala left Abeokuta and returned, via Lagos and then England, to his country, now on the threshold of becoming the United Kingdom of Italy. Here, for the years left to him, he tried to interest his government in his experiences in West Africa and in the commercial possibilities in the area. He carried on a prolonged correspondence about this with Cavour and, after Cavour's death in 1861, with the new Premier Ricasoli and his Minister of Foreign Affairs, Dabormida, and with their officials. He also wrote his *Memoirs*, in which he had the help of a certain Federico Campanella. We know that the Foreign Ministry in Turin had suggested to Scala in 1857 that he should correspond with them in English if he knew it better than Italian.[12] Presumably, therefore, his literary capacity was not great, and it seems likely that a share in

---

[11] Information from Professor J. D. Y. Peel in a personal communication of 14 August 997, citing CA2/0/85, Townsend to Venn, 28.5.58, 28.9.58, 30.4.59 and 2.6.59. See also the appreciation of Scala by the Rev. Samuel Crowther on p. xxii below; and also Smith, *Lagos Consulate*, pp. 39, 79, 82.

[12] Archivio Storico del Ministero degli Affari Esteri, Rome, Protocolli a Lagos, 1857–1869, 17 February 1857, no. 7. Brignardello, p. 64 writes that Campanella agreed to 'correct' Scala's manuscript of the *Memorie*.

the composition of the *Memorie* was taken by Campanella. Copies of the book were widely distributed by Scala himself while, according to one source, a German translation was also published.[13] In 1863 Scala was rewarded by his Sovereign, King Victor Emmanuel II, with a silver medal for 'introducing Civil Industry into Guinea'. He continued to entertain his ambition to forward Italian interests in Africa, drawing up plans for an Italian colony in Egypt and a 'correctional settlement' on the island of Principe. These came to nothing, as did his attempt to form a naval construction company at Naples. Meanwhile he failed to comply with at least two invitations to return to his post at Lagos while his requests for further consular employment elsewhere were refused; for the next few years his office remained in the charge of the Vice-Consul Paggi. At the end of 1876, when he was engaged in ship-building at Sestri Ponente, Scala suffered a recurrence of the fever which he had contracted in Africa. He returned to his home at Lavagna where, after an illness lasting only a few days, he died on 3 December at the age of 59. He was buried at Chiavari, his birthplace.[14]

Brignardello, who first drew attention to Scala and his career, was content mainly to summarize the *Memorie*, assuming the veracity of the narrative and accepting the writer's own estimate of his role and achievements at Lagos and Abeokuta. To this he added his useful account of Scala's early life and of his last sixteen years in Italy. Scala's *Memorie* must, however, be measured against other sources. His seven and a half years (1853–1859) in the south of Yorubaland were all passed within the short period (1851–1861) of the British Consulate in Lagos, that time of 'informal rule' or quasi protectorate[15] which was to lead within half a century to the creation of Nigeria. The fairly full documentation of the consular decade, contained in the official papers at the Public Record Office in London, as well as in the archives of the missionary societies, especially the CMS, provides material for an independent assessment of Scala's career and the reliability of his account. From these it seems clear that Scala, aided and perhaps encouraged

---

[13] No copy of this translation has come to light, nor any reference to it other than in G. Dainelli, *Gli Esploratori Italiani in Africa*, Turin 1960, Vol. II, p. 324, in a brief account of Scala.

[14] Brignardello, pp. 54–78. In his appended notes Brignardello reproduces a selection of correspondence to Scala from the ministries in Turin and Rome.

[15] It is convenient to refer to the period at Lagos from December 1851 (the British intervention there and the restoration of the Oba Akitoye to his throne) to August 1861 (the formal cession of the island kingdom to the British as a colony) as the 'consular decade', although the consulate itself was not inaugurated until the arrival of Vice-Consul Fraser in November 1852. The decade was dominated by the career of Benjamin Campbell, Consul from 1853 to his death in 1859. 'Informal rule' and 'quasi-protectorate' were both terms used by Robinson and Gallagher, for example on pp. 33–34, while Dike, *passim*, uses 'informal rule' to describe the consular system in the Niger Delta.

by Campanella, his collaborator, romanticized and dramatized his years in West Africa and exaggerated the importance of his commercial and political achievements there. In this his aim was seemingly not merely egoistic. One motive, and perhaps the primary one, was patriotic: to arouse the interest in this part of the African continent of the Sardinian and then the Italian governments and of his compatriots and to encourage the new Italy to share in the overseas expansion in which other European countries were already engaged. But the overall impression which results from a comparison of the *Memoirs* with this material is that Scala's work as a source for the history of the period must be used with caution and it is desirable that the English translation which follows should be accompanied by warnings as well as explanations to the reader. Yet the book serves to corroborate at many points and to embellish the somewhat dry and spare account in the official papers as well as the more subjective accounts of the missionaries.

There are a number of matters in this period about which the *Memorie*, for reasons which can only be guessed at, are silent. There is, first, Consul Campbell's allegation about Scala's slave-trading antecedents. Although Campbell seems to have been an impartial witness, the charge remains unproven. Such charges were, moreover, frequently made against Europeans and Americans on the West Coast at this time: Campbell himself had been accused by the French government, perhaps in retaliation for his expulsion of a French citizen from Lagos, of having engaged in the trade earlier in his career in Sierra Leone. In any case, Scala had affirmed to Campbell his intention of confining himself to legitimate trade, and no suspicion of slaving activities attaches to him in the records during his time either in Lagos or in Abeokuta. Then there is the arrangement which Scala made with Oba Dosunmu in or about 1856 to farm the royal customs, that is, the duties paid to the king on the export from Lagos of palm oil and ivory, as agreed with the local merchants under a trade agreement. This arrangement remained in force for a year or a little longer, but is nowhere mentioned in the *Memorie*. Although it was not a matter with which Scala could be reproached, he may have felt that it was not strictly in accordance with his status either as a consul or as a member of the expatriate mercantile community. As Campbell reported to London, it certainly created antagonism between Scala and the other European merchants, and this in turn may have contributed to his decision to remove to Abeokuta. Another source of income enjoyed by Scala was his position, for which he had been recommended by Campbell, as agent for the African Steamship Company of Liverpool whose mail boats had begun to call regularly at Lagos soon after the reduction of the town.[16] He is silent about this too in the *Memoirs*,

---

[16] PRO, FO 84/920, 29 July 1853, Campbell to Clarendon.

possibly because he did not wish to draw attention to his connexion with a British firm. Still more oddly, he fails to mention his manufacture of, or plan to manufacture, bricks and tiles in Lagos for which, according to Campbell, he made preparations in 1857. This reticence about a pioneering venture which could have been of great benefit in a town where the thatched roofs of the houses were subject to frequent and serious fires, may have been due to the trouble which arose over Scala's having covered his own warehouse with tiles which had probably been imported. Oba Dosunmu objected strongly to this since it was local custom that only royal buildings could be roofed in this novel way, a rule which may have had its origin in the tradition that the Palace in Lagos, the Iga Iduganran, had been provided with tiles donated by Portuguese visitors to the town. Campbell, who showed no sympathy for this custom, strongly supported Scala and rebuked the Oba for his 'frivolous pride' so that eventually the order was rescinded.[17]

Another point about which the reader may speculate is the language in which Scala conversed and did business with the inhabitants of Lagos and Abeokuta and those whom he met on his travels. A few urban Yoruba at this time may have known a little English through contact with traders while more would have known some Portuguese, the common language of the slave trade on this coast and also the language of the returning emigrants from Brazil, the Amaro. Scala, as was known to the authorities in Turin (page xvi above), had a working knowledge of English, probably acquired in his seafaring youth. More revealing, however, are his references (in his fifth chapter) to the 'interpreter' who accompanied him to Abeokuta. This was a native of Abeokuta who had learnt good Portuguese while a slave in Brazil and who was now able to pass on to him in Portuguese, a language which Scala apparently also knew, what was being said in Yoruba. Later Scala may have achieved some knowledge of Yoruba itself (as did the missionaries). Nevertheless his linguistic attainments were doubtless limited and it would have been all too easy for misunderstandings to have arisen.

It is presumably this last point, combined perhaps with a somewhat restricted outlook, which accounts for Scala's comparative ignorance of and lack of interest in the general situation of Yorubaland at this time: a situation, involved, confused and giving rise to endless wars, which must have been among the first concerns of the rulers and most of their subjects.

---

[17] Smith, *Lagos Consulate*, pp. 8, 74, 94, 162n. A somewhat similar case had occurred in December 1670 when Matteo Lopez, the King of Allada's representative on a mission to Paris, objected to a clause in a draft treaty between his country and France which allowed French traders to cover their factories with tiles. This may have been due to reasons other than a concern to protect a royal prerogative in the use of unfamiliar building materials. Professor Law has suggested that it may reflect a distrust of any move towards fortification of these foreign premises by making their construction more permanent. I. A. Akinjogbin, *Dahomey and its Neighbours, 1708–1818*, 1967, pp. 30–31.

Scala's account, at the beginning of his Chapter VI, of the foundation of Abeokuta, only some twenty or thirty years before he came there, is obscure and inaccurate (page 64, with note 1), and in general he seems to have been content, like most contemporary European observers, to explain the wars between the different states and towns as little more than slave-taking expeditions. Although he grasps the menace posed by the Dahomeans to the Egba in and around Abeokuta, he shows no awareness of the almost equally pressing dangers arising from the collapse of the important kingdom and empire of Oyo. In particular, he only once, and then incidentally, mentions Ibadan (page 109), the large town some 45 miles to the north-east of Abeokuta which had been founded shortly before the Egba's own federated capital and in similar circumstances, and which was increasingly assuming the role and powers of the former Oyo. Rivalry between Ibadan and Abeokuta was to lead only one year after Scala's departure from West Africa to the Ijaye War of 1860 in which these two towns were the main protagonists and which led to the evacuation of Ijaye, Abeokuta's ally, in 1862, and ended in 1865 in an uneasy stalemate.[18]

Finally, the reader of these *Memoirs* will be aware that the years which they cover, the 1850s, during which the Atlantic trade in slaves was being substituted by the 'legitimate' trade in palm oil and other products, was for the West Africans a time of revolution and challenge. Historians have examined the resulting 'crisis of adaptation' as it affected the different peoples. Robin Law has illustrated, for example, the far-reaching problems posed for the rulers of Dahomey by the transformation of an economy based on the export of slaves to one dependent on commercial agriculture.[19] Scala, although himself an agent of and participant in a similar transformation, economic and political, among the Southern Yoruba, can hardly have realised its wider implications. Nevertheless, the reader will be able to discover in these *Memoirs* indications of the crisis as it affected the rulers and chiefs, the traders, African and European, and indeed most of the inhabitants of Lagos and among the Egba of Abeokuta.[20]

[18] See J. F. A. Ajayi and Robert Smith, *Yoruba Warfare in the Nineteenth Century*, 1971, *passim*. There is a good deal of information about the Ijaye War and its preliminaries in the reports of the British consul in Lagos and by the Christian missionaries who were now spreading northwards into the Yoruba interior. In his own despatches to his minister, Scala expresses the then customary view that the Yoruba wars had as their sole objective the taking of captives to satisfy the overseas demand for slaves. See, for example, Scala's despatches to Turin of 9 February and September (sic) 1857, and pp. 7–8 below.

[19] R. Law, 'The Politics of Commercial Transition', *JAH*, 1997. See also Law (ed.) *From Slave Trade to 'Legitimate' Commerce*, 1995 for instances of slaves as well as former slaves trading in palm oil on their own account. Scala, p. 43 below, estimates that by his time one-fifth of the (native) inhabitants of Lagos were occupied in the growing export trade of ten European firms.

[20] Chapters III and IV, concerning the activities of Madame Tinubu and the career of ex-Oba Kosoko, and Chapter VII, describing events at Abeokuta, seem the most relevant to this theme.

The collection of papers concerning the Sardinian, later Italian, consulate at Lagos filed in the Foreign Ministry archives at Turin and in Rome adds only a little to the information given by Scala in his *Memorie*. Scala's allusions in his reports to the growing influence of both the British consulate under Campbell and the British trading firms, however, are interesting; he refers on occasions to Campbell as the 'Governor', thus anticipating the colonial régime which was to be established in 1861, and he contrasts the neglect with which he felt that he was treated by his superiors in Italy with the support which he himself received from mercantile interests in Manchester in his efforts to forward the African trade.[21] As to Scala's personal reputation among his fellow Italians, there are useful references in the report made in October 1858 by the captain of the Sardinian brig *Colombo*, sent to Turin from Fernando Po. The author had been asked by the Foreign Ministry in Turin and by the Ministry of Marine to report on trade in Lagos generally and then in particular on the Sardinian traders on the West Coast. The captain writes: 'Speaking of G.B. Scala or rather of his conduct and his standing among the Europeans on the coast of Africa, I have usually heard favourable reports and he is generally respected for his intelligence and his skill in matters of trade'. He continues in a passage which possibly reflects Scala's own estimate of his position and achievements as consul and trader as much as the captain's own observation: 'Undoubtedly Sig. Scala has great influence in the Government at Lagos and a large voice in matters of internal government, and his opinion and advice are of the greatest importance. The English Consul, except that his Government has far greater resources, is not as influential as Scala and in the execution of his duties Scala always achieves perfectly good relations...' The report goes on to mention a proposal to form a company operating small ships to be used for communication between the local ports and the interior of the Lagos lagoon. Scala was the chief promoter and would direct this company in which the Sardinian traders were hoping to have the greatest influence and the major shareholding. In conclusion, the captain comments on the destruction of Scala's factories at Abeokuta (earlier reported to Turin by Scala himself and graphically recounted in the *Memoirs*). He considers that this must have been the work of local people and perhaps also of Sierra Leone traders, but adds: 'I would now say that Sig. Scala is on good terms with the people and the government of Abeokuta, so that the great benefits he has in mind for them might have excited the envy and enmity of the King of Lagos and his Court, and those under his influence'.[22]

---

[21] Brignardello pp. 66–67.

[22] The *Colombo* report is filed in the Foreign Affairs archives in Rome: Busta 255, Consolato a Lagos, 1855–60. The signature of the captain is illegible but may be 'Casidico' or possibly Captain Coppello of the brig *Lagos*.

Another appreciative, and more spontaneous, account of Scala is afforded by some notes on Abeokuta by the Rev Samuel Crowther, a Yoruba priest (and later Bishop) of the Church Missionary Society, who visited the town in 1859. He writes:

> Another striking circumstance as regards the general population of Abbeokuta [Abeokuta], is the increased attention to the cultivation of the soil. Many who some time ago applied themselves mostly to war and kidnapping, and others to the palm oil trade, when that trade was newly introduced at Lagos, have, since the introduction of the cotton trade, turned their attention to the cultivation of the land as well, growing not only produce for home consumption, but cotton largely for exportation. Stimulus is given to this now, not only by the Industrial Establishment, but by the appearance of Mr. Scala in Abeokuta, in whose cotton cleaning factory twenty saw gins, with his cotton screw press, are daily at work, except on Sunday, either by hired labourers or those who clean with his saw gins, to sell to him on their own account, and also by the appearance of four Manchester merchants, who were known to come here to buy as much cotton as Abbeokuta can produce.[23]

Scala's exporting and importing business survived his departure for Italy in 1859 for six years and possibly longer. A member of the French-based Society of African Missions (SMA), Fr Francesco Borghero, who made a reconnaissance visit in 1863–64 to Lagos and Abeokuta, acknowledged in his *Journal* that he had received considerable support in Lagos from Scala's assistant, Vincenzo Paggi, like Scala a Ligurian, who was still active in the business and also still acting Vice-Consul: he describes him as a 'man of gold'. Fr Borghero was likewise much indebted in Abeokuta to Scala's agent there, a Brazilian mulatto named Ribeiro.[24] In both towns, Borghero recounts, Scala's memory was alive and respected. At Lagos his 'liberality' was still praised while in Abeokuta he was remembered as 'a very industrious and able man who made himself very popular, was much esteemed by all the chiefs, and generally loved by all'. Borghero was particularly impressed by the quantity of cotton being produced at Abeokuta, which he ascribed to the influence of Scala who had developed the industry there and set up the machinery for processing the raw material.[25]

As the Sardinian consul in Lagos, and thus as the first Italian representative in what was to become Nigeria, Scala seems to have had no official

---

[23] Crowther and Taylor, 1859, p. 444. The British Government was already showing interest in the development of cotton growing in the 1860's as a result of the American Civil War. Cotton exports were always, however, on a very small scale compared to those in oil. A. G. Hopkins, 1973, pp. 137–138; Smith, *Lagos Consulate*, pp. 76, 77, 92–94.

[24] This seems to be the same man who is mentioned on p. 6 above as Scala's 'interpreter' and who is referred to by Scala in his Chapter V, p. 54.

[25] Borghero, *Journal*, pp. 136, 154, 224.

successor until Nigeria's achievement of independence in 1960. However, Vincenzo Paggi was consistently referred to by Scala as his Vice-Consul and, although he apparently never received an exsequatur, continued to act in that capacity during Scala's absence in Abeokuta and after his departure for Italy. After Paggi's death in 1865 the consulate, or rather vice-consulate, presumably lapsed.[26] The Italian connexion was, however, maintained by the presence in Lagos of a small group whose names occur in Fr Borghero's Journal. Of these the most important was evidently Giuseppe Carrena, Scala's trading rival (although his name does not appear in the *Memoirs*). Carrena's 'beautiful mansion' on the Marina (the Lagos waterfront) was remarked upon by Mrs Foote, wife of the last substantive British consul at Lagos and by Richard Burton who described it in 1861 as 'a large pretentious building, white and light yellow ... it is said to be already decaying'.[27]

Apart from Carrena's tombstone, to be seen (at least until the early 1970s) in the Ajele or Consular cemetery in Lagos,[28] there seems to be no other physical reminder of these early Italian residents in this town where they had shared in the opening-up of the West African coast to European influence and 'legitimate' trade. But Giambattista Scala, at least, has a place, even though a minor one, among those who won a temporary foothold in West Africa for the newly united Kingdom of Italy. His *Memorie* assure him of this.

---

[26] The Protocollo Consolate a Lagos, 1857–69, in Rome, examined by Mr and Mrs Packman, contains a letter from the French Ministry of Foreign Affairs dated 6 February 1865 which states that the ministry was unable to look after the Italians in Lagos and Guinea since they could not find a suitable agent for this. Nevertheless Paggi continued to carry out consular duties as well as trading. This is confirmed by correspondence in the Archivio Storico del Ministero degli Affari Esteri (Rome), Divisione della Legazione e Divisione Consolare, 1861–68, Lagos 1861–65. Of particular interest is Paggi's despatch 243, Busta 881, of 5 March 1865, to Count Pasolini, the Foreign Minister, transmitting *inter alia* a complaint from Agostino Carrena (presumably a son of Giuseppe Carrena) against the Governor of Lagos (Freeman). Paggi draws attention to the 'positive refusal of the Governor to recognize this Royal Consulate; in the past he has always kept complete silence about all the solicitations that were sent in written form by this Royal Consulate'. Paggi's death occurred at Porto Novo to which place he, according to Fr Borghero, 'in some way belonged'. Borghero officiated at his funeral but, since Paggi had to be buried in his own house at Porto Novo according to local custom, he omitted the blessing of the tomb. Borghero, *Journal*, p. 230.

[27] Sir R. F. Burton, *Wanderings in West Africa*, London, 1863, pp 21–23; Mrs Foote, *Recollections of Central America and the West Coast of Africa*, London 1869, pp. 190–191; Smith, *Consulate*, pp. 97, 168, note 27.

[28] Carrena's undated tombstone in Lagos has an inscription referring to his sons. It is likely that they carried on his business in Lagos after his death.

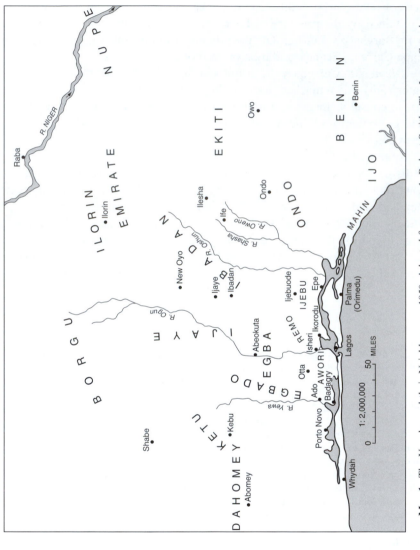

Map 1. The Yoruba and their Neighbours, c. 1850. Adapted from map 1, Robert Smith, *The Lagos Consulate*.

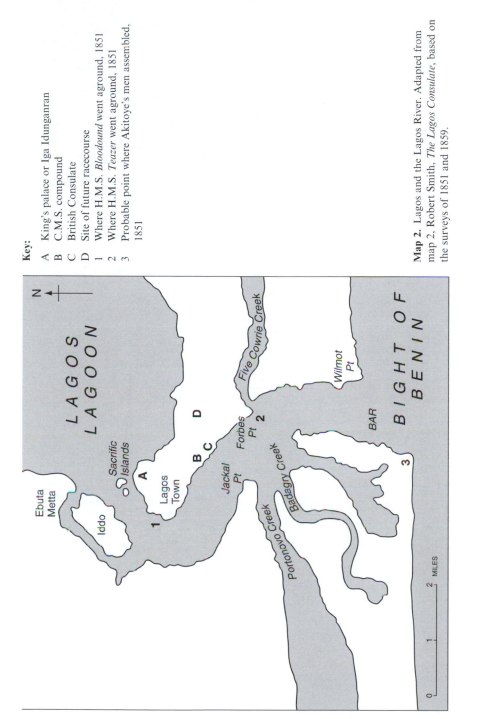

Key:

A King's palace or Iga Idunganran
B C.M.S. compound
C British Consulate
D Site of future racecourse
1 Where H.M.S. *Bloodound* went aground, 1851
2 Where H.M.S. *Teazer* went aground, 1851
3 Probable point where Akitoye's men assembled, 1851

Map 2. Lagos and the Lagos River. Adapted from map 2, Robert Smith, *The Lagos Consulate*, based on the surveys of 1851 and 1859.

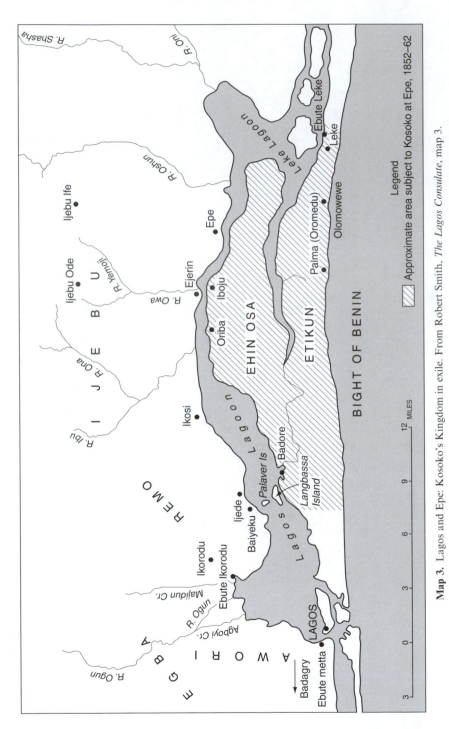

Map 3. Lagos and Epe: Kosoko's Kingdom in exile. From Robert Smith, *The Lagos Consulate*, map 3.

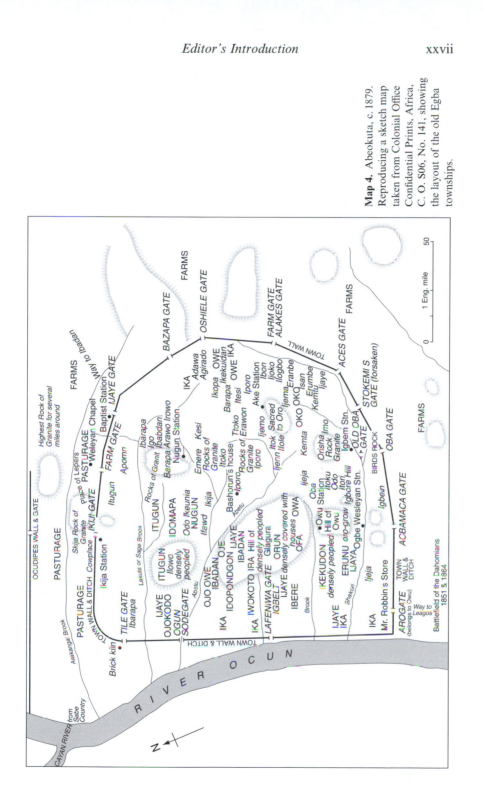

Map 4. Abeokuta, c. 1879. Reproducing a sketch map taken from Colonial Office Confidential Prints, Africa, C. O. S06, No. 141, showing the layout of the old Egba townships.

I

WEST AFRICA AND THE SLAVE TRADE

Among the many regions of our globe that are still a mystery to man, one of the most interesting and worthy of exploration and study is, without any doubt, the interior of Africa. This may seem a strange statement! For century after century successive civilizations of Indians, Egyptians, Phoenicians, Persians, Romans, Arabs and others have spread along the coasts of this vast peninsula, bringing the education and refinement which are reflected in the numerous movements, popular traditions, religious beliefs or super-stitions still to be found today; for century after century invading Europeans have settled at various points along this same coast, erected temples, for-tresses, theatres, factories and establishments of all kinds, and left the imprint of their civilization. Nevertheless the regions of the interior remained untouched by so many years of progress. Not only was the light of so many successive civilizations unable to penetrate this region but it even remained unknown to civilized man and today, as in the time of the Pharaohs, the centre of Africa is still a great question mark for geographers and natural scientists, a problem in the history of humanity and a virgin land still waiting for a Columbus to regenerate it.

Many and various are the reasons which deterred travellers from ventur-ing to explore this unknown region or prevented them from reaching their destination if ever they set out.

The forbidding aspect of the African continent, devoid of roads, with few streams or navigable rivers and not always sufficient water supplies, made penetration to the interior difficult, dangerous and often impossible; there were vast sandy deserts to be crossed, where the only drinking water is in the rare cases situated at great distances from one another. Here it was pain-ful to travel, as one was scorched by the sun's burning rays so blinding when reflected off the sand that they made rest unbearable; the climate was unhealthy and seemed like a zone of fire to those born under gentler skies; there were lethal miasmas and nature was desolate and untamed; fierce beasts were to be encountered at every step and these were even more terrible than the inhabitants; the burning breath of the Simoom[1] raised mountains of sand which submerged men and houses, dried up vegetation and springs, and left in its wake an interminable trail of devastation. Prejudices rooted in antiquity about the inhospitality of this region were reinforced and magnified by the thousand fantastic forms in which the unknown appears to the imagination; these and other causes which it would take too long to enumerate here, prevented the exploration of these lands and retarded their development.

But these obstacles, however serious, were destined sooner or later to disappear with the irresistible progress of science and civilization.

While there is still much to be achieved in the future there are already signs of progress in our own time with the wonderful inventions of the steamship, the railway and the electric telegraph which bring us into contact with the most distant peoples; the perfection attained in all branches of science which makes the way easier and breaks down obstacles hitherto thought to be insurmountable, and the generous zeal and noble competition manifested everywhere by voyages of exploration and new discoveries. One might say that our generation feels shame and remorse at not having yet seen every part of our little globe or spread our civilization among all who inhabit it.

Among the noble tendencies of our age must also be included the solicitude of the most powerful governments, the tireless activities of scientific and geographical societies, the zealous propaganda of the Catholic and the Protestant Churches; the feverish enthusiasms of the scientist, the avidity of the trader ever in search of new sources of profit, and finally the courage of the adventurer seeking fame, danger and excitement. And thanks to all this noble competition in strength and sacrifice and the feverish activity of men of diverse interests, the unknown lands are becoming fewer and fewer every day. In Africa, Asia, America and Australia, in the Indian Archipelago, the polar regions and other parts of the world, new lands rise up from time to time before the astonished eyes of the navigator; rivers no longer conceal their sources, mountains once thought to be inaccessible now bear the marks of human feet, research is being made into the depths of the earth, and nature is being forced to reveal her secrets one by one to man, her sovereign ruler.

But the favoured spot, the magnetic centre on which the eyes of the present-day explorers all converge is without any doubt the interior of Africa whose discovery is of such great interest to Europe. For some years

---

[1] The simoom (spelt 'simoum' by Scala) is a hot dry wind blowing from the desert, known alternatively as 'khamsin' or 'harmattan'. All these words are Arabic. The Yoruba know this wind as *oyé*.

a number of intrepid travellers have resolutely braved the solitude of this desolate land, facing all kinds of hardship and danger in the hope of lifting the veil which covers it, of deciphering at least one page from the book of mystery and taking one step further towards the future development of the land. Like the first pioneers of America who conquered, tree by tree, the virgin forests for future generations, these worthy men are paving the way for European civilization which will slowly but surely invade the whole African continent and redeem it to the life of society. Many of these men have lost their lives there, decimated by the intemperate climate, by fatigue, illness and the rage of men and wild beasts, and science weeps for its martyrs such as Hongthon [Houghton], Mungo Park, Peddie, Campbell, Gray, Dochard, Clapperton, the Landers, Richardson, Overweg, and Vogel,[2] and others no less noble who sacrificed their lives in the cause of humanity.

Other travellers were fortunate and returned from their journeys to set out once again and enrich science and trade by new discoveries and new products. Dr Henry Barth, undeterred by the premature death of his companions Richardson and Overweg, penetrated further than any European before him into the heart of the African continent, pressing on from Tripoli to Timbuctoo and originating a new expedition to complete the discoveries he had begun. The statistical journals (1859) contain interesting information about journeys in these parts made by travellers either privately or sponsored by government missions. The famous Dr David Livingstone, author of an important work entitled *Explorations in the Interior of Southern Africa*, after penetrating and carefully exploring all that part of the African continent which lies between S Paolo di Luanda to the mouth of the Zambezi, returned again to the lands he had previously discovered and with better scientific instruments and apparatus continued his investigations along the banks of the Zambezi.

The Swedish explorer Anderson explored the land of Orompo on the West coast, south of Benguella, following the river Cunene.

Ladislas Maggior of Teresipol in Hungary, after marrying the daughter of the black king of Bihe and being made commander-in-chief of his father's troops, used all his influence and authority, as well as his army, to explore the adjacent lands.

Two English officers, Captain R. Burton and Lieut. Speke, have discovered two great lakes in the centre of the continent, named Tanganyika and Nyanza, the latter lying below longitude 33° and latitude 3° South.

---

[2] This passage lists some of the more prominent travellers in West Africa in the late eighteenth and early nineteenth centuries. Most sought primarily to establish the course of the river Niger to the sea, a quest finally fulfilled by the Lander brothers in 1830.

Massara, a Sardinian missionary, penetrated into the interior of the countries of Abyssinia.

Fritz Windham, Miani, Thomasay and others went up the White Nile in May 1859 in search of its source, the object of so many tireless investigations.

The English geographer MacCarthy travelled from Algeria, where he had lived for eight years, to Timbuctu by routes hitherto unknown.

The English steamer *Rainbow* set out from Bonny in the Gulf of Benin on 6 January 1859 to explore the area along the Niger.

Other excursions no less important are being prepared to East Africa by Pedro del Comitto, Governor of the Portugese forts Tete and Sara on the Zambezi (lands he has already visited and about which he has written a very interesting book entitled *Muata-Cazembe*) and to North and Central Africa by Capt Magnan, Baron Kraft and Yussuf ben Gallabie.

Thanks to these continued investigations and studies, the secrets of Africa are slowly being unravelled and the unknown land gradually discovered. Every day it reveals itself in its true form, very different from the fantasies of the past. Only ten years ago the map of Africa comprised, from its Southern point, i.e. from S Lat 35° to 5°, a vast space either empty or one populated according to the cartographer's whim. Now this immense void, if it has not yet completely disappeared, has at least been greatly reduced by the discoveries of Galton, Anderson, Livingstone, Barth, Vogel, Moffat, Kraft, Burton, Speke and others who describe with care and accuracy the lands they have penetrated, thus correcting the errors of previous guesswork, while the intervening areas which still remain to be discovered are fewer than those which are already known. The same may be said for other empty spaces which have disappeared or are being reduced in other parts of Africa by other travellers. But over and above the treasures they have acquired for science, these travellers have greatly aided trade by learning from the natives about the products of their country and the goods for which they wish to exchange them, the markets where the caravans buy or sell their merchandise, the routes they take, the towns they pass, and the goods which might be sold in them.

This incessant and prodigious labour on the part of governments and private persons is proof of Europe's great interest in finding a solution to the problem of Africa. Over and above a general interest in civilization (the duty which is incumbent upon all civilized peoples to bring a new life to barbarous and savage peoples) the solution raises a further moral problem for Europe, that of the slave trade.

For a long time a universal horror has been manifested in Europe for this violation of the most sacred laws of humanity and everyone has felt a profound pity for all those human beings brutally uprooted from their countries and families, cruelly transported to distant countries and there condemned

forever and through no fault of their own to a degrading and painful servitude which because it is enforced upon intelligent beings makes their
condition even worse than that of animals. Thus a cry of indignation has
risen up everywhere against this ignominy which defiles our century, and a
firm and decisive resolution has been taken by European governments to
bring such savagery to an end.

Already the Dutch, the Danes, the English and the French are freeing the
black slaves in their American colonies, but slavery exists all the same in
many parts of South America as well as, I regret to say, in many states of
North America. Today there is little hope of seeing slavery abolished there
and the shameful mark of Cain wiped off the forehead of American demo-
crats; there has been civil war in their country; they have excited hatred
and contempt among free peoples, and even brought upon themselves the
scorn of crowned despots.

To prevent the continued supply of slaves the European governments
took certain wise measures to bring about the suppression of the trade.
They imposed strict sanctions against slavers, who were to be treated in
the same way as pirates; they established by treaty the right to inspect
ships of the respective nations and they sent numerous cruisers along the
coast of Africa to prevent this infamous traffic and punish those who take
part in it. But these measures, excellent in themselves, are in no way
adequate. The cruisers of the various nations, particularly the English,
more numerous than the others, which tirelessly rove these seas, year after
years in spite of enormous sacrifices of men and money, certainly deserve
the gratitude of all friends of humanity. Undeniably they have rendered,
and are rendering (who can deny this?) great services to the cause every
time they capture ships loaded with human merchandise or divert others
from this loathsome traffic; and if sometimes one complains of the considerable inconvenience their inspections cause, certainly at the present time
nobody would wish to see their vigilance suppressed in these waters. But
are these cruisers, however numerous and active they may be, sufficient to
bring the trade to an end? We do not think so. The coast under their vigilance
is too vast to be supervised with any probability of success; the nature of
these shores, interrupted here and there with cliffs and promontories jutting
out to form thousands of small inlets or bays, with many creeks and waterways accessible to ships and flanked by thick forests, offers many hiding
places to the slaver. He can lie quietly in perfect safety and await his cargo
from the interior, and choosing a propitious time on a dark night or in a
thick mist, he can dart out onto the waves and set his course for America,
leaving the creek as the ship resounds with the agonized cries of the
anguished slaves, perhaps only a short distance from the unsuspecting
cruiser. And not only are the cruisers inadequate for the suppression of the

slave trade, but they even worsen the travelling condition of the unhappy slaves since the slaver, in order to escape the cruisers, is obliged to use light, fast ships which are consequently small and devoted entirely to this trade while the slaves are packed on top of one another in the smallest possible space. Moreover it sometimes happens that when the slaver is chased by a cruiser, in order to lighten his ship, flee more quickly and get rid of his crime so to speak, he fills great casks with human merchandise and throws them into the sea. Besides, the cruisers are generally unpopular with traders and discourage many honest sea captains from trading on these shores, for the right of inspection is not always exercised as courteously or, what is worse, as impartially as it should be. In fact no seaman will deny that the cruisers of one nation prefer to inspect, or one might even say persecute, with useless, over-meticulous time-wasting and discourteous investigations the ships of foreign nations which the treaties have given them the right to search, and appear to aim at discouraging them from approaching these shores so that they can monopolize the trade of Africa for their own ships. Therefore it would be advisable to have a complete revision of the treaties to abolish these abuses and it would above all be desirable that there should be representatives of each nation in these cruisers who would alone have the right, like the Americans, to search the ships of their own nation.

While visiting the many slave markets of South and North America, supplied by the ships which deposit there the sad remnants of their cargoes who have survived the long martyrdom of the voyage, I was profoundly moved by the sight of so much misery and tormented by an overwhelming desire to bring it to an end if ever this were possible. So I set my mind to seeking a more efficacious means of bringing about the solution so much desired by humanity. Since the attempts made up till now by the European governments to suppress the slave trade had not been successful, I thought other means should be tried and to this end it seemed that, first of all, it was necessary to study, at its very source, the origin of African slavery and to discover the motives which induced peoples to sell their own kind.

The Blacks of Africa, like all primitive peoples, have few needs. Their main sustenance comes from grain, roots and vegetables, beef and mutton, milk, eggs, fruit and so on, and with all of these nature has abundantly provided them without their having to do any work. But their long contact with the Europeans and other peoples on the coast as well as those of the interior has given them the desire for inessentials, or should we say luxuries, the satisfaction of which has become a necessity and produced terrible effects. These needs are rum, aquavita, tobacco which they love passionately, brightly coloured cloth, mirrors, jewellery made of beads and coloured glass, and other fancy goods which greatly please their innocent vanity. To procure these objects no sacrifice is too great for the African, but what can he give in exchange to the European trader? The only money in use is the *cowrie* or shell, equivalent to one tenth of our Italian centesimo, and money which is naturally not much valued in other parts of the world; gold dust and ivory which they also possess are too rare and difficult to procure and their other rich natural products they neglect as they have not yet guessed at their use, importance and real value. Therefore lacking any fair exchange for the objects of their choice, the Africans (urged on by the perfidy of the Portugese and Spanish slave-traders and other riff-raff who have settled along their coast) could imagine no better expedient than to fall back on the human coin, so greedily sought by the traffickers in slaves. In a savage country where individual liberty is not guaranteed by social and international institutions, any way of procuring one's wants is good and cases have been quoted of an African who, when lacking one of his own kind to sell has sold himself for a bottle of rum. But in difficult circumstances one falls back on harsh measures. Thus it often happens that if the cellar of the king or chief remains empty of the desired bottles; if the royal pipe lies idle in a corner for want of tobacco; if the favourite of the harem sighs for some ornament thought to be indispensable for enhancing her charms, then the king solemnly calls together the nobles and the people of his kingdom and holds council with them; he explains in pathetic tones the urgent necessity of the state and proposes, as a remedy, that war should be declared on some neighbouring nation, or else a slave raid should be organized against some weak and defenceless tribe.

The proposal, as one might imagine, is always hailed with frantic applause by a rough and fierce crowd, tormented by the same desire for rum and tobacco and determined to satisfy it at all costs without too much thought about the delicacy of the means. Then there is great activity and excitement in the tribe — which usually is apathetic and given to the contemplative life; men, women and children set to work with enthusiasm; arms, ammunition and food supplies are eagerly prepared; the local deities are consulted, sacrifices are made and largesse distributed, and on the day indicated by the oracle, who always agrees with the chief of the tribe, ah, what a pitiful sight! the whole population falls furiously and without pretext upon its neighbours, destroying fields and flocks, setting fire to huts, villages and towns, ruining everything and massacring anyone who resists, all with the one object of taking as many prisoners as possible, men, women and children, and so procuring a given quantity of living money to be exchanged for equivalent quantities of alcoholic drinks or feminine ornament.[3]

[3] Scala equates the wars among the West Africans in pre-colonial time with slave raiding. This had long been the established explanation, and was also the view taken by the Abolitionists. See R. Smith, *Warfare and Diplomacy*, 1988, pp. 30–31.

While the conquered cross the sea in chains, suffering every kind of tor-
ment and hardship, the conquerors carouse joyfully in their villages, drinking
and dancing until, by the law of reciprocity, neighbouring states, inspired by
the same needs or in a spirit of revenge, attack them in their turn and inflict
upon them the same punishment. The whole political life of the African race
is made up of these alternating wars and reversals of fortune.

Would it not be possible, I asked myself, to destroy, little by little, this
iniquitous order of things and replace it with a legitimate and honest trade
which would greatly benefit both the natives and the Europeans?[4]

Africa, as I have said, abounds in products of all kinds, neither cultivated nor sufficiently appreciated by the natives since they are as yet unaware of their use and value. The few items that they know and have for
some time exchanged for foreign goods are very useful to Europe where
they find easy markets. From this it can be argued (and the argument
could be strengthened by the discoveries that are being made every day
of new riches in the African soil and by my own discovery of vegetable
fat,[5] which I was the first person to import into Europe), that other products no less important but as yet unknown to the natives and to us exist
in those lands. If, therefore, civilized man could teach these primitive
people to understand and appreciate the riches of nature and induce them
to cultivate with loving care the many and various fruits of their fertile
soil; if he taught them that the work of man was the true source of the
country's wealth and not the man whom they rob in war or hunt with
such labour and danger to be sold and transported elsewhere, all for the
sake of a bottle of rum per head every now and again; if he proved tangibly
that such labour applied to the cultivation of the land would lead to at least
ten bottles of rum per head, per year, I believe that so simple an argument
and such simple arithmetic, corroborated by the facts, would enter easily
into an African's head.

Inspired by this idea not by any means new although not yet taken into
consideration by those governments who aim to suppress the slave trade, I
resolved to put it into execution, then to prove by example the beneficial
results which could be derived from it, and to initiate (if I may be allowed
the expression) a new era in the social life of these peoples and direct them

---

[4] Scala was far from being the first to advocate the replacement of the slave trade by a 'legitimate'
trade in local products. One of the earliest and most influential of the British humanitarians to
suggest this was Sir Thomas Buxton who published his book *The African Slave Trade and its
Remedy* in 1839. Scala's arrival at Lagos, moreover, had been preceded by other traders seeking
to tap the market in palm oil. See S. O. Biobaku, *The Egba and their Neighbours*, 1957, chapter V,
and Smith, *Lagos Consulate*, pp 31–32, 35–37.

[5] This refers to shea butter. See below, p. 80 and note 6.

towards a better fate. So I decided to go to some point on the coast of Africa and to found a trade establishment there, and to penetrate gradually, as far as I could, into the interior, extending my contacts with the surrounding peoples, studying their character, their customs, their habits and above all the products of their lands and exchanging for these the goods they liked the best.

I had no illusions about the limitations of my enterprise; I knew that such attempts, to be really effective, should be made simultaneously in different parts of this great continent, on a vast scale, with much capital and with government protection and co-operation. They should have the assurance of military stations and fortresses, and be supported by continued scientific explorations into the interior which would provide routes of communication between the coast and the centre. My only ambition was to suggest a way, a means which seemed easy and practicable, to call the attention of governments to its efficacy and to persuade others to attempt it on a vaster scale. I wanted finally to provide a proof, a further argument for the possibility of gradually suppressing the slave trade, to our own advantage and without too many sacrifices on our part.

Can I flatter myself that I have achieved this aim, and suggested the true way and given practical proof of the efficacy of the means I used?

A country is not changed in a day nor are the customs which have prevailed for centuries. The regeneration of a people is a slow, laborious operation to which every generation contributes some improvement. Before the difficult question of the slave trade can be solved there must be long years of careful study, much experiment, tireless work and sacrifices of all kinds.

I do not pretend to have worked miracles, but all the same the prosperity of my different establishments on the West Coast and in the interior of Africa, the numerous cargoes of African agricultural products which I sent in the course of a few years to Europe, the land I cultivated and the new direction which I gave to the savage life of these people, all confirmed me in my ideas, persuaded me to persevere, and gave me confidence to hope for an even better future. When I consider that the many casks of palm oil I sent to Europe would in the past have represented as many black heads destined for the slave market, when I consider the massacres and the destruction that it would have cost to acquire these slaves, while instead a fruitful labour diverted these people from war and man-hunting, and those who would have been either victims or victors, killed or killers, have in all probability been instead employed by me in cultivating the land or working in my factories, then I feel some consolation and even if I have saved only one Black from slavery I shall always thank Heaven for inspiring me with this philanthropic resolution.

In support of my enterprise there was no lack of encouragement or reward from the enlightened Government of the King of Sardinia, always ready to take every opportunity to defend the cause of humanity and to protect and extend the trade of the nation.

A detailed report forwarded by me, some time after my arrival in Africa, to the Minister of Foreign Affairs, C. di Cavour, informed him of my plans, of my establishment and of the advantages which would be derived from them, in my opinion, by both the black population and by our trade in general; the increase which I had brought about in the palm-oil trade had also induced many sea captains of our nation to trade on these shores, and they, by reports and petitions lodged in the Chamber of Commerce at Genoa, begged the government to take the necessary measures to have our flag represented in these parts and our trade protected. The King's Minister was prompt to send me a reply containing words of approval and recognition of my foresight together with my nomination as Consul-General for Lagos and its hinterland.[6] This duty of representing a foreign sovereign greatly facilitated my plans for civilizing these people, giving me greater prestige in their eyes and authorizing me in certain ways to intervene officially and with greater authority in their internal disputes; it revealed to them a power, previously unknown to them, which was interested in their fate and favoured their legitimate trade; it meant that for the first time in this country the name of ITALY was heard and our flag honoured. It was the first of so many European flags to fly in Abbeockuta [Abeokuta], a town in the interior which I was the first to visit and to reveal to Europe.[7]

In offering the reader a rapid and brief account of my journeys and my sojourn in Africa and mainly of my excursions to Abeokuta and the surrounding country, I am not claiming scientific or literary merit for my work. My contribution to knowledge and the information given here are offered in all modesty. I intend simply to draw the reader's attention to an important problem of our time, above all through legitimate trade to promote contact between honest Europeans and Africans, thereby extending our civilization in these parts; I propose chiefly to interest our government,

---

[6] Scala was nominated as a 'consul of the second class', to reside at Lagos, and not as a consul-general. His appointment was dated 11 November 1855 and was confirmed to Professor G. B. Brignardello by the Superintendent of the Piedmontese archives. See also Editor's Introduction above, note 6.

[7] It is possible that when Scala visited Abeokuta in 1857 (settling there the following year) he was the first European merchant to do so but he had been preceded by the Christian missionaries. After an exploratory visit in 1843, the Rev. Henry Townsend, accompanied by the Yoruba convert Samuel Crowther (later the first bishop of Western Equatorial Africa), set up the first missionary station in Abeokuta in 1846 on behalf of the Anglican Church Missionary Society (C.M.S.).

our traders and seamen so that they may develop this trade and derive inestimable benefits for both countries, and to this end I present a general picture of the products and commodities of Africa, and also of the goods which may be imported and which will find a ready market there. In so doing I believe I am performing a useful service to my country and at the same time adding a small stone to the building of a future African civilization.

II

LAGOS

In November 1851 I was in Bahia, in Brazil. There I hired the Sardinian brig *Felicità*, under the command of Captain Raggio, and had it loaded at my own expense with a cargo of rum, foodstuffs and various manufactured goods, and on November 18th I set sail for Africa. After a month of fair sailing I arrived on January 14th of the following year in Accra, a small port situated 60 miles West of Cape S Paolo [Cape St Paul], where I unloaded some of my cargo and exchanged it for gold dust and palm oil; then I went to Keta to seek out accurate information about Lagos, which was to be my destination as this port had become, by reason of its geographical position, the true centre of the slave trade. When I had found out what I wanted, I wasted no time in setting out for Lagos where I arrived on 10th February [1852].[1]

On the west coast of Africa N. Lat. 6°–29°, E. Long. 3°–29°, 360 miles from Fernando Po, 165 miles East of Cape St Paul and 60 miles from Benin is the mouth of a broad river called the Lagos, blocked by numerous sand banks which make access difficult and navigation dangerous since there are only 10 to 11 feet of water there at ordinary tide.

Three miles upstream is the small island of Lagos, almost oval in shape with a promontory on the West. It has a circumference of about five miles and is four miles long by two miles wide. The aspect of the island, shaded by luxuriant vegetation and covered almost entirely in thick forest, is rather pleasing although there is no trace of cultivation. With the exception of the little town the island is entirely given over to stags, zebra, antelope, buck and other wild animals which provide abundant hunting for the

---

[1] Scala, then aged 34, arrived in Lagos one and a half months after the 'reduction' of the town by a British naval force which was accompanied by John Beecroft, British consul for the Bights of Benin and Biafra. This accomplished the replacement on the Lagos throne of Oba (King) Kosoko by Akitoye, Kosoko's exiled predecessor, and was followed by the signature by the restored Oba of an anti-slaving treaty. For Beecroft's career see M. Lynn, 'Consul and Kings', *JICH*, 1982.

inhabitants. Sometimes one sees tigers and other wild animals but they are rare because these animals are loath to cross the river.[2]

The town, also called Lagos,[3] is situated to the north-west of the island on the bank of the river and like all the towns of the Africans has nothing remarkable to offer.

It has about twenty thousand inhabitants;[4] the streets are narrow and muddy and covered in filth; the houses are generally small, about nine feet high and quadrilateral in shape, built of earth which has been dried in the sun and supported by poles. They have one floor at ground level, divided into several rooms, covered with a roof of plaited straw or palm fronds, with an overhang of one or two metres to protect the inhabitants from the rain and the sun, and they are surrounded, at a distance of five or six metres, by trees or a wall, providing the inhabitants with an extremely useful space for domestic purposes and also giving them protection from inquisitive neighbours. These houses, whatever their size, are all architecturally alike; even the king's house, the biggest of all, can only be distinguished from the others by its roof which is made of tiles instead of leaves, a privilege to which he alone is entitled.[5] It is, however, also granted to the Europeans but only for their houses within the city and not outside it. The temple, that is the place of sacrifice, similar to other buildings in form, is only distinctive in that its outer walls are painted with white and red stripes and the single inner room has the floor and walls strewn with grasses and scented plants.

On my arrival in Lagos the town seemed to be a shapeless mass of ruins and there was a feeling of vast solitude. In order to understand the cause of this mournful atmosphere we must go back to the origins of the town and give an account of its history.

To call our account a history is perhaps not very exact and is something of an exaggeration. The African race has not yet produced its Tacitus and even the simple chronicler has still to emerge; there are, however, a number of story tellers who recount legends of their country, and like the poets of antiquity hand down from generation to generation the great

---

[2] Duikers, a species of antelope which resembles a stag or buck, are still occasionally seen in the vicinity of Lagos. Zebras and tigers are not known in West Africa (but the term 'tiger' was often applied to the leopard).

[3] The town and island of Lagos are known in Yoruba as 'Eko'. The name 'Lagos' was presumably given by the early Portuguese visitors and means 'lagoon(s)'.

[4] This approximation accords with observations made by other visitors in the first half of the nineteenth century.

[5] The royal monopoly in the use of tiles in Lagos at this time is well attested. The Oba's palace is said to have acquired its roof tiles as a present from Portuguese slave traders during the reign of Oba Akinsemoyin (1760–c. 1775). Scala omits to mention that in 1856 he was rebuked by Oba Dosunmu for having used locally-made tiles on the roof of his new warehouse at Lagos. Smith, *Lagos Consulate*, pp. 8, 74, 94, 162, and xix above, note 17.

deeds of the nation and keep them alive in popular memory. If such a method is not always the best one to give the necessary stamp of truth to history, if it nearly always happens that successive generations change, add to or subtract from the legends, the Blacks may easily console themselves with the thought that Homer's poem was handed down to posterity in the same way and in spite of the changes made through the centuries has lost none of its divine beauty; they can derive consolation from the fact that the history of great nations has not always borne the hallmark of mathematical truth, and this can be seen in the Histories of Herodotus and in the first Decades of Titus Livy.[6]

However this may be, travellers who wish to learn the history of the Black peoples, must of necessity fall back on the local walking libraries, eloquent enough and available to all for a small consideration of tobacco or acquavita.

According to oral tradition, the island of Lagos was deserted until two centuries ago while the land on each side of the river formed part of the Kingdom of Benin whose capital, also called Benin, is sixty miles east of Lagos.[7]

The kings of Benin, overlords of a great empire and absorbed by various cares in their capital, were not able to occupy themselves with the welfare of all the provinces of their vast dominions. Consequently, they left the most distant in the benevolent care of Providence which fulfilled there as best it could the functions of a king. On one single day in the year the kings of Benin remembered with paternal solicitude all their beloved subjects, and this was the day on which they sent their lieutenants throughout the land to collect tribute. The tribute consisted of shells, corn, oxen, sheep and slaves of both sexes for the royal household. The people of the regions around Lagos, far from resenting being left in the care of Providence for the rest of the year would, on the contrary, have preferred their gracious

---

[6] The written history of the Yoruba may have begun earlier with accounts in Arabic although none has yet been traced. Robin Law concludes that the first serious attempt to write a history of Yorubaland was by Samuel Crowther in the brief introduction to *A Vocabulary of the Yoruba Language*, 1843. See R. Law, 'Early Yoruba Historiography' in Falola (ed.), *Pioneer, Patriot and Patriarch*, 1993. The merits and methods of 'oral history' have been much debated by Africanists, some of whom have attempted to lay down rigid rules for its collection.

[7] The strong tradition of the connection between the Lagos kingship and the kingdom of Benin is supported by the report of a German, Josua Ulsheimer, who visited Lagos in 1603, as well as by ceremonies performed at the coronation and burial of an Oba of Lagos which apparently continued until the mid-nineteenth century. The first ruler of Lagos appointed by Benin is usually named in both Benin and Lagos tradition as Ashipa or Esikpa, whose name comes first in the Lagos king-list. For short accounts of Lagos history see Smith, *Lagos Consulate*, 1978, pp. 4–9, 144, notes 22, 23, or *Kingdoms of the Yoruba* (3rd ed.), 1988, pp. 72–75. For earlier times, see Babatunde Agiri and Sandra Barnes, 'Lagos before 1603', in Adefuye, Agiri and Osuntokun, *History of the Peoples of Lagos State*, 1987.

sovereign not to remember them even on that day and consequently they came together and agreed unanimously to spare him the trouble of sending his lieutenants at the predetermined time.

Thus it happened (I am still speaking of two centuries ago) that the reigning king of Benin sent to these provinces his deputy Kabutu[8] at the head of an army of three thousand men to collect the taxes which were due. On arriving in the heart of the region he expected to find everywhere he went humble, obsequious people prostrating themselves before the king's representatives and eager to deprive themselves of a small part of their possessions in order to contribute to the welfare of their sovereign. He was already imagining the oxen, the cows and the sacks of grain which would enrich the stores of his king as well as those which would fall to the tax-collector; he was already smiling at the thought of the beautiful slave girls destined for the royal nuptial bed and those, no less beautiful, who would be set aside for his own personal pleasure, and carried away by these pleasant thoughts he arrived on the West bank of the River Lagos almost opposite the island.

Great was the surprise of the brave Kabutu when, instead of the well-disposed people he had imagined, he found himself faced with a hostile, menacing crowd, armed to the teeth and ready to repel force by force. He tried to calm the excited people with words of peace and conciliation; he suggested compromises, he begged, he implored but all in vain; his words were received with threats and menaces, his proposals rejected with an obstinate refusal to pay the tribute. In this critical situation, surrounded by a furious armed multitude, in a wild and unfamiliar country, far from the capital and with no hope of assistance, the brave Kabutu cast a melancholy glance at his valiant companions and considering their number and the expression on their faces, he realized how risky it would be to rely on force. So what was he to do? If he returned to the king without the expected tribute he would face certain death; if he used the army against these people, the troops and their general would be massacred with equal certainty. What could he do?

Buridan's ass placed between measures of fodder of the same shape, size, weight, colour and smell, and equidistant from his jaws, in a word absolutely identical, was unable to decide which one to choose so he obeyed the laws of an inexorable logic and allowed himself to die of hunger.[9] Kabutu's logic was more flexible than that of the ass.

---

[8] See note 7 above. But this name is unlikely to be a corruption of Ashipa or Esikpa, and there seems to be no recollection of Kabutu in Lagos or Benin tradition.
[9] This sophism is attributed to Jean Buridan, a French scholastic philosopher of the 14th century.

Placed between two equally certain dangers he bravely made his decision and of the two possible courses chose to become king. Aristotle might have found reason to laugh at a conclusion which did not arise legitimately and naturally from the premises; but the companions of Kabutu, more indulgent than the Greek philosophers in matters of logic, did not mind at all. On the contrary they greeted his decision with enthusiasm and confirmed him king by acclamation. The first thought of the new king was naturally to find for himself a kingdom where his sacred person and his companions in arms, now his subjects, could reside. Too scrupulous to usurp the lands of his former patron, the King of Benin, and seeing by the look on the faces of the people that the times were not ripe for foreign monarchs in these parts, he looked elsewhere and observing that the nearby island of Lagos was completely deserted, he determined to take possession of it with his troops, by virtue of the maxim that occupied land belongs to the first person to take possession.

Having landed on the island, he began to lay the foundations of the town of Lagos, to make laws and to distribute the land among his subjects; to form alliances with the neighbouring peoples and to provide as best as he could for the welfare of his new subjects. As it is the custom of these people to take their women with them into battle, Kabutu's companions were well provided and in order to populate the island they did not need to resort to the vigorous tactics of the Romans so that the fortunate owners of the beautiful Sabines in the vicinity could sleep peacefully in their beds. Kabutu was an excellent king; he fathered numerous children, ruled with justice and after a happy reign of 40 years died at the age of 86, to be remembered with honour. He was the founder of the glorious dynasty of Kabutu, famous among the tribes in the vicinity of Lagos. If the old adage is true that the history of a happy people is the shortest and easiest to recount, then Kabutu's descendants must have been the happiest in the world because local tradition is silent about their deeds for two consecutive centuries. Nothing is said about wars, conquests, battles, discoveries, laws decreed, roads made or monuments erected; nor indeed any of the great enterprises (in the arts of peace or war) which immortalize a nation. The people, without industry or art, lived in the same primitive state as before; the island was uncultivated and as before left to the wild animals, yet nevertheless the prosperity of Lagos increased from day to day.[10]

The secret of this enigma lay quite simply in the slave traffic which the King of Lagos eagerly practised on a large scale, and monopolized, so that it provided the principal income for the State.

[10] This account of the origin and early history of the Lagos kingdom was presumably given to Scala by a local inhabitant. It cannot be reconciled with completely different reconstructions based on the traditions of Benin and Lagos. See note 7 above.

Lagos is situated at a short distance from the sea on a river which penetrates a long way into the interior and communicates with other rivers including the Niger and some very large lakes.[11] It is the centre for all the routes from the slave-producing regions including the immense area which extends to the north as far as Abeokuta, to the east as far as Calabar, and to Portonuovo [Porto Novo] on the west and ends twenty miles east of Ajuda [Ouidah, Whydah], divided by a small tongue of sand, from another river which flows into the River Volta. From all over this vast area continuous streams of slaves of both sexes and all ages come to the various markets of the interior where they are sold to the natives, either for their own service or to be resold to the trade.

The last category, the most numerous, come straight to Lagos from the markets of the interior. There they are bought by the king of the island who has the monopoly of this infamous trade, and are resold for European goods to the Portuguese slavers who come from all over the place in quest of their filthy profit, and shipped immediately to America. The chief slave markets which supply Lagos from the interior are Porto Novo, 60 miles West of the island in the kingdom of Dahomey, Ikorodu in the Ijebu kingdom five miles from Lagos and Igeni [Ejinrin?] in the kingdom of Ijebu 15 miles away; but there are many others no less important even if further away. All these markets are on neutral ground by common consent of the kings or tribal chiefs in whose territory they lie and are protected by special laws for the greater safety and prosperity of such a favoured trade. There are no statistics or certain data as to the number of slaves brought annually to Lagos or shipped to America, but it must be enormous if one considers that until my arrival in Lagos the slave trade had been the only industry and the inhabitants' only means of subsistence for 200 years. Although the kings held the monopoly of this trade they had to employ many men in its various operations, and since the inhabitants all found employment and a sure means of livelihood, they did not deign to cultivate the land or undertake any other work of a legitimate kind.[12]

---

[11] The 'Lagos river' opens into a lagoon which gives access to a vast system of inland waterways; these connect Lagos with Porto Novo and beyond, almost to the Volta estuary on the west and with the creeks a hundred miles to the east. They do not communicate directly with the Niger.
[12] The slave trade at Lagos came into being towards the end of the eighteenth century, probably pioneered by Portuguese traders, and thus some 80 years before Scala wrote these memories. As Scala says, it transformed the economy of the island kingdom; a contemporary observer, G. A. Robertson, estimated in his *Notes on Africa*, 1819, that between 7,000 and 10,000 slaves were sold annually at Lagos in his time. The royal 'monopoly' of the trade implies here not that only the Oba dealt in slaves but that he and, with his concurrence, his chiefs and other leading traders acted as middlemen in the trade. See also Robin Law, 'Trade and Politics behind the Slave Coast', *JAH*, 1983, pp. 343–348.

This flourishing state of affairs could not fail to attract the attention of the English cruisers stationed along the coast and they kept a particularly close watch on Lagos.

A few days before my arrival in Africa, Kosoko, the last scion of Kabutu's line, was on the throne. He is still alive today, but is dethroned and in exile. It has pleased nature to shape in him the true model of an African king. He is tall, of Herculean stature, and endowed with uncommon muscular strength, a quality which is greatly prized in these countries, and which excites the admiration of his subjects and makes him the more respected and revered by all who come into his presence; his bearing is proud and dignified without lacking graciousness and he knows how to maintain the majesty of command in all his attitudes; his features without being regular are rather fine and he can, when he pleases, express his inmost feelings or else remain silent and impassive according to the circumstances. His eyes are black and lively, his gaze is acute, and when he looks into the face of the person he is speaking to, he bores into his heart and easily discovers his secrets. In addition to these physical qualities he has indomitable courage, a strength of character which overcomes any obstacle and will not allow him to be beaten by ill-fortune, and an intelligence and penetration, not only superior to that of the people around him but which can also compete favourably with that of the Europeans who come into contact with him.

If he had been educated in the Arts and Sciences, Kosoko would have been a distinguished man, even in Europe. In Africa among the natives he is, without comparison, an exceptional person.

When he was still a youth, his father died and he had to contest the throne with his cousin, Akitoye, who, taking advantage of the inexperience of the direct heir and relying on the custom by which the collateral heirs of the dead king inherited, claimed the throne against the will of the people, who detested him. Kosoko was rapidly joined by a group of supporters and lost no time in attacking the usurper. After a fierce struggle he succeeded in chasing Akitoye away from the island and forced him to take refuge in Badagry, an ancient little town forty miles west of Lagos. There lived in Badagry at that time an English missionary called Gollmer who, through the intermediary of the English Consul in Fernando Po and the commander of the English squadron, had requested Kosoko's permission to settle on the island and start a mission. Kosoko, having a poor opinion of Europeans who wasted time over religious missions and other matters not concerned with the slave trade, withheld his permission. The missionary then took advantage of King Akitoye's exile to put his religious plans into effect. In Badagry he made friends with the King and promised him that the English authorities would help him to regain his throne if he would allow a mission to be started on the island and the slave trade to be abolished. Akitoye, like all dethroned kings, was full of promises and the missionary started at once to negotiate with the English Consul at Fernando Po and the Commander of the Fleet.[13]

Kosoko, however, once he was peacefully established again on the paternal throne, had followed the example of his ancestors and concentrated all his mental energy, all his knowledge and all his attention on his favourite passion, the slave trade, which had become for him an art, a science and one might almost say a sensual pleasure. His principles in this respect were quite inflexible; to him slavery was by natural law a political institution hallowed by religion, and the sale of human beings was the finest prerogative of his crown and absolutely essential to his state. Anyone who argued against these principles became his personal enemy and no reasoning could prevail against his deep-rooted convictions.

The commercial ventures of Kosoko and Company were in full swing when one fine morning there appeared off Lagos some long boats of the British Royal Navy flying the white flag of truce and manned by a few sailors and some officers. One of these was the bearer of a dispatch from the Consul at Fernando Po, who in agreement with the Commander of the English fleet of cruisers in these waters called upon the King of Lagos to adhere to the treaties made by the European Powers for the abolition of the slave trade. Despite having already heard the content of this message from the Portuguese slavers before it was handed to him, Kosoko was at first amazed and bewildered for he failed to understand how the Europeans could dare to put an end to his *honest* trade or restrict his sovereign powers. Then he became more and more angry and in a fit of brutal rage, without waiting for the message or considering the nature of a messenger (sacred among all civilized people and even respected by barbarian nations) he ordered his soldiers to open fire on the long-boats. This order was immediately carried out and a few sailors and some officers were killed.[14]

---

[13] Cf. Smith, *Lagos Consulate*, pp. 14–26, for the dynastic troubles in the Lagos kingship and the origins of the British intervention, and also the Introduction above, note 2. Akitoye and Kosoko seem to have been uncle and nephew respectively rather than cousins. The consul was John Beecroft and the fleet was commanded by Commodore Fanshawe R. N. and later by Captain H. W. Bruce R. N. The Rev. C. A. Gollmer was a German born member of the Anglican Church Missionary Society (CMS) and presumably a former Lutheran.

[14] Scala's account summarizes, inaccurately, the first of the two British assaults on Lagos. This, on 25 November 1851, ended in the withdrawal of the British force of 306 officers and men, which had been conveyed across the bar of the river (or lagoon entrance) in the paddle-steamer *Bloodhound* towing twenty boats and preceded by a naval gig with Consul Beecroft and Commander Wilmot R. N. on board. In the attack two officers were killed and twelve of the force wounded.

To mark this memorable feat of arms, even more to show his hatred and contempt for the English, the King ordered that the head of one of the murdered officers be cut off and preserved as a trophy in the main hall of his palace. On ceremonial occasions this mournful relic was to be brought with great pomp before the king's seat and served as a footstool whenever he deigned to rest his feet upon it.

So hateful a violation of civil law could not long remain unpunished. Admiral Bruce lost no time in sending his ultimatum, expressed in clear and concise terms: solemn reparations for the injury to the British flag; the treaties to be accepted within 24 hours, or else bombardment of the town. So as not to expose any more of his soldiers to a certain death, he put his ultimatum into a bottle which he placed inside a cask and threw it into the river and in a short time it was carried to Lagos by the current, which on this coast always flows from west to east. There it was picked up by the inhabitants and taken to the King. The ultimatum, written in English, was translated by a Portuguese slave trader and when the King had heard its content he immediately prepared for the defence of his kingdom, determined to finish once and for all with English power, the enemy of his trade.

He barricaded the roads of the town and fortified the entrance with ramparts made of earth or rubble. He had arrow slits made in all the huts overlooking the river and in his own palace, where he assembled his bravest warriors. But his main defence, which was to annihilate the naval power of England, was a battery facing the lagoon from where the English would have to advance. It was hidden by bushes and trees which had been cut down, and consisted of the five or six rusty pieces of artillery which formed his entire arsenal. Thus prepared, King Kosoko awaited his enemy with calm and confidence.

On 25 December 1851 the English fleet entered the Lagos lagoon but because of the solemn nature of the day the attack was deferred until the next morning.

Early in the morning Kosoko's soldiers were all at their assigned posts and with their eyes fixed on the lagoon they awaited the first burst of fire from the English, impatient to measure their strength against the Whites, if indeed they dared to attack. It was already 10 am and there was no sign of the enemy. The Whites were afraid, so it was rumoured throughout the town, and the most impatient warriors wanted to get into their canoes and go out and destroy the enemy wherever they might be, when suddenly an extraordinary sight made these warriors change their minds and somewhat dampened their ardour. Instead of coming up in their canoes as was the custom of the country, the English had been so impolite as to appear in front of Lagos in three gunboats: this was quite unexpected and not very easy to explain in a place where they had never been seen before. At the sight of these great machines which moved without oars or sails, broke through the water with an infernal noise and belched out a long column of smoke, the black men turned white and gazed at one another speechless as they had no words to explain such a marvel. It was obvious to them that these machines were some great magic thought up by the English wizards for the damnation of the Blacks, and thus they came to the immediate conclusion that, whilst it was shameful for a soldier to desert his post in the face of the enemy, it was quite legitimate for any soldier, even one of Kosoko's warriors, to retreat honourably and with a clear conscience when confronted with supernatural powers against which any human force would be in vain. This decision, without being put into words, was reached almost as if by magic, simultaneously and with the speed of electricity by all the men at the barricades, the arrow slits, and the battery, and in the twinkling of an eye they acted upon it with a speed that proved the good faith of these brave soldiers.

So all over the island the defenders of Lagos could be seen, without arms or clothing, either throwing themselves into their canoes or swimming to safety, abandoning women, children, King and country to the good offices of the enemy. It was, therefore, an easy matter for the English with their cannon fire, to destroy the king's palace and so to avenge the insult to their flag and the sanctity of the international laws which had been so rudely violated by these barbarians.[15]

King Kosoko, furious and ashamed at his soldiers' desertion, wanted to bury himself under the ruins of his palace, but a handful of his men who had remained faithful to him dragged him from there and took him aboard the canoes which lay ready in the channel, together with his wives and the few treasures they were able to gather up in their haste.

The fugitives made for Ape [Epe] in Gebù [Ijebu], about sixty miles East of Lagos, where they were soon joined by almost the whole of the population of the island, who preferred exile to the government which the English wished to impose on them.

[15] Lagos had proved to be more strongly defended than the attackers expected, Kosoko's troops, according to the consular reports, having some forty pieces of artillery which were apparently well used. Thus, after their repulse on 25 November the British had spent a month in preparing their second attack. This took place on 26–27 December, to coincide with a march towards Lagos from Badagry of Akitoye, Kosoko's uncle and exiled predecessor on the throne, with a small army of followers. The result was the destruction of much of the town and the flight down the lagoon of Kosoko with his leading chiefs and warriors. On 31 December Akitoye, resuming his kingship, signed a treaty with the British representatives in which he undertook to suppress the slave trade. Scala's exciting account of the two battles accords only in the broadest sense with that given in the British Parliamentary and Foreign Office (consular) papers which do not mention, for example, such details as the display of the murdered officer's head or the ultimatum consigned to a bottle. See Smith, *Lagos Consulate*, chapter 2, and (for the treaty) Appendix A.

The English, certain of victory and having foreseen that Kosoko would either flee or be taken prisoner or be killed, had taken on board his rival, the dethroned Akitoye, the protégé of the missionary Gollmer. They set him down on the island and he took possession of his former kingdom, now reduced to a deserted heap of rubble. He was a weak character, easily led by the people around him and lacking the qualities required to reign over a rough and wild people. Despised by everyone and considered moreover as a usurper he tried in tried in vain by repeated messages and promises of all kinds to persuade those who had fled from Lagos to return to their town and rebuild their homes. His pleas went unheeded and there remained on the island only a very few inhabitants, mostly old men and women who had not been strong enough to follow Kosoko and who were living in appalling poverty.

So it was in these critical circumstances that I arrived in Lagos and to tell the truth the time could not have been more opportune for me to put into practice what I had envisaged. The English, by destroying Lagos, had also destroyed the traffic in slaves which was carried on between the interior and this island and had made the slave trade impossible on these shores at least for a long time to come. But had they destroyed the cause of the Slave Trade and substituted for it another trade, another source of livelihood for this population? Was it not to be feared that once the English troops had gone away the inhabitants would resume their former operations or transfer their trading posts to some other point on the coast, as in fact happened in Porto Novo, which became, after the bombardment, the modern Lagos?

The agents of the English Government in their work of destruction had given no thought to these questions, which however deserved some attention, or else they had thought any solution was impossible for the present, or so at least I decided in the course of conversations which I had on the spot with some distinguished people of this nation. My arrival in Lagos removed all doubt and proved the possibility of a remedy against an evil which had persisted for centuries past.

When I had arrived at the mouth of the river Lagos and before I continued my advance towards the island I went on board the English brig, *Harlequin*, which was stationed there under the command of Captain Willmouth [Commander Wilmot] in order to obtain authorization to land and assistance in off-loading my cargo. There were on board at that moment King Akitoye and two other tribal chiefs. These were secret partisans of Kosoko, as I found out later on, who had been sent by him to the new King for the express purpose of keeping him firmly under surveillance and betraying him at the first available opportunity. They had already insinuated themselves very skilfully into his favour and were following to the letter the secret instruction of their former ruler.

The Captain of the *Harlequin* greeted me with a true sailor's frank and cordial courtesy, and then asked the reason for my visit. I explained to him in detail the object of my voyage and the project which I had formed to establish myself in Lagos and set up a business, trading in the country's natural products as a substitute for the Slave Trade. Captain Wilmot listened to me with the greatest kindness and praised my intentions, and he seemed not a little surprised at the temerity of my plans and informed me that this was not a propitious time for putting them into execution. The bombardment of Lagos, he told me, had excited to the utmost the Blacks' hatred of the Whites and if one of the latter were to appear at this moment on the island he could not fail to be massacred.

Some Portuguese who had been there for a long time and were very well regarded by the Blacks as supporters of and accomplices in their chosen trade, had been unable to follow King Kosoko in his flight, and were put to death by the inhabitants. Much less safe would be a white man's merchandise if it fell into the hands of a starving people. They would throw themselves upon it like a pack of wolves. King Akitoye had neither the authority nor the strength to maintain order and protect the lives of his subjects or any foreigners; without soldiers, without arms and without money, the only way he could make his orders effective was by relying on the support of two or three chiefs who had subjected themselves to him and whose loyalty was more than suspect. The island was in a state of complete anarchy and at any moment an invasion by Kosoko was expected, taking advantage of the departure of the British fleet to regain his lost throne. These reasons given to me so kindly by the English Captain, although they made a serious impression on me, nevertheless did not move me from my intentions. On the contrary I became more than ever convinced that now was the time to act so that the evils threatening these people might be remedied. The Captain entertained me on board that day and I lunched with King Akitoye, the black chiefs and some other officers of the English navy.

King Akitoye, who was racking his brains to find any possible means of keeping his few subjects alive, threatened as they were with death by hunger, greeted my plan with joy and assured me of his royal protection whatever might happen to me. The English Captain did not make any further objections seeing that I was determined to carry out my plans and not only granted me the permission I had requested but also very kindly put at my disposal three boats with cannon to protect my ship, so the next day, 2nd February, I reached Lagos on board the *Felicità* and unloaded my cargo, consisting of 150 casks of rum, 1,000 rolls of tobacco, a large quantity of all kinds of foodstuffs and manufactured articles.

The wretched appearance of this town destroyed by cannon and fire made the saddest impression on me. One could see only the odd inhabitant here and there, wandering among the rubble of the houses to dig out food and other articles which had been abandoned by those who had fled. When I arrived everyone rushed to the beach and I was able to ascertain that out of 22,000 inhabitants of this town only 5 or 6 thousand remained. Most of them were old men, women and young children unable to face the hardships of the long journey they would have had to make if they followed Kosoko. There were extremely few young, strong men. After the advice of the English Commander I expected an unfavourable welcome as I landed in the midst of a people who were so angry with the Whites; I must however admit that the behaviour of the natives towards me was absolutely peaceful and even friendly. King Akitoye had let it be known before my arrival that a European trader was going to settle on the island with a cargo of the goods which they liked most, and instead of demanding slaves would be content to exchange his merchandise for the natural products of the country. This rumour was, at first, though to be a trick of Akitoye's to gain popularity and was not believed by the natives; the wits of the town were asking facetiously what other kinds of products Africa could offer to appeal to the cupidity of the Europeans who were eager only for slaves? But when I arrived and confirmed that I wished to exchange my foodstuffs, rum and tobacco for palm oil or the fruits from which it is extracted and which are so abundant on the island, their incredulity turned to astonishment and their astonishment into the greatest joy. It was not long before men and women were rushing from all around to bring me their products and exchange them for my foodstuffs which they so badly needed.

King Akitoye, delighted beyond measure with these first experiments, hurriedly sent message after message to those who had fled from Lagos, informing them of the fortunate trade which was being carried on in the island and inviting them to return. Attracted by the idea of a new trade which was easier and more lucrative than the former one and moved also by their natural desire to return to their homeland and their dear ones, they gradually began to come back in considerable numbers and to re-build their homes so that in a short time the town took on a more animated and cheerful appearance. These poor natives were very puzzled to know what use would be made by the white trader of all the palm oil accumulated in his store.

On 3rd March, that is about a month after my arrival, the veil which covered the white man's mystery was lifted. On that day I loaded onto the *Felicità* as many barrels of palm oil as I could to send them back to London to the address of Messrs. Cotesworth Powell & Co., explaining that these barrels of palm oil would be exchanged in Europe for barrels of foodstuffs, rum and tobacco which would be sent to me in Lagos for the continuation of my trade; the greater the cargo of oil which I sent to

Europe, the greater would be the cargo of European goods to arrive in Lagos. I added, moreover, that this legitimate and honest trade, far from being opposed by the English as the Slave Trade had been, would on the contrary be favoured and protected by them and consequently Lagos would never again have to fear bombardment or hostile acts from the white men's ships.

This idea produced a true revolution in the social life of these people. It revealed to them the treasures of their land which had up till now been unknown and neglected and it gave them new ideas, new habits and new occupations. People who had been leading a life of idleness every day of the year except when they suddenly became involved in the operations of the Slave Trade, gave themselves to the cultivation of the land and gathered the fruits of the palm tree so as to extract oil from them. But as the products of the island alone would not have been sufficient to supply the needs of the trade, others left for the inland provinces where there were many more plantations of oil palms, in order to come to an agreement with the rulers or tribal chiefs and persuade them to take part in the oil trade. The chiefs of these provinces, which had also been ruined by the interruption of the Slave Trade because of the events in Lagos, gladly took advantage of this opportunity to re-establish their fortunes, devoted themselves to the new trade, and in a short time the old slave markets became palm oil trading centres.

Even the Portuguese slave traders who had followed Kosoko in his flight, now that they found it impossible to carry on their trade, were obliged to mend their ways and become legitimate and honest traders in goods instead of men.

The tree which produces the fruits from which the palm oil is extracted is a palm not unlike a date palm in shape, size and foliage except that its branches have many long thorns. The fruit is a kind of pine-cone covered with a woody skin, oval shaped like a pineapple, about 6 inches thick and 9 inches long, and containing a number of nuts, each about the size of an almond, lying one on top of the other like the seeds in our pomegranates. These nuts contain a kernel covered with a pulpy skin from which the oil is extracted.

The natives gather the fruits from the trees and extract the nuts which they then pound in special mortars to separate the outer cortex from the kernel; they then boil the cortex in great pots of water; then they separate the oil which they collect and put it into casks. This is used for domestic purposes, either for cooking or for anointing their bodies, a common practice in these lands. The kernels are then thrown into the fire and burnt until they carbonize. Then, when they have been ground (as we grind coffee), they are boiled once again until they give an oil of an inferior quality called palm nut oil. The best quality oil is greenish yellow in colour and is much sought after in Europe for the manufacture of candles and soap and it is also used in steamships; the second quality, though less sought after, serves various purposes and still finds a ready market.

The regions near Lagos which are most abundant in palm trees are those of Ijebu to the east and Orobo [Yoruba],[16] within whose boundaries lies Abeokuta to the north; but the oil is only manufactured there for internal consumption and export is not envisaged. When I arrived the total oil trade in Lagos and its hinterland was small in proportion to the production in the whole of the rest of Africa. Annual exports amounted to about 10,000 tons. Today commercial statistics show an annual export of 100 thousand tons and this export could reach 200,000 tons or more if shipping in these waters was not hampered by so many rigorous inspections.[17]

The development of this industry and trade, which must inevitably be followed by agriculture and trade in other natural products still unknown, has meant the beginning of a new era for the people of Lagos, a step towards civilization and the abolition of the slave trade. If one single person of limited means has been able to change in a short time the life of a town like Lagos, who can fail to be aware of the miracles which might be performed by the concerted actions of a large-scale private enterprise with the support of European governments?

---

[16] In modern usage Ijebu, or Ijebuland, is a part of Yorubaland (or, in the phrase used by the missionaries, 'the Yoruba country').

[17] It is not clear whether Scala's figures refer only to exports from Lagos. If so, they must be much exaggerated. According to Consul Campbell, exports of palm oil from Lagos in 1857 were just under 5000 tons. See chapters IV, p. 43 and note 6, and VI, p. 70 and note 10.

III

MADAME TINUBU

For several months I had the sole monopoly of the new trade in Lagos, supplied more and more from the surrounding provinces which had devoted themselves to the production of oil with alacrity and diligence. While my affairs prospered wonderfully, I also had the consolation of being idolized by these people and blessed as a good fetish fallen from the skies to alleviate their present misfortunes. My monopoly did not, however, last.[1] When the English Consul at Fernando Po realized that Lagos had become an important centre for the export of palm oil and that this palm oil was of better quality than had hitherto been known and exported from other places on the coast, he immediately sent Mr Fraser, English Vice-Consul at Whydah, to explore the ground and to facilitate this lucrative trade for his compatriots. In fact, in the course of the year (1852) some English and Hamburg trading posts were set up in Lagos, and English, American, Dutch, French and Sardinian ships arrived here, all drawn by the needs of the growing trade. Finally when the commercial importance of Lagos, had grown beyond measure, the British Government decided to establish a Consul General here and sent to fill this position Mr Benjamin Campbell, a man of intelligence, sensitivity and of exceptional character who was respected by the natives and the Europeans.[2]

---

[1] Scala's claim to a monopoly of trade cannot be accepted even for his early months at Lagos. On 28th February 1852, four weeks after his arrival, five European merchants had already concluded a commercial agreement with Oba Akitoye, providing a scale of customs duties on imports and exports to be paid to the Oba. Of these five merchants, two were British, one an Austrian subject, one a Portuguese, and one a Hamburger; Scala was evidently excluded. See Smith, *Lagos Consulate*, pp. 36, 151 note 13.

[2] The British consulate at Lagos (which was never a consulate-general) was founded as an offshoot from the consulate for the Bights of Benin and Biafra then at Fernando Po. Consul Beecroft sent Louis Fraser in his rank as vice-consul to open up Lagos in November 1852. Fraser was replaced there in July 1853 by Benjamin Campbell who was appointed as full consul. See Smith, *Lagos Consulate*, chapters 4, 5 and 6; Lynn, 'Consul and Kings'; and Introduction above, note 15.

Everything went as well as it possibly could and the Slave Trade seemed to be entirely abandoned and almost forgotten by the natives, but this state of affairs was more apparent than real. The chiefs of the interior, especially Kosoko,[3] could not easily bring themselves to renounce a habit which had been inveterate for centuries and which was sanctioned by their customs and by international laws and was not contrary to their morals and religion. The slave trade therefore continued, tacitly, on a small scale and at rare intervals, it is true, but it still continued. One change only had been made in the sale of human flesh and was making it easier. So as not to arouse the attention of the Europeans living in Lagos, the chiefs of the interior had transformed the sending of slaves to the embarkation points into a rustic idyll. From time to time one saw early in the morning on the hill tops opposite the island, groups of black men and women carrying on their heads baskets of fruit and vegetables or pots of palm oil. Seen from afar they were the 'Melibei' and 'Amarilli'[4] of the district going to the neighbouring town to sell their agricultural produce. When examined more closely the scene was quite different and the idyll took on the gloomy colours of an elegy. The neighbouring town was usually Porto Novo, situated on N. Lat. 8.22, E. Long. 2.30 which they reached after a wearisome march, day after day over crags and swamps. Once the Melibei and Amarilli had arrived there they were relieved of their fruits and vegetables, put into chains and thrown indiscriminately into underground pits until the day came to load them onto the slave ships. In these prisons they were abandoned, often for a long time, to all the torments of hunger, thirst and the inclemency of the weather, decimated by typhoid and yellow fever and too weak to bear the hardships of the long voyage to America. Fortunate indeed were those shipments which managed to arrive at their destination without losing 60% of these wretched people.

And the clandestine trade was carried on not only by the chiefs of the interior but by Akitoye himself, protégé of the English and pupil of Gollmer, the King who had solemnly sworn to abolish the Slave Trade in his Kingdom and, having signed the treaty drawn up by the European powers, wasted no time in starting his own commercial speculations in partnership with two other chiefs, ex-partisans of Kosoko, called Ajenia and Possu.[5]

[3] Kosoko had settled in Ijebu territory at Epe on the northern shore of the eastern lagoon, where he created a miniature state of his own (the Ijebu being apparently acquiescent), with its port at Palma (now Orimedu). For his career, see Smith, *Lagos Consulate, passim*, and G.O. Oguntomisin, 'New Forms of Political Organisation in Yorubaland in the Mid-Nineenth Century: a Comparative Study of Kurunmi's Ijaye and Kosoko's Epe', Ph.D. thesis, University of Ibadan, 1979.

[4] Meliboeus was the shepherd who found the abandoned infant Oedipus; Amaryllis is the name for a country girl used by Theocritus, Virgil and Ovid. This display of classical allusion is almost certainly owed to Scala's literary aide Federico Campanella.

[5] For these chiefs, previous adherents of Kosoko, see references in Smith, *Lagos Consulate*.

King Akitoye, weak and voluptuous by nature, was entirely dominated by the beautiful TINUBU to whom he had given over the government of his Kingdom, the command of his army and the control of all his public and private affairs. While he spent his days in idleness and ignoble orgies in his royal palace, Tinubu reigned in his stead and with her intelligence, energy and activity was able to cope with all the most difficult affairs of state, and proved herself in every way worthy of the throne. Her authority was, in fact, respected and feared by everyone.

Tinubu[6] was *Orobana* [Yoruba] by birth and while still a child had been sold as a slave to the chief of the Ohù [Owu] tribe living in Abeokuta, who treated her and loved her like his own daughter, as was not rare in this country with its patriarchal customs. From the time of childhood she showed no uncertain signs of a precocious intellect and extraordinary strength of character for her age. With her youthful charm she very soon won the heart of her owner and became the idol of the people who willingly yielded to all the whims of the wilful child. Her lack of education and the general servility with which she was treated did not take long to develop in her the seeds of that boundless ambition which became the most important characteristic of her life. Devoured by an overwhelming need to dominate and convinced of her incontestable superiority over the people around her, she very soon came to cherish the idea of rising from the rank of slave to that of a queen, in no matter of what place and by no matter the means. This delightful dream, so cherished in her youth, she still entertained, although the ravages of time and the vicissitudes of a stormy life had diminished her chief means of realizing it, her seductive charms. However, as the years went by she had developed both her personal graces and her mental powers.

Tinubu was tall, slender and well proportioned; her bearing was proud and majestic but not lacking in grace and subtlety; she had the art of expressing by various movements of her body and by all her postures an indescribable voluptuousness which few could resist. The lines of her face were not at all delicate or regular; her nose was rather thick with very wide nostrils, her lips were full, her mouth large and her eyebrows very

---

[6] Scala's (doubtless romanticized) account of Madame Tinubu should be supplemented and amended by reference to Smith, *Lagos Consulate*, and to Oladipo Yemitan, *Madame Tinubu, Merchant and Kingmaker*, 1987, both *passim*. Briefly, she appears to have lived from c. 1805 to 1887, to have been an Egba by birth from the Gbagura district (though with maternal connections with Owu, a town to the east of the Egba Forest), to have been married three times (including marriage to Oba Adele), and to have been expelled from Lagos at least twice possibly in 1845, then in 1853 and 1856. During her stormy career, which involved clashes with the traditional and consular authorities in Lagos, the different groups of merchants there (native, 'repatriate', European, and Brazilian), and the Christian missionaries, she succeeded as a trader in amassing great wealth.

thin: nevertheless these features, combined with two large, black, brilliant eyes which had the fascination of a serpent, and two rows of very white teeth formed a wonderfully harmonious example of African beauty which was immediately pleasing and which continued to hold the beholder's gaze for a long time. It is not therefore surprising that this extraordinary woman, endowed with so many natural gifts and with an uncommon intelligence, soon came to lord it over those rough men and to find numerous supporters and admirers throughout the tribes.

When her first master died, Tinubu, a girl of about 13 years old, had no difficulty in making his legitimate heir Abburaka, the new chief of the tribe and owner of great wealth, fall in love with her. He married her and became enslaved by his slave! This marriage was her first step towards the throne, towards the realization of her ambitious dreams. It should, in itself, have made a woman of her condition happy, but Tinubu was aiming higher and was only mildly pleased to be married to a simple prince and a vassal of the King of Abeokuta. Even before her honeymoon was over, she took a dislike to her husband and to the ties of married life and immediately thought how to get rid of these hateful obstacles which thwarted her ambitions. She began to imagine thousands of strange plots to arrive at her end and finally she threw herself onto that road of adventure and crime which she was to follow for most of her life. Abburaka loved his young wife with a possessive love, the only kind he knew, and he watched over her with the jealousy of a miser. He was a colossal man, a kind of African Polyphemus, whose intelligence was all confined to the nerves of his terrible fist which was strong enough to slay an ox. Against a husband endowed with such fine qualities, an open fight was neither prudent nor possible. Tinubu had to act with care and discretion. But the obstacle of a husband, not insurmountable, even for European women, was for her a simple matter, a pastime and a relaxation. When her plan had matured in her mind she lost no time in putting it into action.

One day the young wife, wishing to relieve the monotony of domestic life, suggested a pleasure trip to the amiable Abburaka, and this was to go to a place on the coast with a troop of 300 slaves and sell them to a slave ship which had arrived there and was ready to buy them. Abburaka could not refuse his wife such an innocent entertainment and gave orders for the expedition. The slaves were collected and the great wooden yokes prepared which would shackle them in pairs by the neck and make any attempt to escape during the journey impossible.

Warriors were chosen to escort the illustrious party and Tinubu took care to pick from them the youngest and strongest men of the tribe among whom, naturally, she had not a few supporters and sincere admirers. These young warriors were eager to prove themselves in the service of their beautiful mistress and seemed sure that their services would be rewarded, and probably Tinubu's eyes had suggested to them the nature of this reward as well. On the arranged day the party set out early in the morning: the procession was led by a chosen group of soldiers armed with those long carbines which were used in Europe two or three centuries ago, then came Abburaka and Tinubu, each lying in a litter slung on two long poles and borne by four slaves. They were attended by numerous servants, men and women dedicated to their personal service; behind the litters followed many more slaves bearing food, kitchen utensils, mats and other domestic necessities and at the end of the procession came another group of young soldiers armed with arrows and swords. Some distance behind followed slowly and painfully the 300 slaves who were to be sold. They were almost strangled by the fetters round their necks which made their progress very difficult; they were surrounded moreover by many guards with muscles like oxen, who whipped them continuously and without mercy, either to goad them on or to stifle their complaints and their pleas.

The journey continued without incident, except that from time to time Abburaka, to amuse himself or to punish some small misdeed, lightheartedly let the weight of his fist fall on the slaves near him, breaking a rib or a jaw here and there and roaring with laughter at the poor wretches' contortions. But this pastime was so natural to Abburaka that no one in the party paid the slightest attention to it.

When they reached their destination Abburaka and Tinubu stepped down from their litters while the slaves set up the canopy which was to shelter them. Then they laid down tiger skins on which they placed two giraffe skin cushions for the royal couple. Some soldiers took up their positions around the tent while others occupied the most important entrances to the site.

The slaves took off the yokes which were strangling them and lay down on the ground to rest. A little way from the tent under a palm tree a lower seat was placed for the illustrious guest who was to come and buy them.

After about half an hour's wait the slave trader arrived followed by his sailors. They too were armed to the teeth with guns, swords and daggers (an evident proof of the confidence which each of the contracting parties had in the other). The trader advanced majestically towards the tent and greeted the royal pair, striking his breast with one hand and keeping the other firmly clenched on his sword. Abburaka replied to his greeting and with a polite smile indicated his merchandise to the trader with a wave of the hand. The trader glanced at them without much interest and replied condescendingly 'we shall see'. Meanwhile he invited the prince and princess to taste some bottles of choicest rum which he had brought with him to render the negotiations less tedious. Abburaka accepted with whatever grace he had and even Tinubu expressed her gratitude to the trader while looking knowingly at her most faithful warriors almost as if to say 'Be prepared'. After the first rather generous libations, the trader, accompanied by Abburaka, inspected the 300 slaves who were lying on the ground and carefully examined them one by one, sitting, as was customary, on the chest of the adults, men and women, to test their breathing, their strength and their health. Those who passed this test were set apart and after a slight altercation over their price boarded the slave ship. As this first operation had taken a long time, the trader requested Abburaka to take a short rest and have another drink of rum. The Prince graciously acceded to such a reasonable request and one which had been made in such respectful terms. More bottles were broached and emptied. Tinubu seemed pleased with this confused scene and was at some pains to be the life and soul of the party. She lifted to her lips the cup of rum which her husband had given her, and then immediately handed it to her husband who tossed it back with evident delight. The heartening liquor began to have its usual effect. Already Abburaka's mind was wandering, his speech becoming somewhat slurred, his gestures uncoordinated. The slaves who were serving him watched with terror every movement of his arm which boded ill for their backs and were careful to anticipate all his wishes with a truly exemplary solicitude. The chief of the Owu people was soon in danger of losing the dignity proper to his rank.

The second negotiation, or shall we say the second batch of slaves, presented greater difficulties. The trader offered a price far below that of the first batch and Abburaka, breathless and furious, demanded the same price as before. Fortunately Tinubu intervened in time to iron out the difference of opinion. With a few cups of rum she calmed the fury of her husband and with her persuasive charm managed to extract a few hundred more *piastres* from the miserly trader, and consequently the second lot went on board.

There still remained about 100 slaves, men and women. These were the 'throw-outs', the old and infirm who would die on the voyage. The trader protested that he did not want such worthless goods which would not stand up to the long journey, but at the most he would agree, he said, to take them on board in order to throw them into the sea after a few days only to get rid of some bales of tobacco which he still had and which he would generously offer in exchange for them. At this Abburaka really became furious and threatened the trader with his fist to teach him that he should respect the Prince's goods. The trader, unmoved by the threat but wishing to finish the deal, made a last effort and added to the tobacco a roll of velvet of such a brilliant scarlet that Tinubu could not resist it and indicated to her husband, with her beautiful black eyes, her longing to possess it. Abburaka, enraged by the fumes of rum and the insulting offer of a derisory price, became more furious than ever and stubbornly refused. Then Tinubu, in a fit of conjugal affection, put her arm around his neck, and offered him a cup of rum, then another and another. Polyphemus looked at her with eyes of lust, drank the rum and burst into stupid, undignified laughter. Then he made a supreme effort to stand up, swayed and fell to the ground like an ox struck by the butcher's axe. Drunkenness had reached its last stage. As swift as a viper underfoot, Tinubu leapt up, looked in disgust at the shapeless lump of flesh stretched out on the ground and after a moment turned calmly to the trader and said in a soft silvery voice 'Oibò' (the Yoruba word for a white man) 'How much will you give me for this man?' (and she pointed to her husband with her foot). The trader, not in the least upset by this scene of conjugal love, looked again at the sturdy limbs of the giant, rapidly counted the amount of work he could do in a day and the price he would get for him on the American markets, and without any hesitation replied 'I'll give you 100 dollars'.

'He's yours'; said Tinubu, kicking her husband and with a whistle she summoned her warriors. At the sight of these fine young men rising from all sides at the command of their beautiful mistress, Tinubu could not help smiling with pleasure and pride. At a sign from her the giant was bound with ropes and carried aboard the slave ship where with great care he was thrown into the depths of the hold.

Passing thus from the arms of Tinubu into those of his fierce guards, from his stool as chief of the Owu tribe to his bench of pain, the unfortunate Abburaka set out the next day across the sea to Cuba among the slaves he had sold who now became his companions in misfortune. *Sic transit gloria mundi.*

As soon as she had taken leave of the trader, Tinubu distributed food and rum among her soldiers and servants and joyfully sat down among them to take part in the feast.

Many were the soldiers who had served her with zeal and devotion and Tinubu could not, in all fairness, choose only one of them to reward; like the good and wise mistress that she was she behaved in such a way as to make them all happy; in fact to judge from the general good humour which prevailed among these fine young men, it seemed true to say that there was ample reward for everyone. Happiest of all, however, were the slaves who had been in Abburaka's personal service, who heartily blessed Tinubu for having freed their wretched limbs from the continual threat of dislocation.

When the feast was over, Tinubu loaded her slaves with the goods received in exchange for her husband, barrels of rum, rolls of tobacco, all kinds of cloth and Spanish piastres. Then, surrounded by her warriors, she set out to return to Abeokuta.

Great was the consternation in the Owu tribe when they heard about the mysterious disappearance of their chief and they called for lawful revenge on

Tinubu whom they accused of parricide, but convinced by the absolute reserve of Tinubu's supporters who had been amply rewarded and by the even more resolute silence of those who still aspired to the prize, the elders of the tribe soon decided that justice had no claim against two beautiful black eyes which could even in certain cases cause a civil war in which the victors might well not be the impotent old men who supported the law.

These considerations gave the elders food for thought and the Tinubu affair was examined more calmly. The proof of her guilt diminished from day to day and her innocence became more evident. In the end, the most politic minds, the *honest* and *moderate* men of the tribe came to offer their most sincere condolences to the unfortunate widow on the premature loss of her husband who had died of phthisis during the journey.

In spite of the good-will of the tribe Tinubu's life in Abeokuta had become unpleasing and one day, when she had converted into cash the great wealth of her husband, led on by her spirit of adventure she set out for Lagos, accompanied by a band of faithful young men, to the court of Akitoye whose reputation for weakness led Tinubu to believe that she could make use of him.

In fact Akitoye was not insensitive to the charms of the beautiful Yoruba and did not take long to fall under their influence. Although he had more than 100 wives, Tinubu won the chief place in his heart, and when he had seen the remarkable intelligence of this woman he handed over to her the reins of government and made her a partner in his slave business which was the favourite passion of them both.

The ambitious woman at last saw the dream of her youth come true; the slave of the Owu had become a queen and ruled despotically over the King and the people of Lagos.[7]

When Kosoko took up arms against Akitoye to drive him off the throne he had usurped, Tinubu had but recently arrived in the island and, not being prepared, could not offer the rigorous resistance which at another time her courage and perception would have suggested. Indifferent to her lover although he was a King, she wanted before resigning herself to the loss of her exalted position, to try any method of harnessing the winner to her chariot, but perceiving that the character of the young Kosoko was quite different from that of Akitoye she felt it prudent to remain faithful to the latter while waiting for a better fate and so followed him into exile at

---

[7] Consular reports describe Tinubu as 'niece' to Oba Akitoye. Yemitan does not mention either this or her association with Oba Akitoye. He does, however, agree that her first husband was an Owu man (*Madam Tinubu*, pp. 3, 7), presumably from the Owu quarter in Abeokuta, but implies that the marriage, although producing two sons (who died young), was of short duration. There is no confirmation of Scala's story of Abburaka and his unhappy fate.

Badagry. There she was at the centre of the plots hatched by the missionary Gollmer and the English agents to substitute Akitoye for Kosoko in the government of Lagos. When she returned with Akitoye to the throne after the bombardment of the island her first thought was to recruit a small army composed of her supporters who would face the invasions of Kosoko and the internal troubles which he would probably have provoked, and in order to demonstrate her authority, she herself commanded them.

The aims of this ambitious young woman were once again realized and she was enjoying all the delights of power when the sin which had caused the ruin of Kosoko, led to her own downfall as well.

Tinubu could not stop being a trader. To advance her slaving business she had created the rustic idylls described above and her ingenious invention was for a long time crowned with the happiest success. The English authorities on the island had, however, their suspicions of this clandestine traffic and remonstrated about it with Akitoye and Tinubu, but they were unable to prove that these two were behind it. They declared that they were as pure as snow and they were naively believed to be so for a long time. Then it happened that a slave trader called Domingo,[8] who had done not a little business with Tinubu in the past, with satisfactory results for them both, quarrelled with her about a transport of living merchandise which had arrived in a state of weariness at Porto Novo. The honest Domingo had asked for a 100% repayment of the price they had agreed upon, but the proud Tinubu, rather than debase her slaves to such an extent, ordered her agent in Porto Novo to drown them in the sea. The disappointed trader, irritated by Tinubu, sought revenge. He had his satellites tie up both the agent and the slaves and took them by canoe to Lagos where he brought them before the English Consul. The offence could not be denied and Mr Fraser was able to take firm action.

King Akitoye was given the alternative of either confessing that he had violated the treaty to which he had solemnly sworn adherence, or seeking out and punishing those guilty of the crime. Naturally he preferred the second course, and thinking that he could escape from the situation by throwing all the blame on his partners, Chiefs Ajenia and Possu, he ordered that they should be immediately arrested and tried. The two Chiefs found this excessive and against all the laws of a well regulated partnership that their partner should share in the profits but not in the losses of the company, so they rallied their supporters and prepared to resist. Poor Akitoye had the mortification of seeing that his partners' supporters were more numerous than his own soldiers, since Tinubu had not yet succeeded in organizing

---

[8] This is the well-known Brazilian slaver Domingo Martinez, who had backed Akitoye's attempts to regain the Lagos throne from Kosoko in 1846 and 1848.

her little army. As a result, his orders remained without the salutary sanction commonly called *ratio regum*. However, encouraged by the English Consul and the missionary Gollmer, he sent his troops to lay siege to the houses where the two chiefs had taken refuge, threatening them with fire and ruin if they did not give themselves up. The people of Lagos were extremely agitated by these events and, as they were divided into several parties, a tribal war seemed inevitable, a catastrophe imminent, when by a stroke of luck the announcement that an English warship would shortly be arriving in Lagos waters had the effect of the *Deus ex Machina* of Antiquity and thus dissipated, almost by magic, the fearful tempest. The three good partners came to an honest agreement between them to save their personal interests and to nominate Tinubu as the victim to be sacrificed for the violated treaty. The cowardly monarch in order to save his crown abandoned his concubine to the just resentment of the English Consul and at his insistence he banned her for ever from the island after declaring her guilty of the whole traffic in slaves.[9]

Tinubu was certainly guilty but not alone in this and not the most guilty, since she had not signed the treaty. Since she was not yet strong enough to avenge the outrage, she took leave of her royal lover with sorrow on her face and anger in her heart and departed threateningly from the island.

Meanwhile Kosoko, who was anxiously seeking any opportunity to regain his lost throne and who had been secretly informed by his numerous spies, including the two chiefs Ajenia and Possu, of the events on the island, considered that now was the right moment to act with speed and determination. Unexpected and very important help came just at the right time to support him in his plans.

A few days before these events, Tinubu had sent messages and money to Abeokuta to summon the young warriors of the Owu tribe to join her in Lagos and swell the ranks of the small army she had been organizing, and as soon as she had left the island she sent new messages to ask the bravest of them to come to her aid. More than three hundred young men armed with guns, arrows and spears came immediately to Lagos and met the

---

[9] The foregoing is Scala's version of 'the Amadie affair' of May 1853, for which see Smith, *Lagos Consulate*, pp. 46–47 and 154, notes 58, 59, 60. Scala's account may supplement that in the Admiralty and consular papers, in particular by his explanation that Domingo Martinez's action in sending the unfortunate slaves to Vice-Consul Fraser was due to his quarrel with Madame Tinubu, who had been the original owner of the slaves before selling them to the 'Hungarian' Amadie and his partner. The 'English warship' mentioned was probably HMS *Polyphemus*. Scala's statement that Madame Tinubu was sent into exile at this point (May/June 1853) is not confirmed in the British official account although it is supported by Yemitan, *Tinubu*, pp. 36–37. If true, her exile was a short one. Soon after these events Fraser was replaced by Consul Campbell, the handover taking place in July 1853; Smith, *Lagos Consulate*, p. 48.

exiled queen, who was waiting with a handful of her faithful servants between Lagos and Epe.

Impatient to repay the insult she had received from the weakling Akitoye, Tinubu, at the head of her troops, offered to support Kosoko and to share with him the dangers and the glories of their common vengeance. The attack on Lagos was arranged by the male and female captains for the 3rd of September.

It was about 1 o'clock in the afternoon, the sky was covered with cloud when suddenly a strange noise and an extraordinary excitement disturbed all the town of Lagos. There was a frantic rush of terrified people, doors were closed, roads barricaded, angry voices, imprecations, oaths, groans, sobs, an infernal tumult broke loose. The King's palace was in great confusion; courtiers and guards were in despair and the King trembled in their midst with his women, unable to give orders or to take any action. Lagos was in the gravest danger. A large fleet of canoes, taking advantage of the darkness, had quietly come up the channel and was surrounding the island on all sides. Kosoko had managed to land with his troops on the East shore while Tinubu at the head of her warriors was occupying the Western shore and had already advanced to a position not far from the King's palace, an area reserved for his dependants. Kosoko's supporters did not remain idle and, rallying the people to arms, now set out to attack the King's palace, combining their operations with those of the troops from outside.

Now Akitoye realized how greatly he missed Tinubu, the only person who was capable of making decisions in such crises, the only person able by her example to call up the few troops who had remained loyal to him. The *love* of his beloved subjects was too weak a thing for him to count on. Akitoye was hated and his ruin would have been certain had not sudden and unexpected help come to keep the shaky crown on his head. An English warship had been summoned by the English Consul in the early days of the dissension between Akitoye and his associates and it arrived opportunely in Lagos waters just at the very moment when the town was besieged. This was the *Antelope* under the command of Captain Phillips.[10] This unexpected arrival changed the outcome of the battle by making it impossible for Kosoko and Tinubu to attack. The English Consul, moved by Christian charity for the unfortunate townspeople, tried with all his might to prevent useless bloodshed and advised Kosoko and Tinubu to desist from an enterprise which had now become impossible and persuaded King Akitoye not to

[10] This mention of the *Antelope* may be due to a lapse of memory by Scala. The naval ships present during Kosoko's attack in August 1853 were HMSS *Waterwitch* and *Polyphemus*, and possibly HMS *Spray*. See note 11 below.

commit acts of hostility against his enemies. But the missionary Gollmer, anxious to consolidate the insecure power of his protégé and to humble the pride of Kosoko and Tinubu, advised Akitoye (with how much evangelical charity I do not know) against losing this opportunity of undoing his rivals and protecting himself forever from their future attacks. Akitoye, like all cowards, had passed from extreme dejection to extreme pride and from extreme fear to extreme ferocity. He gladly welcomed Gollmer's advice and consequently prepared his soldiers who, reassured by the English cannon, had themselves become brave as lions. Gollmer, having previously come to an agreement with the Captain of the *Antelope*, sent to Akitoye his white handkerchief, the sign which they had agreed upon to start the attack. Akitoye's soldiers opened fire on the enemy troops, who replied bravely, still advancing and gaining ground. Tinubu, at the head of her men, encouraging them by her shouts and by her example, was showing great courage and already had penetrated as far as the palace itself, when a few grapeshot, wonderfully well-aimed at the assailants from conveniently sited English gun-boats, put fear and perturbation into the ranks who quickly fell into disorder and escaped in their canoes.[11]

---

[11] Scala's account of Kosoko's armed attempt to return to Lagos, and presumably to dispossess Akitoye once again of the throne, differs markedly from the consular and missionary reports, all of which were written soon after the events described. The course of these events seems to have been as follows. The first hostilities took place on 6 August 1853 and were precipitated by Akitoye's supporters (possibly encouraged by Gollmer) who opened fire on the compounds of Kosoko's main adherents in the town. Pro-Kosoko forces responded in some strength, directing their main attack on the Oba's palace. Fighting was broken off on the arrival of three boats sent by the cruiser HMS *Waterwitch*. Kosoko, who seems not to have been present in person on the first occasion, returned to the attack on 11 August and hostilities continued across the lagoon into September, after the death of Oba Akitoye. Meanwhile Kosoko was joined at Epe by chiefs Ajenia and Possu. (Their descendants remain there.) See Smith, *Lagos Consulate*, pp. 52–55, with p. 156 for notes 18–25.

IV

WAR AND PEACE WITH KOSOKO

Kosoko and Tinubu took themselves off from the island with angry hearts, cursing the English for having snatched an easy and certain victory from them. Lagos became calm again and the missionary Gollmer,[1] thanks to his recent services and the absence of Tinubu, exercised an absolute influence over the feeble Akitoye and was the real ruler of Lagos. It was not long, however, before the King, undermined by illness brought on by the excesses of a sensual life, died a wretched death, more execrated than mourned by his subjects who hated being dependent on a foreigner.

The same dissension as had broken out on the death of Kosoko's father between heirs of the direct and the collateral lines would have recurred had not the missionary Gollmer been able to manoeuvre most of the chiefs into recognizing Dosunmu, the first-born son of the dead King, as the legitimate heir to the throne. He was living far from the court and leading the life of a fisherman in a village some ten miles from Lagos. We do not know what motives had induced the young prince to abandon his paternal home and to choose this precarious and difficult life instead of the one of pleasure and idleness to which he had been born. Perhaps disgust at the example of the court or the certainty of not inheriting the throne or his father's wealth had determined Dosunmu to go right away so that in good time he could return and take them for himself. However this may be, Gollmer sent one message after another to the prince inviting him to take possession of the vacant throne and when he did not receive any satisfactory answer, persuaded the elders of the people to send a delegation of the wisest and most eloquent among them to overcome his resistance. The elders found

---

[1] The Rev C. A. Gollmer had moved up from Badagry to join the Rev. H. Townsend in Lagos in 1852. By origin a German Lutheran (and possibly an adherent of the Pietist movement) he had been recruited, like other Lutherans, into the CMS specifically for the West African mission. Thus his Anglicanism, like that of Townsend and the CMS in general, was Evangelical. He did attain some influence over the Oba and on Lagos politics, but Scala exaggerates: Consul Campbell, who could when he needed call on the Royal Navy for support, was a more powerful figure.

the Cincinnatus of the sea seated in his boat, with a fish-hook in his hand,
singing a barcarolle. According to etiquette they prostrated themselves and
begged the fisherman to leave his boat and ascend the throne. The fisherman
looked at them for a moment mockingly, then burst out laughing and with
one stroke of his oar rowed away from the beach. Mortified and confused
the elders returned to Gollmer and told him how ungraciously they had
been received by this capricious youth. The missionary, wishing more than
ever to keep the ruling power in the hands of the direct descendants of
Akitoye, was not easily discouraged. He was convinced of the wisdom of
the maxim followed by Loyola's disciples that the end justifies the means,
so he thought he would sanctify the (not too immaculate) means of
Tinubu and direct them to the best possible end. He therefore sent messengers to come to an agreement with her on what was to be done about
this important matter of state as well as on what she was to receive for her
services.

Tinubu, after her flight from Lagos, had followed the fate of Kosoko and
was living the life of dethroned royalty. But used as she was to the splendours
of the court and to being in command, she soon came to hate this wandering
life and even Kosoko himself who, besides not being as manageable as
Akitoye, had the additional defect of not possessing a throne, an indispensable requisite for the love of the beautiful African. In this frame of mind she
jubilantly welcomed Gollmer's proposals which opened the way for her to
return to Lagos and to the court and she immediately set off to see Dosunmu.
History does not relate what arguments Tinubu used to win over the
wayward prince, but they must certainly have been irresistible for two days
later the wild fisherman, meek as a lamb, was led by the witch into Lagos
and proclaimed King by the acclamation of the people. To educate the
new King and keep him in a suitable state of docility, Tinubu agreed with
the Reverend Mr. Gollmer that she should occupy the same position at the
court of the son as she had done at that of the father.[2]

Gollmer was convinced that the island would not be at peace unless the
power of Kosoko was entirely destroyed, and meanwhile Kosoko was hover-
ing about the neighbourhood like a vulture over its prey. Gollmer therefore
set his mind to preparing an expedition to destroy Dosunmu's feared rival.
On his orders, numerous canoes were prepared and as many men as could
be collected called to arms. Tinubu sent about three thousand armed men

---

[2] Succession to the Lagos throne was settled by a system of modified primogeniture, reflecting in
this the Benin origin of the kingship. It is unlikely that either Gollmer or Madame Tinubu
influenced the choice of Dosunmu by the kingmakers to the extent that Scala alleges. Instead
it was Campbell who questioned those chiefs who were among the kingmakers on their
preferences and who probably exercised the greatest influence in the matter. See Smith, *Lagos
Consulate*, pp. 6–7, 55.

from her tribe[3] and these, joined with the soldiers of Lagos, made up a force of more than five thousand men. This force was to be supported by four English gun-boats, sent at Gollmer's instigation by the officer commanding the *Antelope*. On 15th October 1853 the expedition set out under Dosunmu's command from Lagos and advanced in an orderly fashion along the lagoon towards Epe, the chief residence of Kososko. Tinubu did not take part. Although Lagos is geographically only forty miles from Epe, the slow progress of the canoes did not allow them to cover the distance in one day and they had to spend the night about ten miles out of Epe. At dawn the next day the fleet set off again and soon arrived in an orderly line of battle along the enemy shore ready to land. Deep silence reigned over Epe and its environs. No preparations for defence had been made, not a living soul moved, not a sign of alarm could be seen. The town seemed to have been abandoned. A dense forest which protected it on the West threw its shadow over this scene of solitude and added to its sepulchral horror. Dosunmu's soldiers landed and boldly advanced towards the town where they found no defences, and so they thought that the enemy had fled in terror at the very sound of their name. Already the bravest had gone into the main streets and were starting to loot, when a volley of musket shots surprised them from behind, one from the right, another from the left, then another and another from every direction. Kosoko had hidden his soldiers in the thick bush which surrounds Epe, ordering them to shoot the invaders as soon as, avid for booty, they fell out of line to start pillaging. This stratagem, which would have brought a pitying smile to the lips of one of our corporals and which the simplest military precaution would have rendered useless, had not occurred to the good Dosunmu who was mortified beyond all words at being caught, and he a good fisherman, in the enemy net like a stupid fish. Meanwhile the unexpected musket shots had completely routed the undisciplined ranks; they ran to escape in their canoes but were pursued by regular and continuous fire from Kosoko's soldiers who were well controlled and caused havoc among the fragile boats. Many of Dosunmu's men were killed and wounded and perhaps not one would have been saved had not the English, who had stayed in their gun-boats and taken no part in the assault on the town, quelled the enemy fire by their shells and protected the retreating canoes. Even so the English lost two officers and five sailors in this battle.

The deplorable result of the expedition greatly upset the people of Lagos and destroyed the popularity of the King who was accused of inefficiency and

[3] This Egba contingent must be that referred to in Smith, *Lagos Consulate*, pp 55–56 and 157, note 33 as 'sent...by the chiefs of Abeokuta despite Kosoko's attempts to buy over their support'. The reported size of the force varies in the consular correspondence from 4000 to 2000.

cowardice. Gollmer and Tinubu felt the need to repair the damage caused by this terrible disaster and to save by some new and brilliant feat of arms the reputation of their protégé. The commanding officer of the *Antelope*, who had so light-heartedly risked the lives of his men in the ill-fated enterprise, felt it his duty, more than anyone else's, to avenge the insult to the British flag and to preserve the prestige of European armies among these barbarians. A second expedition was decided upon but it was to have a different plan of attack.

The beach situated between the West and the north of Epe was covered with factories[4] belonging to Kosoko and other native chiefs who, it was said, had added oil trading to slave trading. Some belonged also to Portuguese slave-traders, accomplices of Kosoko, and served as depots for both kinds of merchandise. So it was decided to destroy these factories which formed the chief wealth of Kosoko and furnished him with the means of supplying his army. The expedition, directed this time by the English, had the desired success and in a short time the factories were reduced to heaps of smoking rubble. Many of Kosoko's soldiers and five Portuguese slave-traders lost their lives in the fighting.[5]

After this vendetta the thirst for blood seemed to be assuaged in Lagos and the frenzy of the people died down. Tinubu's hordes were paid off and returned to Abeokuta loaded if not with glory at least with loot from the factories; the native troops, however, were reduced in number so as not to overburden the finances of the not too flourishing state. Tinubu governed in the name of Dosunmu who was more infatuated than ever with the beautiful courtesan, and these two aimed to accumulate wealth by means of the palm-oil trade, free for the time being from the hateful traffic in slaves. The missionary Gollmer, dividing his time between the duties of his Holy Ministry and the intrigues of the court, had created a very important position for himself in the island and had even become a powerful rival to Tinubu for the King's good graces.

This period of calm on the island meanwhile allowed trade to be carried on freely again and the unfortunate people were able to feel its benefits to a

---

[4] Scala explains in Chapter VIII below that by *fattorie* he means warehouses which in this case of his own buildings also contained machines for cleaning cotton and presses for extracting palm oil. The term 'factory' is used in this translation for *fattoria*.

[5] There are many discrepancies in the accounts of Kosoko's continued attempts to regain Lagos, or at least a footing there, between Scala's memoirs and the consular, Admiralty and missionary papers. The failure of the British to deal decisively with the threat from Kosoko at this time led to recriminations between the Lagos and the Egba (whose traders had been attacked on the lagoon by Kosoko's war canoes) and between the British consul and the Royal Navy, of which Scala seems unaware. There was also some criticism in the English press of Campbell's proceedings. See Smith, *Lagos Consulate*, pp. 56–58.

great extent. Since my arrival ten European trading firms had been set up in Lagos and they exported annually:

> 10,000 tons of oil
> 1,000 quintals of ivory
> 3,000 bales of cotton
> 1,000 tons of palm-nut oil
> 500 tons of grain and various other goods.[6]

The people dedicated themselves to the new trade with alacrity and it can be estimated that 20% of the inhabitants were occupied in it and drew their means of subsistence from it, a number which increased from day to day.

In the meantime my nomination as Consul-General for Lagos and its hinterland arrived which gave me an official status among these people and entrusted me to the protection of my compatriots. It was not long before I had occasion to begin my diplomatic career.[7]

King Kosoko, after the destruction of his factories, devoted all his energy to recovering his lost fortune by trading in slaves and palm oil. His goods, which came from the interior, had of necessity to be transported along the branch of the Lagos River which led to Abeokuta, in order to be shipped at Porto Novo. So it often happened that Dosunmu's canoes under Tinubu's orders gave chase to those of Kosoko and robbed them while he, to avenge himself, then sought reprisals. These acts of hostility kept alive the anger of the warring parties and called for a decisive battle. Tinubu, unable to bear claimants to a throne which she claimed to be hers by right, secretly prepared the elements of a second expedition more impressive than the first. Having heard of this dark plot I resolved to prevent a catastrophe which could be fatal to the country and without any advantage to either side. To arrive at this end it was necessary to open for Kosoko's trade a safe and easy route, secure from the attacks of his enemies. South of Epe a branch of the Lagos River stretches for about thirty miles, almost forming a lake which is separated from the sea only by a tongue of land a few miles long on which Palma is situated not far from a beach where the ships can draw up. It was fitting therefore to concede to Kosoko the territory between Epe

---

[6] These figures which are attributed to no particular year and whose source is not given, are suspiciously large, especially if, as Scala implies, they refer to the early part of his time in Lagos and Abeokuta. The breakdown of items is, however, interesting. The figures may be compared with those provided by Consul Campbell for 1856 and 1857 which, for example, claim that exports of palm oil from Lagos in those years were 3,884 tons and 4,942 tons respectively. See Smith, *Lagos Consulate*, pp. 76–77.

[7] For Scala's appointment in November 1855 as Sardinian consul, see Introduction, pp. xii–xiii and p. 10 above with note 6.

and the sea, which is almost uninhabited except for Palma which has anyway a small population. By advocating this concession I hoped to be able to induce Kosoko to renounce his right to Lagos, to found a new Kingdom, to settle down and dedicate himself to the arts of peace. I hoped to obtain from him a formal renunciation of the slave trade and his adherence to the treaties concerning the trade by means of an annual pension paid by the British Government and the salutary fear of the cruisers which would, if the treaties were contravened, soon have destroyed his new dominions. I made my plans known to the Hon. Consul Campbell and to Mr. Miller, commanding officer of the *Minx* stationed in Lagos, and they, anxious to put an end to these troubles, received it favourably. A treaty between Dosunmu and Kosoko was impossible so they thought of opening negotiations in the name of the British Government, and Mr Campbell sent a message to Kosoko to this effect. No reply came. Then it became necessary to make a show of force to persude the obstinate Pretender to accept the proposals for peace.

On the 10th September 1855 [1854] the British Consul and I boarded the *Minx* for Epe. We were forced to spend six days on a voyage which in other waters would have taken a few hours. The stormy currents, the shallows, the sand-banks and vegetation which obstructed it made the English ship proceed with the greatest of caution and delay. At about 7 p.m. we reached Epe and the ship dropped anchor on the same spot where a year before the English gun-boats had lost seven men. We ran up the white flag and awaited the arrival of Kosoko's emissaries. A vain hope! No one appeared. We held council and it was decided I should land to confer with the King and then, if he refused, hostilities would begin the next day. I willingly accepted this charge notwithstanding the dangers since Kosoko had already proved himself a not too rigid observer of peoples' rights. As soon as the negotiator's launch approached the landing place, a disorderly crowd ran to line up along the beach, shouting, waving spears and giving clear signs of no great liking for the white emissary. At that moment the skull of the English official converted into a royal drinking cup came into my mind and I involuntarily clasped the handle of my revolver. Fortunately the unexpected appearance of the good Tappa [Tapa],[8] one of the King's intimate advisers, who was hastening to meet me, calmed, almost as if by magic, the excitement of the people and entirely dissipated my fears. He was a sensible, honest man of considerable experience. From his long contact with the Portuguese he had

---

[8] For Oshodi Tapa (Scala's 'Tappa'), Kosoko's leading chief and war captain, see Smith, *Lagos Consulate, passim*. Tapa was a Nupe ('Tapa' in Yoruba) from the Niger and a former slave in the palace at Lagos. His descendants have erected a monument to him outside the family compound in Epetedo, Lagos.

learnt to appreciate the European's power and he wisely counselled Kosoko to be prudent and moderate. He welcomed me politely and cordially and when he had given me the greeting of peace invited me to accompany him to his dwelling.

At the sight of Tapa's courteous reception the people's attitude towards me changed and from being threatening it became peaceful and one might say almost benevolent. We walked in the midst of a thick crowd of onlookers only held back with great difficulty by Tapa's guard of honour composed of thirty men armed with guns, who only just managed to make a way for us. These good men whose duty was to guard the King's minister let off shots into the air every few minutes and at only four or five feet from us with the laudable intention of frightening off the evil spirits who, they believe, wander through the air waiting for a suitable opportunity to enter their master's mind. Letting off guns seems to be in African liturgy as effective an exorcism against evil spirits as holy water is in the Catholic faith. The shots were let off one after another without interruption by the guards who took careful aim at some object in the air which was invisible to the profane but definitely seen by these believers; and from this it might be thought that evil spirits abound like flies in the African climate.

Amongst the crowd numerous musicians could be heard, praising the glory of the great minister to the accompaniment of a certain instrument shaped like a clarinet, made out of the bark of a tree and covered with coloured skins. This instrument sounds like a hunting horn and when the bard sings verses every syllable can be clearly distinguished. The Africans delight in these melodies which are not very pleasing to the European ear. The office of bard is greatly sought after in Africa. The King, the tribal chiefs and great men all have their own special bards, chosen from among those who are most attached to themselves and their family just as the feudal princes of the Middle Ages had their troubadours. These musicians accompany important people when they go out for a walk, when they travel, and when they visit the courts of other tribes. Their job is to tell the public about the great deeds and the fine qualities of their masters and this calls for no mean imagination on their part. Hyperbole and pomposity are the rhetorical qualities essential to every good praise singer in order to make the multitude applaud them. Tapa's men must have used the highest grade of rhetoric since they were applauded most enthusiastically. Our procession was made gay with dances which wove around us to the sound of fifes and little drums. Five or six of these dancers came out from their respective groups from time to time, ran about fifty paces away and lay down on the ground. They then came rolling towards us at an incredible speed. Five paces from us they stood up rapidly and repeated their gymnastics without becoming the least bit tired. All this serio-comic display was put on in honour of Tapa and his guest.[9]

At last, after an hour we reached the minister's dwelling, although it was no more than three hundred feet from the landing place. My host invited us to sit down on a sort of bench or couch against the wall of the house, made of dry swamp grasses and covered with fine mats and cushions all along the wall on which to recline. The minister sat down next to me. Then the war chiefs came to prostrate themselves before the minister greeting him with the word *quabo* (welcome) to which the minister replied *ocu,ocu* (greetings also to you) or else *amer-omer* (amen or verily):[10] when the greetings were over the chiefs returned and sat down on a mat laid for them on the floor. The people made their salutations either from outside or from the threshold of the house and then sat down on the ground. After the men came the women, first the mother and then some of the wives, the youngest and most beautiful. The others, looked upon rather in the light of highly-prized furniture, do not generally take part in these solemnities of pomp and ceremony and live in retirement. The women's form of greeting is different from that of the men. First they take off the head scarf or cloth which they wear round their heads, then they remove the cloth which covers their shoulders and wind it round their waist, then they kneel down, sit back resting their left arm on the ground, inclining their heads and clasping their hands three times. When this ceremony is over they rise and retire. However, four of the youngest stayed with Tapa, lavishing their caresses on him and fanning him with a kind of banner of dried skin fixed to the end of a piece of cane.

First of all my host had two glasses of water brought in and offered me one. I drank half of it and the servant drank the other half according to etiquette, to convince me that it had not been poisoned. It is customary to drink water first since, as they say, no other drink can do any harm afterwards. Then various bottles of rum and other liquors were brought out, served always first to me and then given to the rest of the company.

After these preliminaries, I could at last explain to Tapa the object of my mission and the proposals for peace which were brought to him from the

---

[9] Johnson, *History of the Yorubas*, p. 121, gives some twenty names for Yoruba musical instruments, both wind and percussion, but see also Akin Euba, *Yoruba Drumming: the Dùndún Tradition*, Bayreuth, 1990. For the *Oriki*, meaning both descriptive names and praise-songs, there is a useful introduction by Chief J. A. Ayorinde in Biobaku (ed.), *Sources of Yoruba History*, chapter V. Articles on Yoruba music may be consulted in *African Music*, a journal published in the Transvaal, 1954–1987. For general studies, see A. M. Jones, *Studies in African Music*, 2 vols, London, 1959 and chapters in J. Murray (ed.), *Cultural Atlas of Africa*, Phaidon, Oxford, 1981.
[10] These words are usually spelt in Yoruba as kábó, ókú, and àmín, and it is likely that the Oyo dialect of Yoruba was being used. Scala's translations into Italian have been amended with the help of Professor J. F. Ade Ajayi.

representatives of the British Government. He listened to me attentively and replied that he would convey everything to the King. In the meantime he made me his guest for the night, putting at my disposal the reception room in which we were then as it was the best one in the house. He ordered his war-chiefs to be in charge of my safety and posted sentries all round the house to protect me from any danger.

Left to myself I began to study the furniture in the room. This consisted of the bench or couch previously described, a wooden table and some stools of wood. On the walls hung two pictures (if such an expression can be allowed) in which the black artist had wished to represent in one the commerce and in the other the agriculture of the country. In the first was depicted a man armed with a spear. He was the vendor in the act of displaying to the buyer (who was not shown) two unfortunates, a man and a woman, lying in chains on the ground, and these were the goods. Agriculture was represented by a palm tree and a few blades of maize springing up out of the ground as best they could. If from the artistic point of view the two pictures did not equal the worst examples from our own studios, they could however compete favourably with the pictures drawn with charcoal by the children on the walls of houses.

In the meantime, while songs, dances and gunshots followed one another without interruption around my dwelling to fête the minister's guest, a more serious scene was being played out at the King's palace where Kosoko had called a council of all the tribal chiefs and high priests. There they were debating the peace proposals I had brought and deciding on the fate of the country. After a long debate lasting all night, peace was unanimously decided upon and the fetishes were consulted to find out whether they too had enough good sense to give a favourable answer. The people of Epe were very concerned about these things and, remembering the destruction of Lagos by the English cannon, were terrified at the idea of a war with the Whites. A sad event which had come about a few days previously increased their terror and made the power of the Europeans yet more fearful in the eyes of these superstitious men. An unexploded bomb which had been discharged by the English in Lagos was picked up by a native who brought it back to Epe and sold it to a smith. He used it as an anvil and, not knowing what was inside it, one day placed it too near the fire. The bomb became hot and suddenly exploded with a terrible bang, sent the house and the smith up into the air, killed between ten and twelve people and wounded many more. From this simple fact, popular superstition came to believe that the White men possessed the secret of making bombs explode whenever they wished.

Men and women were seen running through the town in the greatest alarm, throwing themselves at the feet of their fetishes and begging them to advise the King to choose peace and to remove the threat of war from the town. At nightfall, when the council was still meeting, the old men, women and children went out of the town and hid in the nearby forest, leaving behind only the young men with fighting skill. This move on the part of the townspeople made a profound impression on the king and his council and they decided to accept the proposals for peace.

The next morning Tapa came to wish me good day and to tell me of his sovereign's decision. At the same time, he added, as Kosoko was the father of the people who had elected him to be their chief he did not feel he had the right to sign a peace treaty without first consulting them. This vain formality was necessary to Kosoko's pride to prove that he had not been forced into a peace which was repugnant to him. At daybreak, the King's heralds with trumpets, flutes, horns and drums went all round the town and the neighbourhood calling the people to a meeting. In a short time the people of Epe gathered in the market place where a pavilion had been erected for the King and his family.

Kosoko advanced majestically, surrounded by his guards and followed by dignitaries of the kingdom and everyone prostrated himself respectfully as the King passed. He took his seat under the canopy and ordered the priests to pray that Heaven might bless the decisions of the Assembly. Then an ox was sacrificed to Oro[11] and when the palm nuts had been thrown it was evident that the God was in favour of peace. These results were announced to Kosoko.

Then I was presented to the King and took my place on a small stool opposite the Royal pavilion. At Kosoko's request I read aloud the message from the English Consul and it was immediately interpreted by the King's interpreter. Then Kosoko rose to speak and a religious silence reigned over the Assembly. 'My sons' he proclaimed in a deep voice charged with emotion, 'you have heard the proposals of the Whiteman, our terrible enemies who have driven me from the throne of my fathers and have given it to the enemies of my line, who have laid waste my factories, destroyed my power and taken away all the means by which I could assert my rights. If the strength of our army were equal to the justice of our cause, I would reject with scorn the proposals for peace and would never lower myself to exchange the land of my fathers for a deserted territory. You well know that my heart does not shrink from battle, you know my zeal and my constancy in defending your interests and my own. If we had only to fight Tinubu's fierce hordes or the soldiers of that weakling Dosunmu, whom we have defeated and destroyed many times, I should waste no time in vain words but should lead you straight to Lagos in triumph, trusting in your glorious deeds; but we have to face the Whitemen, Dosunmu's protectors, who, as you know, fight

[11] For Oro, see pp. 92–94 below with note 8.

with weapons greatly superior to ours and against whom any resistance becomes vain. So, to assure ourselves of the days of peace and rest which we so badly need, to prevent our houses being destroyed and the blood of dear ones shed to no purpose in an unequal fight, I advise you to accept the Whitemen's proposals and under the protection of our Gods to hope for better days to come'.

A murmur of approval followed this speech and the crowd, eager for respite, shouted from all sides 'Let us accept the Whitemen's conditions'. Then an English flag was raised above the royal pavilion (perhaps the same one that had been stolen from the English gun-boats three years before when the emissaries were massacred) and at this sign of the acceptance of the treaty the *Minx* fired a twenty-one gun salute in honour of the King and the town. The Consul and the Commander landed and went to the King's palace to sign the treaty. Kosoko signed all the conditions relative to the treaty and even agreed not to make war on the King of Lagos without provocation, but he firmly refused to make a formal renunciation of his right to the island saying that the bones of his ancestors rested there and so his own must rest there too. To this effect he rejected scornfully the English offer of an annual pension of one thousand colonnati[12] in return for his renunciation. As no better terms could be obtained matters were left at that and the treaty drawn up. Palma, the capital of the new Kingdom, was renamed Port Kosoko.

The rest of the day was spent in feasting and gaiety in which everyone took part and I more than anyone else, because I was delighted with the happy outcome of my mission of peace.

Next day the commanding officer of the *Minx* invited Kosoko and the most important people of the town to a banquet in their honour on board. The King, either out of shyness or dislike for the English, refused and only the two chiefs Tapa and Ajenia and their retinues accepted.

They were pleasantly impressed by the polite and cordial manner in which they were received on board by the officers and men of the British Navy. Their pride was visibly satisfied and they showed that they were grateful for this. They visited with childlike curiosity all parts of the ship, particularly the engines although they could not understand the secret of their motive force in spite of the scientific explanations given them by the obliging engineer. The cannon and the mortars were objects of terror rather than wonder for the black chiefs and their officers, especially the cannon balls which they believed could explode at a sign from the Whiteman. They

---

[12] This probably refers to the Spanish peso or 'piece of eight' (*peso de ocho*), which was intended for circulation in overseas territories and whose reverse depicted the Pillars of Hercules (Gibraltar), hence called *colonnati* by the Italians. See Adrian Room, *Dictionary of Coin Names*, 1987.

were regarded with holy terror and nobody dared go near them. Abagii, Captain of Tapa's retinue and the bravest of the company, encouraged by the sailors, plucked up courage to go to the mortar shells and tried to pick one up. At this display of superhuman temerity his companions fled below decks. Seeing that the ball did not explode in his hands Abagii became braver and asked the captain if he might fire one from the mortar to see the effect of the explosion. The Commander kindly agreed to his request and had a mortar loaded, then he invited Abagii to fire it. He, having now become as brave as a lion, accepted this offer and with a fairly steady hand brought the fuse to the touch-hole. The explosion made a salutary impression on Tapa and Ajenia who had stayed on deck out of a sense of *noblesse oblige*, cursing in their hearts Abagii's foolhardiness. '*Oibo Oibo*' (whiteman), Tapa exclaimed after thought, 'with these means of destruction no African nation can stand up to you. What do you think, Abagii?' 'It is true' the captain replied, 'The White men are better armed than we are'.

After the mortar experiment Abagii's companions came out of hiding and congratulated the hero of the feast on the miracles he had performed. The captain had grown greatly in the estimation of his companions in arms. Then a sumptuous banquet was laid for these good people and the two chiefs Tapa and Ajenia lunched with us at the Commander's table. Toward evening they all returned to Epe, delighted by the treatment they had received and enthusing over the power and courtesy of the White men.

The next day, early in the morning the *Minx* took us back to Lagos.[13]

When Tinubu found out that a peace treaty had been concluded between the English authorities and Kosoko, the proud woman was furious and found it a hard pill to swallow that the fate of her country had been decided against her wishes and without her knowledge. In truth the position of the Lagos Government was humiliating since it was now totally dependent on the English. But could it be otherwise? National independence is the supreme good of civilized nations and without it they can neither prosper nor

---

[13] Scala's account of these negotiations, which resulted in a treaty under which Kosoko renounced his ambition to regain the Lagos throne and his participation in slave trading in return for British recognition of his port at Palma with the right to charge specific export duties there, is more colourful and less accurate than the sober account in the British official papers. He confuses or conflates the conferences with Kosoko's representatives at Palma on 7 January 1854, at Epe on 13 January, on the Palaver Islands in the lagoon on 27 January, and finally at Epe on 26–28 September 1854 (not September 1855 as Scala writes) when the treaty was signed. Although Scala describes himself as playing a major role, he seems to have been present, as one of the representatives of the Lagos merchants, only on the last two occasions and there is no confirmation of his preliminary encounter with Tapa which he describes so vividly. His name appears ('Geo. Batt. Scala, Merchant of Lagos') as one of the seven witnesses to the Treaty of Epe. See Appendix B for the text of the Treaty, and also Smith, *Lagos Consulate*, chapter IV.

progress, but for uncivilized peoples it is a misfortune, a danger, a deadly weapon in the hands of children. To them independence means a lack of progress, that is to say remaining in an abject state of idolatry, superstition, ignorance, polygamy, idleness, slavery, continuous warfare, man-hunting and selling their own kind; they need the guidance of civilized men to free them from barbarity and bring them to their seat at the banquet of independent nations. Only, this guidance must be given in a benevolent and disinterested manner, making itself felt as little as possible so as not to offend their pride. The treaty concluded between the English Government and Kosoko did not exceed the limits of a wise intervention; it did not violate anyone's rights. It assured for Kosoko the possession of land which was almost uninhabited and did not belong to any other sovereign, as well as assuring the peace of those people and removing a formidable rival to the throne of Lagos. They did not think it wise to bring the King and Tinubu into the drawing up of the treaty because they were certain that their hatred and intrigues would have hampered it and, moreover, Kosoko would not have accepted from his enemies terms of peace, which he could accept without any humiliation from England.[14]

Tinubu was furious at what she considered an insult to her authority and turned her anger against the English to whom the King owed his throne, thinking up the means of a terrible revenge. To resuscitate the racial hatred which had completely died down, she sent her many emissaries to spread a report secretly to the people that the White men wanted to take over the government of the island from Dosunmu and extend their dominion over the whole of Africa, taking possession of the country's riches, monopolizing the trade, and reducing all black men to servitude so that they would farm their land for them. These treacherous rumours, repeated everywhere, could not fail to be believed by a credulous and ignorant people and gave rise to great excitement all over the island. The anger of the Africans against the Europeans grew from day to day and began to manifest itself in threats and acts of aggression. Our lives and property were in danger and, alas, the cruiser, believing that the island had been pacified, had left Lagos waters. To ward off the threatening storm a meeting, over which I presided, was held at the Sardinian Consulate and the chief European merchants attended it. We

---

[14] Cf. Smith, *Lagos Consulate*, p. 64 : '... the treaty [of Epe] was intended as an instrument for the pacification of the lagoon, and Kosoko's renunciation of the Lagos throne was its first, and probably in the consul's view its most important, clause'. Apart from the consul and representatives of the Royal Navy and the Lagos merchants, there had also participated in the meetings four chiefs from Lagos, representing Oba Dosunmu and the traditional interest, and the captain of the Egba force sent from Abeokuta to support the Oba. Although it recognized Palma as Kosoko's 'port of trade' (that is, of legitimate trade), the Treaty accorded no specific recognition of Kosoko's position as an independent ruler at Epe.

agreed on means of defence in case we were attacked and decided that I
should go immediately and seek help from the first cruiser I should meet.
Straight away I boarded the Sardinian brig *Lagos* which was anchored in
the roads and told the good Captain Copello what had happened. We
immediately set sail and after two days we met an English brig with twelve
cannon, the name of which I cannot remember. She accompanied us to
Lagos and at once sent launches to the shore, dropping anchor in front of
the King's palace. Then the English Consul, who had returned in the meantime, decided to put an end once and for all to the machinations of Tinubu
and provide for the safety of the Europeans. He went to Dosunmu and
demanded in clear and definite terms that this woman be exiled.

The King hesitated for a long time and could not make up his mind to
abandon one whom he loved so much and who had become so necessary
to him in the government of the state, but the cannon of the English ship
and the threat to recall Kosoko were arguments too strong to be resisted
by the weak monarch. Dosunmu gave in fearfully and like his father Akitoye
sacrificed his beloved for the good of the state.

This measure had to be carried out with speed, secrecy and prudence.
Tinubu had more than a few supporters, mainly among the troops, and it
was feared, not unreasonably, that the proud woman would oppose the
ban and bring about a civil war. It was agreed, therefore, to give her that
very night a sleeping draught made of some drug used by the natives, to
tie her up securely and to throw her into the bottom of a canoe and thus
convey her to her home town, Abeokuta. Six strong men carried out these
orders and in their custody the enraged Tinubu was taken off to meet her
fate.[15]

---

[15] Consul Campbell eventually succeeded in persuading Oba Dosunmu to banish Madame
Tinubu from Lagos in March 1856 after her involvement for a second time in a plot against
his life. This action by the consul antagonized the merchants since Tinubu was heavily in debt
to them for palm oil which had been supplied to her under the credit system used in this
trade; this also explains the Oba's reluctance to take action against her. See Biobaku, *The
Egba*, p. 57, and Smith, *Lagos Consulate*, pp. 73–74.

V

JOURNEY TO ABEOKUTA

Five years had passed since I settled in Lagos and inaugurated the era of legitimate trade. The happy results I had achieved and the growing preference of the people for their new means of livelihood decided me to go further afield and to take the civilizing element of legitimate trade into the very centre of slavery. So I thought I would move to Abeokuta, capital of Orobù [Yorubaland], situated one hundred and forty miles North of Lagos,[1] a great slave market which had not yet been visited by Europeans apart from one English missionary. I told the Hon. Mr. Campbell of my project and he, actuated purely by affection for me, did his utmost to dissuade me from the journey, saying that it was crazy and assuring me that I would lose my life and substance there. Even greater was Dosunmu's opposition, apparently for the same reasons of affection but in reality because it was not to his interest that the white men should make direct contact with the natives of the interior, where he himself monopolized the trade. These arguments were based chiefly on the ferocity of the people who lived in the country through which I had to pass, and this had been made worse by the hatred of the Europeans aroused by the suppression of the slave trade in Lagos, but these arguments made little impression on me. I had learnt from experience that the reputation of the Africans was not always in accordance with their merits or faults, and 'the devil is not as ugly as he is painted' seems to be a proverb invented for them. However, although many times I asked the Consul and Dosunmu for the safeguard of their staff or ring (a sign of command which the natives respect) and a small escort, they refused and the King even forbade any of his subjects to act as my guide.

[1] Abeokuta (which is actually only about 60 miles from Lagos) should instead be described as the capital of the Egba people whose three distinct groups or provinces had abandoned their towns in the Egba Forest as a result of the prolonged wars of the early 19th. century in Yorubaland. After many vicissitudes, including a sojourn by a number of the fugitives in the recent, mainly Oyo, settlement of Ibadan, they concentrated on the northern edge of the Forest in c. 1830 in a large federated city 'under the rocks' (thus, Abeokuta) on the east bank of the river Ogun. Here they were joined by a fourth Yoruba (but non-Egba) people, the Owu, and in 1862 by a fifth group, also non-Egba, the Ijaye, from the Oyo kingdom of northern Yorubaland.

In spite of these obstacles I equipped a large canoe 7 metres long and 90 centimetres wide, on which I loaded about three tons of merchandise, made up of the usual rum, tobacco, cloth, hand-guns, powder and different manufactured goods, besides my luggage, provisions and utensils necessary for a long journey. The canoe was manned by six strong and expert oarsmen, natives of Abeokuta and therefore not subjects of the King of Lagos, and on 10th September 1857 I boarded it with my interpreter and left Lagos, to the sorrow of my friends, who disapproved of the foolhardy undertaking, and to the amazement of the crowd. My interpreter was also a native of Abeokuta. He had been sold into slavery when very young and taken to Brazil where he learnt quite good Portuguese. He was freed when his master died and had come to Lagos in order to return to his homeland.[2]

We quickly crossed the larger torrent which flows from East to West in the direction of Porto Novo and came into a small river, going up-stream towards the North. This is a branch of what is known as the Abeokuta river. Alluvial sand deposits and floating tree trunks block parts of the river, and enormous masses of rock sticking out of the water make this a miniature archipelago where navigation is very difficult. The chief duty of the oarsmen is to study the currents which vary according to the configuration of the banks with their numerous creeks. For some miles we travelled with great difficulty, in danger all the time of being overturned by the enormous floating masses which we met every few yards. We arrived at an old village called Abui [Aboyi] on the border between Lagos territory and that of Abeokuta. This village is about a mile in circumference and consists of about 100 huts situated on different islands, separated from one another by a lagoon which winds around them. It is a grotesque parody of the Queen of the Adriatic, unhappy Venice.[3] The inhabitants told us that the village had been founded three centuries before by a chief called Sabah [Saba, a title] who had taken up residence there with four or five hundred soldiers. He laid waste to the surrounding countryside with impunity, safe in the isolation of his exceptional position. It is probable, however, that the ancient village was destroyed by the flood waters gradually eating away the banks and forming little islands. It is interesting to note that some recently-built houses are in fact on piles of about ten to fourteen hands long driven into the mud by means of great stones attached to a lever which is worked by hand. We went towards the village to look for

---

[2] This is almost certainly Ribeiro, the Brazilian mulatto whom Fr Borghero met in 1863–4 in Abeokuta. Ribeiro was then acting as Scala's agent there.

[3] Scala calls Venice 'unhappy' because the city remained in Austrian hands after the unification of Italy by the Peace of Villafranca between France and Italy in 1859. It was ceded to France and passed by France to Italy in the arrangements which ended the Austro-Prussian war of 1866.

provisions. Trade there is carried on entirely by women. These, in their fragile canoes with one and sometimes two babies tied on their backs, row with speed and skill, cope with the currents, carry their wares from the beach to their houses, and go backwards and forwards a hundred times a day. Water is their natural element. Men, women and children are all excellent fisherman and swimmers.

After an hour's journey we reached the confluence of the channel and the stream called Abeokuta. This rises in the mountains of Yaribba [Yoruba], crosses the province of Dahomey and loses itself in the Lagos River one hundred and fifty miles from Abeokuta.[4] Here we found another village built in the same way as the first and were delighted by this picturesque place with its fertile soil and extensive cultivation.

At 6 p.m. we reached a small town situated on the Eastern bank of the river. It is about three miles in circumference and is divided by a canal which seems to have been skilfully made to irrigate the land round about. My interpreter, who had until now been quite indifferent to the beauties of nature, suddenly came to life at the sight of Goom [Gaun, Igaun] (as the town is called) and pointed out to me with pride its line of fortifications consisting of a surrounding wall four metres high. Then he pointed to a large quadrilateral compound surrounded with thick shrubs and acacia trees, situated on the right bank and dominating the whole landscape. This, he said, is the home of Aburah, Chief of the Igaun and a dependant of the King of Abeokuta. Then he told me the history of the town of Igaun.

A witch who had been driven away from the company of her sister witches because she loved a young man from the high regions of Abar who was a follower of the Koran and an enemy of fetishism, had her beloved spirited away while he slept and deposited on the spot where Igaun now lies. There the lovers built a city and gathered into it the wild people from the surrounding country, gave them laws, and founded the dynasty of the Kings of Igaun which was later overthrown and extinguished by the King of Abeokuta. As the interpreter finished his story, our canoes, with the national flag flying, came up to the beach. We landed and were immediately surrounded by a vast crowd who rushed up from all over the place and were amazed at the arrival of a White man. But when my interpreter explained that the White man was the representative of a powerful European monarch and had come from Lagos to visit their town, reverence and respect for me was added to their astonishment. They helped my rowers to beach the canoe according to the custom of the country and after a few minutes I saw the Chief coming towards me accompanied by the most important

---

[4] This is presumably the river Ogun or one of its tributaries. In its course northwards from the lagoon the Ogun does not traverse the territory of Dahomey.

officials and escorted by his guards. When he heard the object of my visit and my wish to spend the night there, he greeted me affectionately and took me to his house.

There I was given a frugal dinner consisting of a piece of roast goat in a plate of yams cooked in ashes, with other vegetables, and a kind of pap made with cassava flour and honey seasoned with a strong dose of hot pepper. I was given a corner of the house covered with a fine mat to sleep on and I was looking forward to a good night's rest to prepare me for the next day's trials but, alas, the townsmen sinned by an excess of zeal. To honour their guest, these good people were kind enough to play, all through the night, horns, pipes, drums and other 'harmonious' instruments and to let off guns and make an infernal noise which made it quite impossible for me to close my eyes. Zabarah the Chief of Igaun[5] had understood that I planned to set up a trading station at Abeokuta and told this to the important people of the town. These immediately held council and seeing the advantages that such trade would bring to their country asked me to set up a depot in their own town, and to this effect they decreed that I should be assigned a piece of land big enough to build it on. I promised to fulfil their request as soon as I possibly could and should certainly have kept my word had not persecution from my enemies prevented me. In the meantime they solemnly set about preparing the property, that is to say they burnt the grass, trees and everything covering the piece of land I had been given and put up posts to mark the boundary. The people of Igaun heartily approved of this gift of land and shouted at me not to forget my promise. A few days later, when I arrived at Abeokuta, I sent these good people a demijohn of rum and eleven heads of cowries (twenty two thousand in number) in appreciation of their generosity. When I passed through Igaun on my return to Europe, I found the piece of land cleared just as I had left it and still at my disposal.

The next day at dawn, I took leave of Zabarah and his family, deeply touched by the affection they had shown me. The people gathered in the big square to greet me and accompanied me to the shore where my canoe was waiting for me. We travelled all that day, going from one bank to the other to avoid the currents or rowing in the middle of the stream to avoid the ropes laid along the banks to which the local people attach nets for catching crayfish, their favourite food. The countryside up to now had been a vast and monotonous plain cultivated for the most part with maize and yams and shaded by thick clumps of palms or acacias some distance apart. Although grazing land seemed rich and abundant there appeared to be no cattle

---

[5] This appears to be the same man who is identified on the previous page by the interpreter as the chief of the Igaun, Scala not noticing, or at least not explaining, the inconsistency in the names — Aburah and Zabarah.

about, only a few scattered sheep and goats and other small beasts. I could not understand the reason for this lack of animals so useful to mankind. There are many monkeys and different kinds of birds, chiefly parrots, which are nearly all grey. There are also elephants and wild animals but these are rare in all countries where firearms are used. After Igaun the Eastern bank of the river becomes hilly and deserted while the Western plain is still under cultivation and is animated by rural habitations whose occupants ran from the fields to see the white man pass, wading up to their waists into the water. When we drew the canoe up to the bank to rest and prepare our meal they brought us wood, yams, vegetables etc. in a disinterested and spontaneous manner which we appreciated. A small mirror, a copper necklace and some strings of glass beads with which I rewarded them for their gifts and services gave them the greatest joy which they repaid by further acts of kindness.

In the evening we stopped for the night at the village of Obi, on the Western bank where we found the same surprise and respect from the people and the same affectionate reception from the chief that we had experienced in Igaun. A little way from the shore we found, heaped under a tree, a number of cowries, currency of the country, which seemed to have been abandoned not only owing to the effects of the weather but also to the greed of passers-by. Naturally we asked for an explanation of this phenomenon and were told that under this tree was the shrine of Amasi, one of the most venerated Fetishes of the African people and the special patron of Obi. When the fierce hordes of the Dahomians, a tribe bordering on Yorubaland, advanced from the East to sack the village on one of their usual men-hunting expeditions, the defenceless people of Obi prayed to their favourite Fetish and begged him to save them from this peril.[6]

The Fetish received their prayers favourably and when the Dahomians advanced in their canoes made especially to cross the river and invade the village on the opposite side, he made himself invisible, stood in the middle of the river and then with a single breath blew the canoes back to the other side where they were overturned in the waves. The attack was repeated several times but always with the same result; many Dahomians were drowned in the waves, others swam to safety and abandoned the unlucky shore, giving up for ever any hope of attacking Obi, so miraculously

---

[6] This abortive attack on the village of Obi seems most likely to have occurred during the advance of the Dahomean army towards Abeokuta in 1851, six years before Scala's journey described here. 'Amasi' has not been identified among the members of the Yoruba pantheon; probably he (since Scala refers to the god as masculine) was the patron deity (*orisha*) of the village. For the wars of the Dahomeans against the Egba and the neighbouring Egbado, see J. F. A. Ajayi and Robert Smith, *Yoruba Warfare in the Nineteenth Century*, second ed., 1971, chapter 6, and Smith, *Kingdoms*, pp. 133–134.

protected by an invisible deity. Meanwhile the fame of the miracle spread all around and no canoe, either friendly or enemy, dared come near for fear of being overturned.

Such widespread interpretation of the miracle was not altogether to the good of the villagers for it ruined their trade, nor to the good of the Fetish himself for it drove the faithful from his shrine. To prevent any misunderstanding the priests consulted the deity as to his intentions and the reply was what one would expect from a wise and reasonable god. He intended to drive off enemy canoes on condition that a small contribution be made to his shrine. The first to make the experiment was a trader from Abeokuta who brought a rich cargo of goods and, delighted at not having been driven back, left twenty per cent of it at the foot of the sacred tree. Then others came and each one made an offering according to his means. I felt I should not be exempted from the sacred tribute so I left my shells amid shouts of approval from the crowd and thought to myself that as far as miracles are concerned wild Africa has no need to envy our civilized Europe.[7]

Early next morning we went on our way and I lay back in my usual place in the canoe, a position which was beginning to fatigue me. The canoe was pretty well filled by my merchandise and by the oarsmen so that I was forced to lie without moving between two barrels of rum and dared not stand up for fear of upsetting the balance and overturning the fragile boat. To while away the time I let my imagination run wild and thought lovingly of the future African civilization of my dreams. Now it grew to gigantic proportions in my mind and was very pleasing to my pride. I, the first man, I said to myself, to have ventured into these wild regions, shall show the natives how to farm the land and shall teach them the arts and industries of civilized nations. I shall teach them how man's labour when applied to agriculture, trade and navigation is the real source of a country's wealth because it increases the products of the land and transports them from one place to another on the globe and exchanges them for others, thus making life comfortable and easy for everyone and creating a sure means of subsistence. I shall explain how the slave trade impoverishes the country by depriving it of products and corrupting the people, making them insensitive to the sufferings of their own kind. I shall set up a commercial and industrial firm at Abeokuta where I shall employ as much labour as I can and open this new market to Europe as I have already done in Lagos. Just then a violent shock brought me to earth and I found that we were close on the shore of Tapana, a village about twenty-five miles from Abeokuta.

---

[7] Scala uses the words 'Fetish', plural 'Fetishes' (Feticcio, Feticcii), throughout the *Memorie*, these words deriving from the Portugese *feitiço* a 'made thing' (Verger). Modern usage discards these terms, preferring, for example, 'nature gods' and for the smaller inanimate objects 'charms', 'amulets' etc. Scala also refers to 'God' and 'Idol' without making any distinction.

The sun was setting and tinting with rosy light the dense clouds which were piling up on the horizon. Tapana, situated on the West bank, is on the slope of a small promontory which dominates the river. It is surrounded by pleasant country very well cultivated and covered in rich vegetation, mainly of palm trees. These trees, apart from their intrinsic value, are of the greatest use in a country subject to rains almost every three months. Since the land is often flooded and could be washed into the river together with the seeds which have been planted in it, the various clumps of trees which have sprung up here and there form a natural protection from the force of the floods. The local people, to help the providence of nature, have adopted a method of cultivation which would not be unsuitable in parts of Europe subject to long seasons of rain which make them swampy. They do not plant grain as we do on the tops of furrows, but they build up an infinite number of small mounds about six to eight inches high, around which they make a wall of tiny stones. Each of these mounds, about twenty to thirty centimetres in diameter, contains four or five plants. The rain water thus finding a ready-made drain does not damage the roots of the plants and flowing gently down the natural slope of the ground collects in artificial canals which lead it into the river. I could not gaze long enough at the vast fields and pleasant hills decorated with long rows of grain, yams, beans and other vegetables.

The arrival of the White man set the whole village in motion. Men and women rushed to the shore and the children climbed like monkeys into the trees and on the roofs of their huts in order to see me better. I was received by the village chief, Igiai [Ajayi?] by name, who showed me the same cordiality and generous hospitality that I had experienced at Gaun and Obi; and this repeated proof of the gentle customs of the Africans confirmed me all the more in my opinion that all that was said in Lagos about their ferocity was slanderous and intended to prevent the Whites from making direct contact with them. Then the following morning I set off at daybreak for Abeokuta which I was eager to reach as soon as I could.

I shall spend no more time in describing villages and landscapes like those of which I have spoken. At mid-day on 13 September, I arrived at Agba-maya, a little market town five miles from Abeokuta, where I stopped the canoe and sent my interpreter with my stick and my ring to the King (Alake) to tell him of my arrival and the reason for my journey. Meanwhile, I lay under a tree to await the messenger's return. Everything presaged a favourable reply from the King of Abeokuta, and the welcome I had had from the different chiefs and people up till now promised a successful result. In fact, at about 5 p.m. I began to hear in the distance a cheerful sound of drums and pipes, then I caught sight of my interpreter followed by several distinguished people, among whom the inhabitants pointed out to me, with signs of deep respect, Basorun Ogabona [Ogunbona] and Sokenu,[8] chiefs with great authority and favourites of the King. They were mounted on the little horses of the country, like those we have on the island of Sardinia. A slave lad led another of these by the bridle, fully harnessed and intended for me. After the customary greetings, which consisted of bowing to the ground three times and rubbing one's arms with dust, we went on to Abeokuta where we arrived late in the night.

The King's messengers led me to a house which had been specially prepared for me by order of the King and told me that they would return the next day to present me to His Majesty when I would explain to him the object of my mission. Then they politely departed, each leaving me his stick, according to local custom, as a safeguard. The furniture in my house consisted of a kind of couch completely attached to the wall, quite wide enough to sleep upon with comfort, on which woollen cushions covered with cotton made in Manchester were spread. On a rough wooden table, palm oil burnt in a jar serving as a lamp and casting a feeble light over the room. The floor was covered with mats made of palm leaves and the walls were bare and blackened with smoke. Next morning the two chiefs, Basorun Ogunbona and Sokenu, came as they had promised to take me to the King.

We were followed by a dense crowd and after half an hour's walk reached the royal dwelling, situated almost in the centre of the town. I was shown into the Audience Chamber where the King[9] surrounded by his courtiers was seated on a kind of throne composed of a small carpet spread on the ground and two cushions of red velvet with gold fringes. I was invited to sit on a stool opposite the King; then through our interpreter, we held the following conversation.[10]

'White man,' the King said to me, 'Is the country where you were born blessed by a beneficent sun like this one and is your land fertile enough to provide enough food for its people?'

'The sun's rays are more temperate in our country and make the climate more mild and healthy. Our lands are fertile and produce all kinds of fruits in proportion to their cultivation.'

---

[8] Scala confuses names and titles here. Sokenu the Basorun had commanded the Abeokutan army which drove back the Dahomeans in the battle for Abeokuta in 1851, while Ogunbona the Balogun, or war captain, of Ikija had commanded that part of the army which operated outside the walls of the town.

[9] By the 'king' Scala indicates the senior of the three rulers (Oba) of the different sections of the Egba. This was the Alake, Oba of Ake, and at this time the title was held by Okukenu who reigned from 1854 to 1862. His predecessor, Alake Okikilu, had died in the Egba Forest during the wars. See Biobaku, *The Egba*, and Chapter VI, note 4 below.

[10] Scala does not reveal in what language this conversation (and others like it) was conducted, but it seems likely that his interpreter, an Egba, relayed to him in Portuguese what the Alake had told him in Yoruba. See p. 54 above for Scala's interpreter and also remarks on this subject in the Introduction, p. xix.

'Is your King as powerful as I am and are his people happy under him?'

'The King of my country possesses a great deal of land and a great many subjects who, compared with other peoples, can say they are happy because they are free.'

'Who makes the law for your country?'

'The King and his Parliament, that is the representatives of the nation.'

'Why do the white men of Europe want to stop our slave trade with the Portuguese?'

'Because this traffic is an abominable violation of the rights of our own kind, contrary to the laws of God who made all men free...'

At this heresy the King smiled at the priests standing by him who gave signs of definite disapproval.

'Then all men in your country are free? You have no slaves?'

'No, slaves do not exist in our country; we are free to do anything that is not forbidden by the law.'

'When your King wants to make war on his neighbours, are you free to refuse to do military service?'

'The King does not declare war just when he feels like it or without the consent of Parliament. This consent is not given unless the war is for a just cause and in the interest of the nation. Then all the citizens voluntarily take up arms and become soldiers.'

'Is the man who has nothing to live on free to work or not to work?'

'All men, even the rich, must work according to their ability to be useful to their fellow creatures; but the man who has nothing must work more than anyone else to keep himself and his family.'

'Then he is a slave as regards his work?'

'That is true, but he is compensated by a corresponding gain, all of which goes into his own pocket, not into that of an idle master.'

'The King and rich man of your country, do they not have servants?'

'The King and rich people of my country have domestic servants whom they pay an amount agreed between them, but they cannot maltreat them, nor beat them, nor sell them, and the servants are free to leave them when the contract between their masters has been completed.'

These distinctions between the forced labour of slaves under the whip for the sole benefit of the master and the free, paid labour for the domestic servant and the artisan, evident to us Europeans, were perhaps too subtle for the intelligence of His African Majesty, who seemed only partly satisfied with my answers and not very impressed by the power of the monarch I had described, who was forced to pay a wage to his servants without being able to beat them or sell them when he felt like it. To divert the King's mind from these impressions I asked leave to explain the object of my mission. Hardly had I expressed this wish when the King, interrupting the interpreter, said to me:

'I know that for some years White men have settled in Lagos and are trading in palm oil, cotton, ivory and other products of our country. Are you one of these?'

'I was the first,' I answered, 'to settle in Lagos after the bombardment of the town, and to exchange with the Africans their products for those of Europe. The town was completely ruined not so much by the English cannon as by the stopping of the slave trade which had been made impossible by the cruisers. The impetus which I gave to the new trade, supported by the competition of other Europeans, whom my example had encouraged to settle on the island, brought new life to the city and made it more prosperous than before.'

At these words the King became calm again, took on a grave expression and appeared to be thinking hard. Ogunbona gave me a look of approval and the other chief looked at one another in surprise or doubt. Only the priests remained silent and suspicious. After a brief pause the King went on:

'The advantages of your trade are greater than those we get from the slave trade?'

'Certainly,' I replied. 'The wars you fight to capture slaves for export impoverish the country, depriving it of the men needed for agriculture. If the thousands of men sent every year to America were employed in cultivating the land, in picking cotton, in making palm oil, in hunting elephants, in building canoes on the European system, in making roads, bridges and canals for the transport of merchandise, you would increase an hundred-fold the riches of the soil which as yet only produces a thousandth part of what it might produce and would procure for everyone an easier and happier existence.'

'Who would buy our surplus products?'

'The European merchants.'

'I have a lot of cotton, palm oil, ivory, grain and other things. Do you want to buy them?'

'Yes, at once!'

'And if any one of my subjects also had similar things to sell, would you buy them?'

'Certainly. I should exchange them for cowries, rum. tobacco, gunpowder, guns, cotton cloth, etc.; and when my stocks have run out I shall bring other goods from Europe to exchange with you.'

'All right. You can stay for a while with us under the protection of my ring. The priests will consult our Fetishes as to the advisability of admitting the white man among us; if their answer is favourable you will share the

Kola[11] with us and be our guest. In eight days I shall recall you to my presence and give you a definite answer.'

So saying he rose from his seat, handed me his ring and retired. I was taken back to my dwelling by Ogunbona amid the same crowd who had been waiting in the main square.[12]

[11] Kola is a bulb similar to garlic and like it is made up of cloves. It tastes like a crab apple and is used as a sacred symbol in religious ceremonies, marriages, peace alliances, etc. The parties concerned each break off a clove and eat it, thus making a contract inviolable. (Scala's note). The kola nut is the fruit of the West African tree (*Cola acuminata*) cultivated in the South and Central American tropics. It contains caffeine and is imported for use in beverages.

[12] Fr Borghero's visit to Abeokuta in 1864 may be compared with Scala's account in this chapter of his first visit there in September 1857 towards the end of the wet season. Both followed the route northward up the river Ogun, but while Scala accomplished the journey in three days Paggi's canoes, loaded with merchandise and 'armed', on which Borghero was a passenger, took 'six days of painful navigation' in May, also during the wet season. Borghero's journey was rendered eventful not only by bands of undisciplined soldiers but also by the dangerous passage of 'the rapids of Titi', somewhere south of Aro but not mentioned by Scala whose canoes may have followed here a minor branch of the Ogun. Borghero's short stay in Abeokuta took place only a few months after the fierce Dahomean assault of March 1864 on the town, and he gives a detailed and graphic account of the battle as well as an excellent description of the fortified walls of Abeokuta. Apart from their resistance to repeated Dahomean aggression the Egba were now involved in the Ijaye War (1860–65) against Ibadan. Meanwhile Alake Okukenu, who had received Scala, had died. A leading chief, Somoye, Basorun of the Egba, had assumed the regency, and it was he to whom Borghero brought gifts and who gave the missionary help and attention. It is also evident from Borghero's account of his visit that in the intervening five years since Scala had left the town the European and American population there had grown significantly. Borghero, *Journal*, pp. 167–186 *passim*.

VI

ABEOKUTA

As I had to wait eight days before I could learn the answer of the oracle which was to decide my fate, and as I was not allowed to transact any business, I thought I would use the time to explore the town and its surroundings.

Abeokuta, which means 'Under the Rock' in Yoruba, is situated on Latitude N. 8.32 and is the most important town that one can find not far from the coast on the Western side of Africa. The natives say their town is about one hundred and fifty years old and was founded in the last century when numerous fierce tribes migrating from East to West burst into Yorubaland and forced the inhabitants, who could not stand up to them, to seek exile around the Abeokuta River. The abundance of water and the fertility of the land persuaded the fugitives to set up their homes there and build a town surrounded by strong walls to protect them from future invasions. Then there happened again in Africa what had happened in Europe when the hordes from the North descended on the Latin peoples to take possession of their lands; with this difference, however, that the invasions of Europe mark a tremendous step in human progress through those barbarians being influenced by Latin civilization, while in Africa, as conqueror and conquered are both barbarians, the invasion is a terrible calamity without any benefit to humanity. The salvation of Africa depends entirely on a peaceful invasion by the Whites.[1]

Abeokuta town is about twenty miles in circumference and is surrounded by very strong walls with a gate at each of the four points of the compass,

---

[1] The history of the wars in Yorubaland, lasting for much of the nineteenth century, is complex, involving the collapse of the Oyo empire in northern Yorubaland and the overrunning of much of the countryside by the Hausa-Fulani armies from what became Northern Nigeria in their jihad. This movement, one of conquest rather than a 'migration', was from north to south so far as Yorubaland was concerned, while the general Fulani movement in West Africa, beginning much earlier, was from west to east. The classic account of the Yoruba wars is in S. Johnson's *The History of the Yorubas*, 1921; see also Ajayi and Smith, *Yoruba Warfare*. For Abeokuta, see Chapter V, note 1 above, and Biobaku, *The Egba*. The town was probably founded in the late 1820s; c. 1830 is the date usually assigned. See map 2.

according to the African system. Its population, calculated approximately for want of statistics, is about one hundred and twenty thousand, some of whom are Moslems and some Pagans. One can observe three distinctive types characteristic of the three different races from the North, West and East and these suggest that the population has been formed by successive invasions from Timbuctu in the North, from Ethiopia in the East and from the Coastal regions of the West. The Eastern race is tall, strong and muscular with a low forehead, high cheek bones, a flat nose with wide nostrils and a prominent lower lip. They are Moslems. The Timbuctu race, considered the best of the three, have more regular features and are lighter in colour. They are more intelligent and docile and less warlike. They make friends easily and are more inclined towards commerce and industry than towards war. Those people provide the best and most sought-after slaves; those who have returned from the American plantations after being freed because of their good conduct are almost all from this race. Their religion is a mixture of Islam and paganism which are rather difficult to reconcile. The third race belongs to the West Coast and is the worst of all. They are not very different from the Easterners in physique and colour but are much fiercer and given to war and plunder. Frequently they invade the neighbouring tribes, sacking, capturing slaves and committing all kinds of atrocities. They are pagans and excessively superstitious.[2]

The provinces of Ashanti, Dahomey and the Selah[3] are occupied by these people. Although in Abeokuta the three races are ruled by the same political laws under the same King, they live nevertheless in separate districts and each conserves its original character, the customs and religions of the respective tribes. Each tribe has a special Chief dependent on the King of Abeokuta. The Northern tribes are occupied in commerce and industry and the others are soldiers or undertake raids for them. Slavery is in full force and is considered as a political institution. Slaves form at least half the population of Abeokuta.

The city is built on several small hills which make as many separate districts. The streets are narrow, winding and indescribably filthy. There

---

[2] The circuit of the eastern wall of Abeokuta (which can still be traced) was about 15 miles in length while Scala's estimate of the population seems still more exaggerated: the number of inhabitants in 1857, according to Bowen, an American missionary in the town, amounted to some 50,000. These included about 3,000 'emigrants', mostly freed Egba slaves arriving from Freetown. References to invasions from Timbuctu and Ethiopia derive probably from the partly understood accounts of local informants relating a mixture of tradition and myth, and should be discounted. By 'paganism' Scala stigmatizes the indigenous religion which otherwise he makes a quite serious attempt to describe in chapter VIII below. By the time of Scala's first visit to Abeokuta in 1857 Christianity had been introduced to the town; mission stations were set up there by the Anglicans in 1846, Wesleyans in 1847, and (American) Baptists in 1850. Islam had been introduced into Yorubaland much earlier and more gradually.
[3] 'Selah' is unidentified.

are four big squares bordered by double lines of acacia trees, where the people go to rest at the hottest time of day. These squares and the main streets are crossed by gutters which supply water to the houses for various domestic purposes. The houses are made of mud and are not unlike those in Lagos which I have already described. The Royal Palace at the Eastern end of the town consists of a vast terrain surrounded by a wall seven or eight metres high, inside which one building stands higher than the others. This is the King's own residence and around it are many buildings like private houses except for the roofs which are made of tiles instead of thatch. They belong to members of the King's family, his wives and his numerous slaves. There are said to be more than one hundred royal concubines and each woman has her own house where she lives with her children. Opposite the Royal compound stands a small hill on top of which is an enormous tree considered sacred by the townspeople. Every time the King marries a new wife, we can see, the next morning, a flag of one colour or another flying from the branches of the sacred tree. The different colours signify the degree of the King's satisfaction with his spouse. A white flag is the brightest praise that an intact and immaculate flower can hope for.

The government of the Kingdom is in the form of a modified elected Monarchy.[4] On the death of the King, the priests call together all the people of the towns and villages in their market place and after offering the requisite sacrifices to the local Fetiches, invite them to nominate a Chief as an elector to choose the new King. Those nominated are usually the wealthiest men of the region from whom the people hope to receive largesse and benefits. The chiefs thus nominated come to Abeokuta from all parts of the region and after a solemn three days of prayer, fasting and sacrifice etc. go with great pomp to the square where in the presence of all the populace they proceed to the election of the new King, who is chosen usually from the rich class of the *Ogboni* (nobles),[5] rarely from the family

---

[4] Richard Burton, who visited Abeokuta some three or four years after Scala had left, used similar words in describing the government there; it was, he wrote, 'a weak constitutional monarchy, blighted by the checks and limits which were intended to prevent its luxuriance': *Abeokuta and the Camaroons Mountains*, 1863, pp. 275–278. The Alake, Scala's 'king', exercised influence but little real power. He was and is traditionally chosen by the heads of the five major towns of the old Ake province in the Egba Forest. In the early days at Abeokuta, however, the title lapsed. It was revived in 1854, mainly under the influence of the Rev. Henry Townsend of the CMS, and Okukenu, Sagbua of Ake, was chosen. See Biobaku, *The Egba*, pp. 4, 5, 52, 73, 86. An interesting comparison can be made between political arrangements in Abeokuta and in 'republican' Ibadan, both founded c. 1830 as a result of the Yoruba wars.

[5] Apart from the sectional (previously provincial) organization which survived in Abeokuta, there were town chiefs, in particular the Ogboni, a society composed of rich and influential men and a few old women, exercising political and judicial powers, and the Parakoyi who oversaw all commercial activities. Both these bodies met every seventeen days.

of the deceased King and never, until now, from the warriors. Then there is a sort of Chamber of Representatives whose members are chosen by acclamation, rather than elected, according to a list drawn up by the tribal Chiefs, who are clearly the *de facto* electors and most of the time the elected as well. The priests also elect their representatives from their own ranks and the King nominates his ministers, three in number: the minister of finance called *Appesi*, the minister of finance called *Barakui* [Parakoyi] and the minister of war called *Bolongun* [Balogun].[6] The so-called representatives of the people have one vote, the priests of the second order have two, and those of the first order three. The ministers are considered to be of equal rank to the last and also have three votes.

The King has the power of absolute veto. In times of war, civil uprising or public disaster he dissolves Parliament, chooses from his close supporters seven councillors for public administration, and assumes a dictatorship until order is restored. In spite of this apparently constitutional system the King may be considered as absolute ruler and he is surrounded by all the apparatus of almost divine power and prestige that man's adulation can invent for despots in any country. No subject may have access to the monarch without first going through the supreme Appesi (staff-bearer) and he can only be approached through two councillor-sergeants who have power to accept or reject the postulant's request. When the King rides in the town or suburbs, everyone has to stop what he is doing and prostrate himself while the King passes. The King cannot speak to anyone outside his own compound. An old deep-rooted suspicion would have one believe that the evil spirits, while harmless in the area presided over by the Fetish, will chose the moment when the King speaks to anyone outside to steal his mind, corrupt his soul, and make him a tyrant and an enemy of the people.

When the King is ill, the priests order public prayers, fasting and sacrifices. All work stops. If he recovers his health the days of penance are followed by days of rejoicing and revelry. Private and public buildings bear garlands of flowers, men and women put on their best dresses, and in the squares and streets gun shots, the sounds of pipes and drums and joyful songs can be heard. Public entertainments are improvised all over the town. In some places there are wrestling matches like those of the Ancient Greeks, in which sturdy youths, their limbs anointed with oil, fling themselves at one another, each trying by many different means to throw the other to the ground. In other places there are races, the children's favourite sport, and elsewhere again, archery at which Africans of all ages show great skill.

---

[6] '*Barakui*' is a corruption of *Parakoyi*, the trading title-holders. '*Bolongon*' must be '*Balogun*', war captain, a title which was originally used only in the Oyo empire and kingdom but which came to be applied more widely in Yorubaland in the nineteenth century.

The most popular entertainment and the one which draws the greatest number of spectators is dancing. The African dances are original, expressive and, in so far as I can understand them, highly allegorical. I have watched, several times, one of those which is the most often performed and which seems to me to depict a poem or rather a résumé of the wandering, precarious and arduous life which these unfortunate people lead. About twenty or thirty men, almost entirely naked, with a stick or battle-axe in their right hand and a coconut in their left, take their places one behind the other in a circle previously drawn on the ground. At a given signal all leap to their feet and stamp twice on the ground, then they start dancing, sometimes fast, sometimes slowly but always rhythmically, or advancing in a squatting position. They keep in their circle all the time and utter terrible cries. These are tribesmen who, bearing weapons and food, emigrate to more favourable regions, now bursting forth, now hiding quietly in the bush to surprise the enemy. At another signal, one of the men in the circle starts to beat his neighbour with a stick, shouting *Ulani selabu* (Away with you, accursed one),[7] and the latter, without losing his place in the circle, turns towards his assailant and returns the blow, and these reciprocal blows accompanied by the same shouts are repeated in succession by all the dancers. It would seem that the emigrants have reached the territory of the other tribe who, unprepared for the attack, are forced to flee from the invaders. It is interesting to note that each man is both pursuer and fugitive, an evident symbol of the terrible cycle of African life. For the rest, the steps and blows are the only movements carried out to a regular rhythm: those of the head and arms as well as the facial expressions are left *ad libitum* to the artist's fancy, and the Africans make great use of the freedom given them by the ritual. Their screams and shouts enjoy the same privilege. The dance is accompanied by pipes and drums and coconuts beaten against one another. These instruments are for the most part played by children who carry out this duty, I shall not say conscientiously, but in a real frenzy. The women seated in groups around the circle also accompany the dance by clapping in time to it and intoning a sort of plaintive, monotonous chant which gives to the celebrations all the gaiety of a funeral. From time to time one of them comes out of her group, goes into the circle of dancers, makes some movements, gesticulates violently, utters a terrible cry of despair, and retires. It is she, perhaps, who gives warning of the invasion, exhorts her people to resistance or reproaches the fugitives for their cowardice. Whatever we Europeans may

---

[7] The words in brackets translate Scala's translation, *fuggi via maledetto*, of *ulani selabu*. These last are presumably Yoruba but have not been recognized by Yoruba speakers, native and non-native, nor can such a phrase be traced in the dictionaries of Crowther, Wakeman and Abraham.

think of the merits of these dances, the natives are unanimous in declaring them the *nec plus ultra* of art and believe that there can be no more beautiful dance in any other part of the world.

By a strange contradiction, though one not difficult to explain, on the death of the King public exultation and entertainment is doubled. Hardly has the King breathed his last when the halls of the palace echo with the cheers and festive shouts of the priests. Thereupon the people, in mourning for the illness of their beloved monarch, run to the palace and join their joyful songs to those of the priests. The corpse, washed and perfumed by the high dignitaries of the Kingdom, is clad in ceremonial dress and displayed for his subjects' contemplation on a death-bed richly adorned with silk and velvet cloths with gold fringes. Meanwhile the supreme *Appesi* (staff-bearer), assisted by the ministers and royal councillors, proceeds to make an inventory of the deceased's estate. The cowries (small money) and the furnishings are immediately distributed among the indigent classes and priests (herein lies the secret of their joy) and the immovable property is transferred to his successor, if he belongs to a not very wealthy family, or else sold and the proceeds used for the public good. A primitive law not only excludes the sons and legitimate heirs of the King from the right to succeed to the crown but also deprives them of the right to inherit any wealth which the King possessed at the time of his election. In this way the people are guaranteed against the greed of their Kings and any desire on his part to prefer private to public interest and accumulate treasure for his family. The position of the Abeokuta princes is not in fact enviable. Having nothing to hope for from their father they are forced to become soldiers, merchants or farmers and to make their own living. Such a law would not be out of place in certain European states, particularly in Rome where barefaced nepotism has always been rife and has caused the people great poverty and misfortune.

The Yoruba Kingdom has a population of about two million. Its confines extend to the East as far as the Kingdom of Ijebu, to the North up to the Yoruba mountains, to the West as far as the Dahomey Kingdom, up to Porto Novo on the Gold Coast border, and to the South as far as the Kingdom of Lagos.[8]

Meanwhile the day was approaching on which the King, according to his promise, was to pronounce my fate. I knew quite well that the Fetishes had to be consulted about me and appreciating that these terrible divinities do not

[8] Scala's population figure for Yorubaland seems a reasonable guess but his description of the 'confines' of the 'Yoruba kingdom' clearly refers to the area formerly controlled by the Oyo kingdom and empire rather than to the whole Yoruba linguistic area since there is no 'Yoruba kingdom' known to history or tradition other than the occasional application of the term to Oyo. The 'mountains' must be the Yoruba highlands from the Ibadan area northwards.

like to be overlooked, I asked the priests to offer them, on my behalf, some
cowries, tobacco, rum and other small things which might please them. The
effect was as I had expected. Edified by my piety the gods gave a favourable
reply. On 21st September [1857], I was accorded an audience with the King
and was received with the same pomp and ceremony as before. The King
greeted me graciously and, when he had told me the oracle's reply, conferred
on me the title of his guest. Then the chief priest took a magnificent Kola nut
which had been placed on the so-called table of the oracles, and breaking it
into three parts, presented one of them to the King, another to me, and kept
the third for himself. The King ate his first, then I mine, and finally the priest
ate his. This ceremony not only confirmed me as the King's guest but also
consecrated me, in the eyes of the people, almost as an inviolate member
of the royal family.

I immediately started to lay the foundations of my trading station. The
King generously gave me quite a large piece of land on which to build a
factory. In a very short time, thanks to the voluntary help of the inhabitants,
I was able to build a temporary wooden shed to protect from the weather my
personal belongings and my merchandise which had not yet been unloaded
from my canoes as well as that which I should immediately order to be
sent from Lagos. Then I began to build my house and a big factory with
stores, according to my own design. To do this I employed daily from two
hundred to three hundred people whom I paid at the following rate: boys
100 cowries (about 50 centesimi); women 200 cowries; men 400 cowries.[9]

During this time I managed to collect from the inhabitants the greatest
quantity of cotton and palm oil[10] in exchange for my goods. The same
enthusiasm was shown here as in Lagos at the opening of my business,
which was in direct contact with the people who no longer had to deal
through the intermediary of monopolists. It was at everyone's disposition,

---

[9] Comparative information about wage rates in Lagos at this time may be found in A. G.
Hopkins's article on 'The Currency Revolution in South-West Nigeria in the Late Nineteenth
Century', *JHSN*, 1966 and in J. Hogendorn and M. Johnson, *The Shell Money of the Slave
Trade*, 1966. The exchange rate between cowries at Lagos in 1857 was 4s.2d. (50d.) for 2000
cowries (one head or two strings) (Hopkins, p. 476), from which it appears that Scala paid
his boys, at Abeokuta 2s.5d. a day (17s.5d. for 7 days), the women 5d./35d., and the men
10d./70d. During the 1850s the value of cowries at Lagos was falling steeply, following the
breaking of the monopoly of supply by the Hamburg firm of O'swald. Cowries, supplemented
by barter, continued to be the main medium of exchange in Lagos and its hinterland until
about 1880, after which they were quickly replaced by sterling.

[10] Exports from Lagos in 1857 included: palm oil, 4,942 tons at £222,390; ivory, 24,118 lbs at
£4,220; cotton, 114,848 lbs, at £3,590; manufactured cotton fabrics, £25,000. (Smith, *Lagos
Consulate*, p. 76). Biobaku, *The Egba*, pp. 58–59, describes the growing importance of cotton cultivation in Abeokuta and Consul Campbell's efforts, in co-operation with the missionaries, to
promote this (including the use of machinery for processing), in response to the rising prices
of raw cotton from America.

even the smallest traders, and also attracted the general population of Abeokuta who flocked to my wooden shed and soon realized the need to cultivate the land and increase its productivity.

Meanwhile news had reached Lagos of my arrival in Abeokuta and the emphatic report which my rowers gave of my solemn and flattering reception from the King and the inhabitants aroused the greatest surprise all over the island and a very natural curiosity to hear more details about me. An unforeseen circumstance gave me the opportunity to satisfy their wish by my return to Lagos. My building had not been completed when I received a message from the Hon. Mr Campbell which told me that Kosoko was once again threatening the island and asking me to return and help maintain the peace. This news, arriving at such an inopportune moment, saddened and worried me very much. On the one hand were my personal interests, the establishment of my firm in Abeokuta and the building of my factories on which my fortune depended. Both these required my presence on the spot. I did not hesitate for long. I left all my interests in the hands of my trusted agent in Abeokuta and after taking leave of the King who wanted to honour me with the protection of his staff I left hastily on 29th October for Lagos where I arrived on 4th November [1857].

King Kosoko, still tormented by the idea of regaining the throne of his ancestors, had prepared arms and canoes for a third invasion. Having been requested by Dosunmu and the English Consul to go to Epe and prevent this storm, I had no difficulty in convincing Kosoko of the folly of his plans by bringing to his notice the fact that Lagos was under British protection against which he could not possibly hope to be successful. I added that the British were determined to put an end once and for all to these attacks and that he would lose not only his arms and canoes, property and Kingdom but very probably his freedom or his life. These arguments prevailed upon the King; hostages from both sides were exchanged and peace restored, at least for the time being.[11]

The feelings of jealousy which had made Dosunmu oppose my going to Abeokuta were now shown very forcibly by the traders along the coast, particularly the Sierra Leonians. Abeokuta, situated between the Kingdoms of Dahomey and Ijebu, a short distance from the confluence of the Niger, was the central depot for the slaves and natural products to be sent to the coast and from there European goods were sent into the interior. The

---

[11] No confirmation can be found of Scala's claim to have played this role. Kosoko's presence on the lagoon did, however, constitute a menace to Lagos and to some extent also to Abeokuta, which necessitated a warning visit to Epe in February 1858 by Consul Campbell. Eventually Kosoko returned to Lagos in 1862 as a pensioner of the colonial government which had replaced the consular regime in 1861.

Lagos people and the Sierra Leonians or, to be more exact, the King and a few of the tribal chiefs who held the monopoly of this lucrative trade, were very anxious to prevent others from undertaking it on their own account without its passing through their hands. Besides this, my active co-operation in the abolition of the slave trade in the various transactions between the English and Kosoko clearly made me a sworn enemy of their favourite trade.[12] There was a strong motive, therefore, for those at Lagos to prevent me from returning to Abeokuta and to lessen my reputation among the inhabitants there. They resorted to their usual cunning. They repeated the same old insinuations against the greed and tyranny of the whites. These rumours, vain and ineffective at first, when repeated every day by hundreds of lips, were in the end believed and subsequently brought dismal consequences for me. Although I noticed these plots against me, I persisted in my plans to return and prepared seven canoes on which I loaded eighteen tons of the usual goods. On 20th February, 1858, accompanied by the same rowers and interpreter as before I left Lagos for the second time to go to Abeokuta, leaving the Sardinian Consulate in the care of the excellent Vice-Consul, Sig. Vincenzo Paggi.[13]

My first thought for my return to Abeokuta was to ensure the good-will of the King and the people so as to protect me from the insinuations of my enemies. For this purpose I had brought with me some presents which I proposed to distribute among them. For the King I had brought a rich mantle of crimson velvet lined with satin and decorated with gold fringes, a close fitting jacket of the same material with silver stars, a Damascene sword with a gilded hilt, a double-barrelled English sporting-gun with the necessary cartridges, and a six-chambered revolver. The King was uncommonly pleased with my gift and to prove his gratitude kindly granted me free access to the Royal Palace, the privilege of being admitted to his table, a privilege not granted to any of his subjects except the high dignitaries of the Kingdom on days of great national importance. He also gave me some land a few miles from Abeokuta and another piece in Agbamaya and Aro on the bank of the river, and authorized me to use his slaves for my building operations. I then gave the King's three ministers and the most important court dignitaries, silk scarves embroidered in gold and silver, various brocades in different colours and some toilet articles for them and their wives. The

---

[12] The quarrel between Scala and the Lagos merchants arose in part from Scala's offer, accepted by Oba Dosunmu, to farm the royal customs, mainly the duties paid on palm oil exported from Lagos. A secondary matter was the association which was alleged between Campbell and Scala. Scala's most prominent antagonists were the European merchants but the Sierra Leonians (or 'repatriates') also took an active part, their committee citing Scala in January 1857 to appear before their court for alleged non-payment of debt. Smith, *Lagos Consulate*, pp. 77–80.

[13] Vincenzo Paggi, like Scala a Ligurian, was Scala's business assistant as well as Vice-Consul.

people too could not be forgotten and had a share in my largesse. I had eleven
sacks of cowries corresponding to fifty-five Spanish 'colonatti' brought into
the public square and asked the priests to distribute them. They took a tenth
part, according to custom, and distributed the rest among the indigent
classes, shouting from time to time in emphatic tones, 'Here is the White
man sent by a powerful European King to make us his allies and friends
and help us to exchange our products for those of the Europeans. In
appreciation of our hospitality he is making us a present of his cowries.
Come and take them and may the protection of our god extend over him
and you.' The people replied 'Amen'.

From that moment I was considered a person of importance locally and
was consulted in almost all administrative activities. The minister of
commerce, anxious to find out about the techniques of European trade
which brought the white men such wealth and power, came almost every
day to ask me to explain the most effective methods for developing a
commercial spirit in his country. 'The primary basis of commerce,' I replied,
'is agriculture, particularly in countries where there is no industry. Two-
thirds of the lands within one hundred and fifty to two hundred miles
radius of Abeokuta are uncultivated and belong to a few leading families
who completely neglect them. A third of your people are warriors, that is
to say that they are idle. Now divide the land into equal parts and have
each part rented out for a small sum to be paid to the owner each year or
given to single families of warriors to be cultivated by them, and thus you
will have two advantages: (1) You will increase an hundredfold the national
riches of your soil and exchange them for European goods. (2) You will
reduce the pretexts for the wars which the warriors require for their livelihood.' Against these proposals three strong objections were raised: Would
the land-owners agree to surrender part of their land to the warriors?
Would the latter, used to the free and idle life of soldiers, settle down to
become farmers and to live by manual labour? In the third place, would
they not have to fear more frequent attacks from an enemy always on the
look-out, now that the region was deprived of its defenders, to which was
added the attraction of rich booty?

To these objections I replied that the land owners would maintain control
of their lands and would be pleased to see some return where they previously
had none; that the warriors would not be forced to work the land with their
own hands but could employ their families and the slaves that they took from
their enemies and sold to the slave trader. (There being as yet no hope of
abolishing slavery, it was better to restrict it to internal use and to reduce
it considerably by removing the profits derived from export.) With regard
to the fear of frequent invasions I pointed out that the presence of the
warriors was not indispensable on the lands which were cultivated by their

families; instead they could be mustered in separate companies at the points on the border that were most threatened and so protect them. In the event of an attack they would fight better if they had families and farms to defend. These arguments impressed the minister, a man of sense and experience, and after a few days I had the satisfaction of seeing my plans discussed and approved in the Parliament.

Meanwhile I made every effort to launch my business not so much for my own personal profit as to make the people realize its advantages. In two months I had exhausted all the town's supply of cotton, palm oil and ivory and sent it by river or land to Lagos where it was exported to Europe. Now I had to put Abeokuta in direct contact with the chief towns round about and then continue my good progress.

To this effect I sent accredited agents to Abrecudo [Iberekodo], twelve miles North of Abeokuta, the centre of cotton cultivation for the whole of the Western area up to the Dahomey border, and to Ikorodu on the South East on the river in direct communication with Epe, and I formed two depots, one in Agbamaya and the other in Arro [Aro], a small village West of Abeokuta, as centres for the transit of goods from the areas of production.

This plan did not escape the knowledge of my enemies. The distribution of the land decreed and carried out according to my suggestion by the Assembly, Abeokuta's becoming the import-export centre for a vast area, and the increasing importance of my factories excited the rancour of the powerful few who had monopolized this trade and they formed a coalition to ruin me. It was not long before I felt the effects of their secret plots.

VII

PERSECUTIONS

The attacks from my enemies were at first directed against my property. On April 4th [1858], I had sent to my Lagos house six canoes loaded with ten bales of indigenous cotton, twenty barrels of palm oil, and some crates of ivory. After a few days I received news that a fleet of pirates from Lagos and Sierra Leone had lain in wait near Obi and had made a surprise armed attack on my canoes, stolen my goods and forced my rowers to swim to safety. I complained to the King of Abeokuta on whose territory this act of piracy had been committed and he expressed sincere regret at the incident, adding that for a long time he had been receiving messages from the King of Lagos asking him to banish me from his state. A month later I sent another batch of canoes loaded with goods and this too was attacked, near Arri [Aro?]; my goods were stolen and my rowers, although bearing the protection of my staff and ring, were tied to trees and savagely beaten. Their lives were spared only on condition that they swore to their god to leave my service and take no more part in the transportation of my goods.

I was certain that some Lagos canoe-men were taking part in the raids and that these were actually planned in Lagos so as soon as I heard the news I wrote to King Dosunmu and to the English Consul asking for satisfaction in the form of punishment of the guilty parties and of guarantees for the future. The former replied by casting all the blame on the inhabitants of the locality where the acts of aggression had taken place, and he told me that as I had ventured rashly among a savage people where such cases occurred daily, I should be prepared for even greater misfortunes if I continued in my project. The second deeply sympathized with my misfortune which was, in his opinion, inevitable in present conditions and he added that my story had strengthened his conviction that Abeokuta was not yet prepared for European settlement. He advised me to return to Lagos and look after my Consulate where my presence would be more valuable in furthering the cause of African civilization which I had promoted. These letters far from weakening my resolution made me more determined than ever to fight against these increasing difficulties. Alone, isolated and thrown back upon my own resources, I found a sort of poetry in thwarting the dark plots of my powerful enemies and coming out victorious from such a bitter struggle. So I surrounded myself with trusted and experienced people who went to the markets in the interior to buy the products before the Sierra Leonians got there, offering prices with which they could not, in any case, compete. The products were then sent by land to various points on the lagoon near Lagos, and from there loaded onto canoes and swiftly taken to the island and then to my house, to the extreme surprise of King Dosunmu, the English Consul and the people of Lagos.

Disappointed in their hopes of committing more robberies at my expense, my enemies resorted to calumny and depicted me to the King and people of Abeokuta as a secret emissary of the King of Dahomey who had been sent there for the express purpose of facilitating an invasion of the region, a plot which had been long in prospect. They said that I had cunningly suggested the removal of the warriors so that the city should be left undefended and exposed to attack. They worked on people's superstitions and spread the news everywhere that the local oracle had predicted that when a White man came to the town, the Kingdom of Abeokuta would fall and pass into the hands of their natural enemies, the people of Dahomey.[1]

This kingdom, whose capital is also called Dahomey, lies to the West of Abeokuta, covers an area of three hundred miles and has about six million inhabitants, most of whom are warriors or more exactly raiders. Its borders are the beach from Badagry as far as Grand Popo on the South, the Yoruba Kingdom on the East, the Ashanti Provinces on the West and the Yoruba mountains to the North. It possesses fertile lands and rich palm plantations, but as the people are inclined towards plunder and war rather than agriculture the yield of maize, yams etc. is not very large and hardly sufficient for the needs of the people. When they need European goods, which they feel are absolutely necessary to them, they undertake great slave raids into the neighbouring countries, transport the slaves to Porto Novo which has succeeded Lagos as the great slave market, and sell them to the Portuguese.

The King of Dahomey has a regular, permanent army of twenty thousand men, easily doubled in the case of war by the voluntary service of the idlers and tramps of the Kingdom (and there are many) who are attracted to the army by the hope of rich booty. But the real strength of his military force

---

[1] There are numerous accounts in English of the Kingdom of Dahomey by travellers, writers about the slave trade, and more recently historians and anthropologists. See, for example, R. F. Burton, *A Mission to Gelele*, 1864, W. J. Argyle, *The Fon of Dahomey*, 1966, and R. Law, *The Slave Coast*, 1991.

is the Royal Guard, composed exclusively of women.[2] The Abeokuta people assess the number of these Amazons at thirty thousand, but this figure is doubtless an exaggeration. Reports from travellers who visit this Kingdom make the number vary from three to five thousand. These female warriors wear a close-fitting jacket of blue cloth and a Greek-style tunic of striped cotton going down almost to their knees. They have a copper breast plate and armlets of the same metal. Their heads are covered with a turban; to this is attached a strip of cloth which flutters over their shoulders. Their arms and legs are bare. They are agile, swift, brave and very skilled at handling bows, spears and carbines. In battle they are the first to rush at the enemy and play the same part as our *Bersaglieri*.[3] They attack with great force and are savage and fierce in the mêlée, giving no quarter. They are chosen from among the youngest and strongest maidens in the country and are enrolled for three wars or for three years, since the nation is obliged by its laws to fight one war each year. During their military service they cannot be married and any infringement of the laws of chastity is severely punished. An Amazon who becomes a mother will be put to death and so will be her seducer. They live in special barracks where they receive splendid board and lodging and are waited upon by many slaves. They hold exercises in the public squares and so greatly are they feared and respected that the men prudently keep away from the place where they exercise. Their military training is entrusted exclusively to former women warriors and promotions are given, according to merit, to the bravest and most skilled. In peacetime they guard the Royal Palace and escort the King when he goes out or at public ceremonies. They alone have the privilege of carrying His Majesty on a richly adorned litter, the voluptuous monarch's usual means of locomotion. Then their service is over, the King chooses those who have most distinguished themselves in war, without bothering about their being beautiful or ugly, and accords them the honour of joining his harem. This position which in their opinion assures a rich and honourable retirement, is naturally sought after by them all and is a great incitement to valour and training.

This regiment of women has rendered the Kingdom of Dahomey formidable and has terrified all the inhabitants of the surrounding countries. The Yoruba and Ijebu people and those of the provinces bordering on them, with the exception of Kosoko who had cleverly made an alliance with the King of

[2] For a review of the evidence about the female soldiers (or 'Amazons') of Dahomey, see R. Law, 'The "Amazons"', in *Paideuma*, 1993. Law concludes that this force originated, probably in the eighteenth century, as a royal bodyguard, and was therefore not normally engaged in battle. It was converted into a fighting force under the warrior king Gezo (?1818–1858). During this reign the force was enlarged and for a time foreign captives were recruited to it. Numbers varied, with a possible maximum of about 2,500.
[3] An élite force within the Italian army, literally 'sharp-shooters'.

Dahomey by opening a port for him in his small territory,[4] live in continual
terror of being attacked and plundered by their feared neighbour. The time
of year when they were used to make their raids was in March, April and
May because of the drought which made the tracks passable and allowed the
army either to ford the streams and rivers in these regions or simply to cross
them when they were dry. This season was approaching and the unrest of the
people, increased by the sinister rumours spread through the town about my
presence, had reached its peak when suddenly news was received that Aro
was in flames. Consternation and terror were rife, while the crowds, gathered
in the square and in the King's compound, screamed and wept.

From time to time imprecations and threats were heard against the White
man, the emissary of the Dahomians. Night was approaching and adding its
horrors to this picture of woe. Already a furious crowd had gathered round
my house ready to attack; already those most excited had penetrated into my
factories and started their work of destruction; in another few minutes I
should certainly have fallen a victim to these wretched people whom superstition had made fanatical, if a strong group of élite soldiers sent by the
King had not forced their way through the crowd and cleared the area.

In the meantime a reddish light and thick columns of smoke were appearing on the Western horizon and a distant, confused noise was reaching the
ears of the terrified townsmen. Their imagination was heightened; fear
transformed their purpose. There was no longer any doubt. That light
meant that Aro and the neighbouring villages were in flames; that noise
must be the trumpets and war cries of the Dahomians as they advanced to
destroy Abeokuta. There was no time for delay. The King hurriedly mar-
shalled his troops, joined by many volunteers who owned weapons. Others
ran to the walls and posted cannon at the most vulnerable points. The
King placed himself at the head of his troops, followed by a vast train. I
took my position next to the war-chiefs, armed with an excellent carbine
and two revolvers in the saddle holsters, and we hastened towards Aro.

We had not gone a mile when a grotesque spectacle presented itself to our
eyes and explained the mystery of these alarms. Instead of the terrible
warriors from Dahomey we were confronted with a delirious crowd of
Furies, naked, dishevelled and carrying clubs and darts, furiously waving
resin torches in the air as they uttered desperate yells. I thought I had
fallen into the midst of those horrible assemblies where witches and infernal
spirits perform their sacrilegious mysteries. The glow from the torches
throwing an eerie light on the forest trees, the smoke from the resin which

---

[4] G. O. Oguntomisin examines relations between Kosoko and the King of Dahomey in his thesis
'New Forms of Political Organization', 1979, pp. 301–305. These relations were close and frequent, and although Oguntomisin concludes that the King lost interest in Kosoko as an ally
after his removal to Epe, Scala's report here seems likely to be true.

enveloped men and things in a dense cloud, the yells and gesticulations of these obscene Bacchante, the sinister black faces which surrounded me, all made this scene a true pandemonium bringing to mind the orgies of Satan's Kingdom. These poor women truly thought that they had saved Aro and were coming to save Abeokuta. Some priests, bribed by the people of Lagos and the Sierra Leonians, had given them to believe that the white man who had settled in Abeokuta and Aro was an agent of the King of Dahomey and that his factories were strategic points for helping the enemy when the invasion took place. They had, therefore, to destroy everything in order to force the white man to leave the country. Half their duty had already been accomplished. My factory at Aro containing goods to the value of more than two thousand *Scudi* had already gone up in flames and was no more than a heap of rubble. Some Africans, like jackals gathering round a corpse, were salvaging the few articles which the fire had spared. There still remained my factory at Abeokuta and the saviours of the home-land were hurrying towards it.

The King had difficulty in pacifying these good women and persuading them to return to Aro. Although I had suffered grave losses I felt deep pity for those innocent victims of superstition and of the malignity of a few envious people. The Africans are for the most part well-meaning but religious fanaticism in every country makes men blind and fierce.[5]

I was not defeated by this new misfortune but re-doubled my zeal, activity, determination and sacrifices. I rebuilt my factories on the ruins of the former ones, set up machines for cleaning the cotton and numerous presses for extracting palm oil. The various operations of my work shops employed more than one thousand people a day and the population having recovered from the calumny of my enemies blessed me as they had done before. Fate smiled on my enterprise and unexpectedly offered me a great compensation for my losses.

---

[5] Aro had been on the line of approach of the Dahomian army in their attack on Abeokuta in 1851, and the first phase of that battle was fought around the Aro (or Badagry) Gate in the walls. See Ajayi and Smith, *Yoruba Warfare*, chapter 6 and p. 155 (plan). Recollection of this, combined with rumours about and prejudice against Scala, may explain the misapprehension which resulted in the burning of Scala's warehouses. This action by the mob is retained in the childrens' song at Abeokuta: *Enia ko jagun ko j'owo* 'You can't fight us or beat us with money' *Awa la'peki Sikala lo* 'We are the ones who drove Scala away' (Information from Dr G.O. Olusanya). References to relations between Scala and the people of Abeokuta in the reports of the CMS missionaries confirm the resentment aroused, especially among the Parakoyi (trading chiefs), by Scala's presence in the town and the subsequent opposition to his trading activities. They do not confirm the women's movement described here. T. King (CA2/0/61); T. B. Macaulay (CA2/0/65); J. A. Maser (CA2/0/68), and the Rev. H. Townsend (CA2/0/85) (Information from Professor J. D. Y. Peel.). This information contrasts with accounts by Fr Borghero and others of Scala's good reputation in Lagos and Abeokuta, for which see the Editorial Introduction above. In the text Scala's spellings of Aro as Arro, Arri, have been amended.

There are near Abeokuta, along the banks of the river, enormous trees just like our chestnuts. They produce a fruit oval in shape and about two inches thick by three inches long, covered with an oily sugary rind, identical in taste to unripe dates. The inside of the fruit is composed of a pistachio-shaped kernel covered with a brown skin as soft as that of our chestnut. The blacks eat the outer rind and when they have peeled the fruit, pound it in a mortar and make from it a paste with which they oil their bodies to cure them of rheumatism. I had an idea that this fruit might be of use in the manufacture of soap, candles etc. and anxious to increase African exports, I had a number of them collected and sent immediately to England for chemical analysis. The reply came that this fruit, hitherto unknown in Europe, did indeed contain large quantities of fat which could be used in making soap, candles etc. and was unanimously pronounced 'vegetable fat' by the chemists. It is possible that other qualities may subsequently be discovered in this plant which may perhaps supersede animal fat as a powerful cure for rheumatism, the only quality for which it is known in Africa. These trees are abundant in the Yoruba, Dahomey and Ashanti provinces and one can obtain large quantities of their fruits for almost nothing. Before long I had sent four hundred tons of them to England.[6]

Two months passed by quite peacefully and I took advantage of them to develop and increase my business as much a possible until new persecutions and new events arose to hamper the progress of my commercial venture. A formidable enemy who had been hidden in the shadows and almost forgotten by me, suddenly appeared in opposition to plans for legitimate trade, and one fine day I found myself confronted with Tinubu. The famous agitator, after her exile from Lagos, had returned, as I have already said, to Abeokuta bringing with her great wealth and exerting a more disastrous influence than ever over the men of her tribe.[7] While still waiting for a situation to

---

[6] Here Scala refers presumably to shea butter, obtained from the nuts of the shea tree (*Butyrospermum*). Consul Campbell had tried to interest the authorities in London in this product in 1857. Small quantities were eventually exported and in the commercial agreement of 1859 between Oba Dosunmu and the European and Saro (Sierra Leonian) merchants a duty of two heads of cowries was fixed for every ton of shea butter exported.

[7] Scala does not exaggerate the importance of the position which Madame Tinubu held in Abeokuta. Numerous references to her occur in consular and missionary reports; of these Fr Borghero's account is perhaps the most vivid. Calling on her in the course of his visit to Abeokuta in 1864 he found her on the point of leaving for the Egba war camps to which she had been called. Nevertheless she received him in an unhurried and gracious manner, alluding to Scala as she did so. She then left for the front, moving among her escort of some 40 soldiers armed with guns with great natural dignity. Tinubu is still remembered in Lagos and Abeokuta, and in the latter her Iyalode (First Lady) compound, which contains her tomb, is an attraction for visitors. Until a few years ago portions of her landed wealth were still the subject of litigation among her descendants. Biobaku, *The Egba, passim*; Yemitan, *Tinubu*, chapters 7 and 8; Borghero, *Journal*, p. 182.

arise which would once again bring her onto the field of action where she could pursue her boundless ambition, she had taken up her favourite passion of slave trading on a large scale. Soon after I arrived in Abeokuta this lady came to visit me, evidently wanting to know what my intentions were, and I told her frankly that I planned to substitute legitimate trade for the slave trade as I had already done in Lagos. Moreover, I asked for her cooperation in this enterprise, pointing out that her capital would be more advantageously used in the new kind of trade since the slave trade was becoming ever more uncertain and dangerous because of the vigilance of the British cruisers. Tinubu did not take very kindly to my proposals and in a mood more angry than friendly she took her leave. From then on I lost sight of her until an extraordinary circumstance put her once again in touch with me.

At that time, the famous English expedition directed by Dr. Baikie was exploring the course of the Niger on behalf of the British Government and was proceeding with alacrity in this scientific search. The expedition had reached the confluence of the River Blas [Brass?], but, surprised by the dry season which usually lasts from February to September and during which the river becomes unnavigable for lack of water, now had to return to Lagos to wait for the rains. On hearing about my journey, Dr. Baikie decided to travel by way of Abeokuta to Arubu [Raba], the point at which the great caravans from the interior cross the Niger and where there is an English Protestant mission.[8] He divided his expedition into two parts, each taking a different route and, taking command of the first party himself, set out for his destination. On the way he was met by a ragged band of seventy to eighty Black slaves, destined for the trade, who had fled from Porto Novo and the surrounding places and who begged for his protection and permission to follow him so that they could return to Osa [Hausaland?] and Tappa [Nupe], their homelands. The second party, commanded by the brave Lieutenant Glover, a man of great energy, had left a month after the first and was likewise met on the way by other fleeing slaves. The Sierra Leonians, owners of these slaves, hastily armed their men and came along the road from Abeokuta to intercept Glover and recapture their slaves. They met him a short distance from Lagos and fired at his column but were energetically repulsed by the English and dispersed into the forest.

When the Sierra Leonians saw that their attack had failed, they sent a message to Tinubu telling her of the incident and offering her half the slaves if she succeeded in wresting them from Glover's hands. She gladly accepted their proposition and having won over the guards at the [town] gates, ordered

[8] Raba was the former capital of the Nupe, replaced by Bida. The 'English Protestant mission', however, must be that at Lokoja, founded by the Rev. (later Bishop) Samuel Crowther during the Niger Expedition of 1857–1858 at the confluence of the Niger and Benue rivers.

them to stop the men of the first expedition on some pretext or other before
they entered the town [of Abeokuta] so as to have time to warn her of their
arrival. In fact as soon as the advance guard, made up almost entirely of
fugitive slaves, reached the gates, Tinubu sent her trusty warriors to bring
them to her together with any supplies they might have. Lieutenant Glover
had remained some way behind with the main strength of the party. It
must be noted that Tinubu had a large number of slaves belonging to the
same tribes as those who were captured at the gates and it was therefore
quite easy for two of the latter to escape with the help of their tribesmen
and take refuge in my house, where they told me what had happened.
They still wore the chains which Tinubu had ordered to be put round their
necks and ankles. I immediately ran to the King and explained to him the
gravity of the matter and the consequences which could follow from this
insult to an officer of the British Royal Navy. The King and his ministers
were greatly vexed by this affront from Tinubu and sent a large body of
soldiers to free the captives. Meanwhile I went out to meet Lt. Glover and
asked how many men were in his party.

Tinubu, seeing she had failed and warned of the storm gathering over her
head, had already released the slaves and given them back some of the provisions she had taken from them, protesting that she had never intended to
appropriate them for herself. Then she incited her own slaves to mingle
with those who had been freed and to say that they too wished to follow
Lieutenant Glover. The slaves obeyed and then Tinubu let it be known
throughout the town that the English White man who had already stolen
the slaves from Lagos and Sierra Leone now intended to steal those of
Abeokuta. She drew attention to the loss of her own fugitive slaves and
tried to arouse the people. In fact very great unrest was evident all over
the town and already some groups of resolute men, roused by Tinubu's emissaries, were preparing to attack Glover's house where the slaves had taken
refuge. This brave officer laughed at the vain threats of the crowd, knowing
quite well that the carbines of his men could keep them quiet. However he did
not wish to cause bloodshed nor to bear the heavy responsibility for arousing
a civil war by arming slaves against their masters in a foreign country. He
came to consult me. I told him that I knew Tinubu and that she was capable
of anything but that she also knew me and feared me because she was not
unaware of my great influence over the King, Chiefs and people of Abeokuta
who called me their father and benefactor. If I threatened to leave Abeokuta
because of her, she would certainly not want to be responsible for my
departure, for fear of stirring up the anger of the people which could have
dismal consequences for her. So I asked Glover to leave the matter in my
hands and advised him in the meantime to make no preparations for defence,
to open the doors of his house and disarm the Africans, ordering them all to

refuse to respond to the enemy's provocations and threats. He promised to follow my advice.

Without losing any time, I sent a messenger, bearing my ring, to Tinubu, asking for an explanation of the rumours about an attack on the English officer's house and adding that, if the attack were to take place, I should immediately leave the town and hold her responsible for my departure. The messenger found Tinubu seated in the courtyard of her house, holding council with her war-chiefs. As soon as she saw him, she stood up, took him by the hand and led him into a separate room to hear the message. When she returned to her people she said: 'My friends, Scala sends us a message. He has seen through our plot and threatens to go away if we put it into operation. You know that everyone considers Scala as the father of the people, sent by the God to give us our livelihood. Now, what will happen to us if he leaves through our fault?'

A murmur of disapproval greeted these words but a threatening glance from the proud lady was enough to calm any spirit of rebellion and deep silence reigned all around. Tinubu dismissed my messenger, saying, 'Tell Scala I have understood', and she sat down majestically again amid her warriors. A large distribution of Aquavita and other small considerations managed to reassure the rebels and compensate them for the loot they had hoped for. All ended in blessed peace and harmony.

Next day Lieutenant Glover came to visit me and expressed his most grateful thanks for the peaceful solution to this unfortunate affair. He set off for Raba with all the slaves to whom he had promised his protection, except those of Tinubu who had insinuated themselves into the ranks for strategic purposes. When he reached Raba, he wrote me an extremely kind letter, renewing his thanks and mentioning my friendship and influence with the African people to whose progress I had dedicated myself. Dr Baikie also wrote to me in very flattering terms.

The Abeokuta people, recognizing that the wiles and intrigues of Tinubu in this affair had all been directed towards appropriating half the fugitive slaves, equally expressed their gratitude to me for having saved the town from a bloody conflict which might have had disastrous consequences for their country.[9]

---

[9] The episode of the slaves is summarized in Smith, *Lagos Consulate*, pp. 107–108 and notes 78, 79 on p. 170. The sources for this account are the British consular papers, Crowther's *Journal* in Crowther and Taylor (1859), and extracts from Glover's diary reproduced in Hastings (1920), pp. 206, 207. None of these refer to any part played by Scala in the affair. William Balfour Baikie (1825–1864), a Royal Naval surgeon, commanded the Niger Expeditions of 1854 and 1857. Sir John Hawley Glover (1829–1885), then a Lieutenant R.N., was a member of the 1857 expedition. After leaving the Royal Navy in 1862 he served as Governor and Administrator of Lagos between 1863 and 1872; under him the colony began its slow expansion into the interior.

But Tinubu, bent on revenge, was not so easily beaten. Being unable to fight me overtly she thought up a far-reaching plan for a terrible, infernal revenge which, had it succeeded, would have involved not only myself but all the innocent people of the Yoruba Kingdom as well. It is possible that, as well as wanting her revenge on me, she still hoped to fulfil the dream she had never forgotten of gaining the throne of Abeokuta by means of some such political confusion. In agreement with the fanatical priests who had roused the women of Aro and Abeokuta to burn my factories and who were still awaiting in trepidation the punishment for their misdeeds, Tinubu sent secret agents into the Kingdom of Dahomey to incite the Dahomians to take advantage of the dry season and invade the Yoruba Kingdom. To the desire for loot, so powerful among these fierce and rapacious people, religious fanaticism was now added. Tinubu's emissaries, nearly all priests, spread the rumour among the Dahomians that I was not a European merchant who had come to Abeokuta to set up legitimate trade, but a religious missionary who had come for the express purpose of overthrowing their idols and subjecting Africa to European dominion. Strange contradiction! Only a few months before I had been denounced as the secret agent of the Dahomians and now I was the enemy of their religion and independence. I need not say that this calumny was believed and inflamed the people who did not, in any case, need any incitement to go to war. The invasion of Yorubaland was decided, prepared on a large scale and this time it assumed the character of a religious crusade.[10]

As soon as a vague rumour of this reached Abeokuta, the people, armed and fearful, left their work in the fields and their business speculations to prepare themselves to face the enemy army which the usual exaggeration had increased to almost fifty thousand men. I too closed my factories and put myself at the King's disposal for the defence of the country. If I had believed that my presence was the only motive for the invasion, I should have left immediately to save those poor people from such a terrible calamity, but I knew very well that once the spur to action was applied there was no lack of pretexts, and moreover, periodical wars were quite normal for the Dahomians. In such circumstances my leaving Abeokuta

---

[10] Two major assaults by the Dahomians on Abeokuta took place during their wars with the Egba (c. 1844–c. 1874): in 1851 (six years before Scala visited the town) and in 1864 (five years after he had left). None of the authorities substantiate Scala's description of a major Dahomian expedition against Abeokuta in March (or any other month) 1858 or 1859. Nevertheless there was general nervousness in the Egba capital in these years; the Dahomians continued to raid the intervening countryside, burning Egba and Egbado villages, while Consul Campbell in Lagos reported warnings sent to Abeokuta from Ketu in early 1858 that the King of Dahomey intended to move imminently against Abeokuta. Campbell attributed these internal disturbances to a revival of the slave trade at Whydah: F084/1061, Campbell to Malmesbury, 3 March 1858, 7 April 1858.

would be cowardice and shameful desertion in the face of the enemy. My first thought was to send trusted agents to Dahomey to gather precise information about the enemy's strength and movements and to ask my firm in Lagos to send all available weapons. My agents reported, among other things, that there was some wavering among the Dahomian troops on account of the bloody defeat inflicted upon them by the Yoruba ten years earlier, entirely due to the stratagems of Anoba, the King of Abeokuta's most practised warrior. He was still alive, though a very old man venerated by King and people and he could once again save the country by his marvellous stratagems.

Knowing that the national army was insufficient to face the great hordes of the Dahomians, he had for a long time been working out a plan of defence which had been suggested to him by the very nature of the country. He had observed that between Tapuna and Abeokuta there was an area of high ground rising on both sides of the river and thus making so narrow a channel that only four canoes could pass through it one after the other. On this high ground, some metres from the river, was a cave hewn by nature from the living rock, about one hundred metres deep by three hundred wide, which seemed made to serve as a reservoir from where, by means of a convenient opening below, the water could hurl itself down on the land beneath and flood it. A few miles from this place rose another small stream called the Serra which flows into the Abeokuta river about seven miles to the North of the town, while all the land in between these two rivers forms a deep valley which, in the rainy season, is always flooded as the rivers overflow. Anoba tried to take advantage of the favourable position of this valley and had dykes constructed at intervals along both rivers so that at an agreed signal the valley could be flooded. The difficulty was to draw the enemy to this fatal spot, and the good Anoba himself took charge of this important operation.

On 13th March the armed forces of Dahomey, commanded by the King himself, had invaded the Yoruba territory and were advancing towards Abeokuta, destroying and plundering everything as was their wont. Anoba had ordered the strongest units of the army to occupy the heights which dominate the town, from where, heavily fortified, they could with advantage resist the enemy's charge and protect the capital. Then, at the head of a strong body of experienced troops, he set out on foot to meet the enemy whom he found encamped in a forest a few miles from Samina. The Dahomian vanguard, composed for the most part of women, did not hesitate to hurl themselves upon the Yoruba who offered strong resistance until gradually they retreated in good order. Encouraged by this first success, the Dahomians pursued them with growing ardour and continued their victorious progress as far as Gobon [Gbogun?]. There, a separate body of women who had ventured further into the forest were unexpectedly attacked by Anoba. There was a long and desperate fight and the women proved to be quite worthy of their reputation for indomitable courage, but in the end they had to surrender, leaving on the battlefield about a thousand of their companions dead or wounded and a large number of prisoners. The others fled towards the north, perhaps too ashamed to return to the camp after their sad defeat which would bring upon them the scorn of their companions and ruin the reputation of the corps. From then on, no more was heard of these fugitives.

The King of Dahomey, hearing of the women's defeat, grew furious and swore not to halt his advance until he reached Abeokuta, a two day's journey from where he was. I do not need to say that the unfortunate city was destined to be sacked and burned. Meanwhile the astute Anoba, still pursued and still in flight, allowed himself to be seen in the distance, exchanging a few blows with the enemy's vanguard, so as to draw the enemy into the ambush he had prepared. Finally on 21st March, the King of Dahomey with the flower of his army came to camp on the exact spot Anoba had foreseen. The trials of the hurried march through forests and swamps necessitated at least one day's rest before the town could be attacked. While the waiting army was enjoying the delights of a recuperative sleep, Anoba, as evening approached, secretly sent his men to the dykes and ordered them to loose all the floods simultaneously on the stroke of 6 o'clock. The waters, pouring out of so many openings opposite one another, flowed down the slopes and came together in the valley of the sleepers. The effects were soon felt. Suddenly awakened by the invading element which continued to rise, astonished to find themselves surrounded by water, under a clear sky and after so many months of drought, the Dahomians arose in terror and disorder, uttering piercing shrieks. Struck by their usual superstition they believed that the flooding of the camp was the work of hostile Fetiches so that they threw down their weapons and hurriedly escaped in all directions. But the Yoruba army stationed on the heights above Abeokuta, sure now of the success of the strategem, had moved towards the valley and, joining with Anoba's force, surrounded the enemy on all sides. It was easy for these fresh and disciplined troops to disperse the terrified and disarmed hordes who opposed them. Horrible was the massacre, enormous the loot and thirteen thousand the number of prisoners.[11]

[11] See note 10 above. No other reference has been found to this ingenious flooding of the valley and the Dahomian encampment, and it is unlikely that the Egba at this time had the technical expertise and equipment to carry out these works. Professor J. Anthony Allen of the Department of Geography, School of Oriental and African Studies, University of London, in a conversation on 17 September 1996, agreed, while pointing out that Scala's account could possibly derive from the recollection of a particularly heavy rainfall which might have enabled some local diversion of the waters. Examination of the Ordnance maps of the area (Sheet 260, 1 : 100,000) revealed no defile on the river Ogun in the vicinity of Abeokuta such as Scala describes. Nor could Tapuna, Samina and Dasron be identified on the maps.

The King of Dahomey with a body of three thousand men and five hundred women hastily escaped to Dasron and when he reached there started immediately to erect fortifications and defences at which he worked with his own hands. But being without food and fearing that at any moment he would be attacked by a victorious enemy who now had greater numbers, he sent messages to the King of Abeokuta to treat for peace. As humble in misfortune as he was proud and cruel in triumph, he said that he would offer himself and his family as hostages if his people might be spared. But this offer was doubtless a pretext for gaining time.

A council was held in Abeokuta over which the King presided and in which all the important people of the Kingdom took part. It was almost unanimously decided to show no mercy to the defeated, to make the King and his family prisoners and to burst into Dahomey burning and killing in order to avenge the injuries they had suffered and to protect themselves for the future. But the wise Anoba who knew, better than the others perhaps, the strength of the Dahomians and how difficult it was to destroy them, or else was moved by humane feelings, very natural in such a good and honest man as he was, expressed different opinions and advised gentler treatment. 'You have repulsed an enemy', he told them, 'who was unjustly attacking us for no reason at all, and this success is owed to the protection of our Fetiches who always favour the cause of justice. But you cannot abuse this victory without losing the protection which you have enjoyed. The Kingdom of Dahomey is vast, immense and inhabited by a warrior population greatly superior to our own. You can take advantage of this moment of terror we have inflicted to invade their country and devastate a part of it, but to occupy it completely and destroy or enslave all their population is impossible for us just as it is contrary to our principles of justice. If you inflict too harsh a punishment on the Dahomians, you will perpetuate the hatred of these fierce people and their desire for revenge will bring them sooner or later back into our land. If, on the contrary, you are generous and offer them peace with honour, you will make them a friendly people with whom, from now on, you can live in peace and trade freely.'

These words were greeted with a heavy disapproving silence, quite natural to these rude men who were drunk with victory and more inclined towards blood and plunder than to feelings of generosity and justice, but the authority of Anoba was so greatly respected that no one dared to contradict him openly.

So they accepted the King of Dahomey's proposals and sent messages inviting him to come to Abeokuta to consecrate with solemn religious rites the peace treaty which they were to draw up. But in the meantime the King of Dahomey, escaping the vigilance of his enemy, had succeeded in escaping from Dasron with the remains of his army and had regained his own territory. Peace was not made and the two peoples became even greater enemies than before. Nevertheless the people of Abeokuta celebrated their victory for three consecutive days.

VIII

RELIGIONS, LAWS, CUSTOMS AND THE ARMY[1]

The dominant religions of those parts of the West Coast of Africa which I have visited, being the Kingdom of Lagos, Yorubaland, Ijebuland, Benin, Dahomey, Ashanti and Sierra Leone, are Islam and Idolatry. It is true that there are, here and there along the coast, some English Protestant Missions which apply themselves zealously to spreading the true gospel, but no Christian Church can yet boast of having laid any solid foundation. There are only a few Protestant converts of uncertain faith, and attracted by the gifts and the protection of the missionaries rather than by any true convic-tion. It is rare for an African to abandon entirely the old superstitions and fervently embrace the new faith. The catholic missionaries have been even less fortunate for they have not succeeded in founding a single church in those regions in spite of their many attempts. Some were killed by the climate and others chased away by the fanaticism of the people. One of the chief obstacles to the propagation of the Gospel is undoubtedly the practice of polygamy, so contrary to Christian morals yet so dear to these hot and lusty people. However, religion and civilization must in time triumph over even this difficulty and in the end, the law of God will reign over all the earth. We shall learn from travellers' accounts that some tribes of the interior

---

[1] Scala does not identify his sources for this chapter, but it seems likely that he found many of his informants among his fellow traders including the Saro (ex-Sierra Leonian) and Amaro (ex-Brazilian) emigrant communities rather than from the native Awori of Lagos and the Egba at Abeokuta. Much information is now available about Yoruba society in general. The bibliography prepared for Darryl Forde's book on *The Yoruba-Speaking Peoples of South-Western Nigeria*, 1951, contains some 300 items and the list could well be doubled today. Useful comparison with the information in this chapter might be made with the first part of Samuel Johnson's *The History of the Yorubas*, 1921, and also with the works of two American missionaries, T. J. Bowen, 1859 and W. H. Clarke, 1972 who were both in Yorubaland during the 1850s. Modern works are G. J. A. Ojo's *Yoruba Culture*, 1966, J. D. Y. Peel, *Ijeshas and Nigerians*, 1983, and, for the Lagos area, Sandra Barnes, *Patrons and Power*, 1986.

have embraced Christianity and spontaneously renounced their vile, inveterate customs. Sooner or later the good seed will bear fruit.[2]

Islam was brought into Africa by the peoples of the Northern coast,
Arabs and Moroccans,[3] but it has degenerated and the purity of the
Koran has been corrupted by confusion with pagan superstitions. Whilst
the Koran teaches that there SHALL BE NO OTHER GOD BUT GOD and makes
the unity of God the basis of religion, the Moslems of Africa have found a
way of adding to the ONE God the company of other deities, of an inferior
order, it is true, but of considerable importance to them. So, while the devout
Moslem fulfils the obligations and recites the prayers laid down in the Koran,
he runs immediately afterwards to offer sacrifices to the Fetishes, to propitiate them and placate their wrath when some misfortune has occurred.[4]

Idolatry is the true religion of the interior of Africa: the others are only
foreign importations. African paganism is difficult to define and varies
according to country and tribe. In general the Africans have no concept of
a Supreme Being, creator of the Universe and impartial judge of men's
actions after their death. They worship a number of invisible spirits called
Fetishes,[5] which have various supernatural powers and preside over all
their domestic and social activities. The Fetishes are innumerable and of
various orders, higher or lower according to the miracles they perform, or
it would be better to say according to the cunning of the priests devoted to
their special cult, for they are adept at drawing greater or lesser benefits
from the credulity of the faithful. Each town, village and household, each
tree in the forest and, we might even say, each individual has a guardian
Fetich with its own particular worshippers. However much the existence of
an invisible being may strike the imagination of the ordinary people and
fill them with terror, particularly in the forest or in the darkness of the
night, the priests, on the other hand, consider it wiser to give some sort of
form to their idols so that they may act on the senses of the worshippers.
These forms vary greatly according to the imagination and the ability of
the priests. Some take the form of a single shapeless block of stone, as
huge as Druids' stones; others are small stones or pieces of wood, equally
shapeless, and portable for the greater convenience of the faithful; others
represent all kinds of animals, lions, oxen, snakes, crocodiles etc and these
are de luxe fetiches used by well-off families. Very wealthy people can even

---

[2] This prophesy could be assessed against, for example, J. F. A. Ajayi, *Christian Missions*, 1965,
and E. A. Ayandele, *Missionary Impact*, 1966.
[3] Examination of Arabic-derived words in Yoruba suggest that Islam was brought to this area
from the Western Sudan, probably by merchants moving down the Niger. Even today Moslems
in Yorubaland are sometimes called *Imale*, 'people of Mali'.
[4] But see T. G. O. Gbadamosi, *The Growth of Islam among the Yoruba, 1860–1908*, 1978.
[5] For Scala's use of the terms 'Fetish' and 'Fetishes', see Chapter V above, note 7.

acquire for themselves fetiches which more or less represent human beings but these are only found in big towns where such art flourishes. I have been able to obtain one of these, a small grotesque head of a creature somewhere between a man and a monkey, and have brought it back to Europe as an example of African sculpture. Fetishes of the first order, those that are worshipped by a whole town or village, have special temples and a large number of priests to serve them; those of the lower orders, the proletariat, are placed in a corner of the hut or in the trunk of a tree until some miracle happens which raises them from obscurity to a higher rank.[6]

The temple of the Fetishes is a vast building shaped like a private hut, built of wooden posts with a floor of dried earth and the outer walls painted in red and white stripes. Inside there is a huge square hall with walls and floor strewn with scented grasses which make them a dirty green colour. The ceiling is made of the most precious wood in the area and the roof is tiled like that of the King's dwelling. In the middle of the temple is a wooden table for the sacrifices and against one of the walls draped with a white cloth stands the Fetish, on a wooden three-legged stool made out of a single tree trunk. For great festivals the temple is decorated inside and outside with garlands of flowers and branches of trees; the interior is lit with many lamps or rather earthenware bowls filled with palm oil and placed on three-legged stools along the walls. Incense and aromatic herbs are burnt, food of all kinds, and rich cloth is thrown on the floor around the idol and at the set time the sacrifice is offered. The lesser priests stand along the wall draped with the white cloth and those of higher rank assist the high Priest at the sacrificial table. Then the victims are presented, generally goats, lambs, hens and other domestic animals; the high priest kills them, his acolytes nail them to the wall covered with the white cloth beside the Fetish, and priests and people dip their fingers in the blood which flows from the victims and reverently smear it over their foreheads and other parts of their bodies. Private sacrifices are carried out in the same way but with less ceremony.

---

[6] Samuel Johnson, 1921, chapter III, gives useful information about the Yoruba religion; he bases this, however, almost wholly on his knowledge of Oyo and Ibadan, attributing, for example, little importance to the cult of Oro. In contrast to Scala, Johnson asserts (p. 26) that the Yoruba 'believe in the existence of an ALMIGHTY GOD, him they term OLORUN, i.e. LORD OF HEAVEN'. For this Creator God, or High God, see also E. B. Idowu, *Olodumare — God in Yoruba Belief*, 1962, and Pierre Verger, 'The Yoruba High God — a review of the sources', and Robin Horton, 'Conference: "The High God in Africa"', both in *Odu*, New Series, 2, 2, 1966. For more general accounts, see G. Parrinder, *African Traditional Religion*, 1974, Oyin Ogunba, 'Ceremonies' in S. O. Biobaku (ed.), *Sources of Yoruba History*, 1973, E. B. Idowu, *African Traditional Religion: a Definition*, 1973, and Sandra Barnes (ed.) *Africa's Ogun*, Indiana, 1989.

In cases of illness or misfortune or before any enterprise, a priest is called
to consult the Fetish. The priest comes hastily or not so hastily, according to
the wealth of the postulant. He hears about the matter and then decides upon
the sacrifices which must be made to obtain a reply from the god. No self-
respecting Fetish will put himself out for one or two hens. When the price
has been agreed upon the priest proceeds to the sacrifice according to the
ritual and consults the oracle by casting palm nuts. The oracles do not
always reply when first consulted and the people concerned run the risk of
having to try two or three times. Since the answer is infallible, whatever
happens, whether the petitioner dies or lives, whether he succeeds in his
enterprise or not, the fault is never with the oracle but with the simple
souls who could not properly interpret the fateful instructions.

When the country is threatened by war or any other public disaster, the
King and an assembly of the people demand that the oracle be consulted
before they come to any decision. In such a case the most senior priests
proceed with great ceremony to throw the sacred palm nuts (the black priests
have no other method of consultation) and the required oblations and
sacrifices are in proportion to the gravity of the circumstances.[7]

A very important divinity greatly honoured by the Africans is the God
Oro who is responsible for justice. This God has his own temple and his
image, whether real or imagined, I do not know, is shut up in a tabernacle
in the temple and is never exposed for the contemplation of the faithful. It
is therefore not known in what physical form he may be represented.
From the spiritual point of view, he is an invisible being endowed with
extraordinary powers and very great integrity, who has chosen to live in
this tabernacle in order to judge all civil and criminal cases which are brought
to the court. His judgement is final. If anyone is accused of any crime or if
there is litigation between two or more persons, the parties are free to
follow the regular course of justice, or else, even if only one of the parties
so wishes, to bring the case before the God Oro who will absolve or condemn
without appeal. The God has one thing in common with the ordinary courts:
he does not render justice free of charge but accepts fees from both parties; his
decisions, so the priests say, are always just and infallible and are never subject
to the ignorance and frailty of human nature. The priests of the God are all
chosen from the Ogboni (noble) class. Since they alone can understand his
language they act as his interpreters and transmit the sentence.

But there is no limit to the attributes of this terrible and mysterious deity;
in addition to his judiciary duties, which are already numerous and lucrative
enough, he has other police activities which give rise to a court of inquisition

---

[7] This describes the practice of divination according to the cult of Ifa, the Yoruba god of
divination. See Chapter IV by Wande Abimbola in Biobaku (ed.), *Sources*, 1973.

not unlike our Holy Office of unhappy memory and to the Venetian Council of Ten. If a person fails in his religious duties, does not make the prescribed sacrifices or fails to consult the oracle in any important matter of his domestic life, he is cited by the priests at the court of the God and punished according to the gravity of his crime. From the King down to the lowest slave, all are subject to his terrible jurisdiction.

In a village near Abeokuta there lived a very old man, father of a large family and owner of a huge piece of land to the cultivation of which he had given his whole life. He was a good man and a true patriarch of the olden days. He was adored by his family and by his many slaves whom he treated as his children. He was respected by his neighbours to whom he was very generous and blessed by poor people and travellers who accepted his hospitality. But this old man was, as we say a *spirito forte* [strong character], the Jean Jacques Rousseau of the village. He was a son of Nature and he worshipped Providence through its works and its creatures and offered his prayers and sacrifices directly to God without the intervention of the priests. He was his own family priest and had little faith in the sacred palm nuts. If his first-born son became ill, if his wives were pregnant or his farms threatened by the inclemency of the weather, he did not consult the Fetiches but tried by thought and loving care to remove the ills for himself. This ran contrary to religious practices and was inevitably noticed by the God Oro who, faithful to his duties as Chief Inquisitor, had him gently warned by his priests to be in future less irreverent to the religion of his fathers and so avoid any scandal in the district. The old man, his conscience clear that he had harmed no one, paid little heed to this warning and continued to live as he had done before. One fine morning he was formally summoned to Oro's court to account for his behaviour. The simple country man, surprised to find himself called to the presence of so formidable a God, hurried to obey the summons, and when he entered the sanctuary the God, speaking through his priests, enumerated one by one his sins, and his sacrileges, scolded him sharply for his obstinacy and ordered him to pay into the treasury of the temple 20 bags of cowries, 100 sheep, 10 bales of cotton and 50 pots of palm oil. The old man, not very impressed by the God's moderation, bowed deeply to him and his priests and returned quietly to his fields. Days passed, then weeks, then months, but the treasury of the temple was not enriched by his fine. He was summoned once more. This time there was an atmosphere of gloom in the court. From the faces of the priests it was clear that the God was extremely angry and in fact, after some minutes of pregnant silence, the impenitent sinner was told briefly and unconditionally to hang himself from a tree of his choice; if the sentence was not carried out within a month the God would have him struck dead with all his children, wives, relatives, friends, slaves and animals and all his goods would be burned.

The peasant bowed even more deeply than before and once again returned quietly to his fields. A month went by and he had not hanged himself. Then, one night when everyone was asleep in his great house, a terrible cry was heard and from all sides came dense clouds of smoke and hungry flames. The God had kept his word and destroyed in his revenge guilty and innocent alike. No one was saved. Men, animals and possessions were devoured by the fire which also destroyed most of the village. Next morning the unhappy wretch was found hanging from a tree, and no one knew how it happened!

On certain solemn occasions when great sacrifices are to be performed, the God Oro forbids everyone, even his adherents, to walk about round the temple or even inside the town. This prohibition gives rise to certain suspicions as to the nature of the sacrifices and many people think that the victims may be human beings. However this may be, during my time in Abeokuta a poor old mad woman was slaughtered mercilessly in the street because she defied the God's command and went out of her house.[8]

Another lesser Divinity widely worshipped, or rather feared, by Africans whether pagan or otherwise, is the snake.[9] This reptile, harmless however in Africa, symbolizes in African belief the incarnation of the spirit of evil and exercises a direct influence on all the events of their domestic and social life. Births, illnesses, deaths, winds, rain, harvest and the success of any enterprise are subject to its influence. But in particular it has power over a woman's heart. If a hut burns down, an epidemic breaks out among the domestic animals, the harvest fails, a baby is born deformed, a mother's milk dries up, children rebel against their parents, masters maltreat their slaves or chiefs their subjects, a fierce battle takes place, a judge is corrupt, a person is ill, wounded or dies, then the snake is responsible. A neglected or ill-treated snake breathes the venom of discord into the family, the village or the tribe; it weakens the mind, excites hatred and destroys the peace of the family. In a word, the serpent is their evil genius and therefore every effort is made to placate and propitiate it by treating it well and offering it sacrifices.

---

[8] Oro, as Scala realizes, was (or is) a cult of unusual importance among the Egba of Abeokuta. In fact, Oro was less 'a god' than a designation of the collective ancestors of the community. Its cult organization was used by the Ogboni (see p. 66 and Chapter VI, note 5) as their agent in enforcing their government; criminals, for example, were executed by them in the Oro grove and a curfew was proclaimed by their symbolic 'bull roarer': Biobaku, *The Egba*, pp. 6–8, 11, 23, 62, adding that each town in the federation had its own patron *orisha* (local deity). The ban on public participation is usually said to apply specifically to women who are kept indoors during Oro ceremonies.

[9] Veneration is accorded to snakes in many parts of West Africa. Snelgrave, *A New Account of Some Parts of Guinea and the Slave Trade*, London, 1734, pp. 10, 13, adduces an example of a 'particular harmless Snake' which the Whydah regarded as 'their principal God'. Scala errs dangerously, however, in believing that African snakes were generally harmless.

From Sierra Leone to Fernando Po, snakes are generally indolent, placid and harmless; they are easily domesticated and therefore contribute to everyone's well-being. Each family has its guardian snake just as the ancients had their household gods. These snakes live on the roofs of the houses and are treated as members of the family, kept warm and well fed, caressed and adored. When out walking or at the market, the Africans carry their snakes wound round their arms or hanging from their necks as a kind of talisman to protect them from danger. Woe to anyone who molests or kills a snake; such sacrilege will be regarded very seriously by these superstitious people.

The Africans, as I have already said, do not have well-defined ideas about the immortality of the soul. Some believe that they will be born again after death in happier lands where they will enjoy all the material pleasures of the earth, the only ones they know. This belief is held mainly by the warriors and enhances their courage since those who die in battle have more right than anyone else to these pleasures. Others believe that after death they are transformed into lions, crocodiles, elephants etc. and will eventually, in another country, take up the human form again. Others still believe that the spirits of the dead hover around the place where their bodies lie. Most of them, however, have no idea of the immortality of the soul and take little thought for the life after death. Amongst such confused beliefs one thing alone has struck me and that is their absolute lack of any idea of human responsibility towards the Creator, by which I mean any belief in reward or punishment in the next life according to one's behaviour in this one.

The Africans have no written laws. Their languages, which are deficient, figurative and symbolic, do not lend themselves to the definition of a Code of Law.[10] After the Divinity Oro, the King, the Assembly and the Chief Priests are the supreme administrators of justice. In the provinces governors delegated by the King perform the functions of judges. Each tribal chief has moreover a special jurisdiction over the members of his tribe with regard to minor offences and civil litigation. Cases of civil law are examined and judged by a panel of five or six persons chosen by the King, or in the provinces by the tribal chief, from among the most respected members of the community, and sometimes these are chosen by the contending parties themselves if they can come to some agreement. In serious cases there are at least ten or twelve judges. The condemned man in a civil case is allowed

[10] For Yoruba laws, see T. O. Elias, *The Nature of African Customary Law*, 1956, and works by P. C. Lloyd, especially *Yoruba Land Law*, 1962 and his chapter on 'Conflict theory and Yoruba kingdoms' in I. M. Lewis (ed.), *History and Social Anthropology*, 1968. A. K. Ajisafe (E. O. Moore), *The Laws and Customs of the Yoruba People*, 1924, is relevant but narrowly reflects the author's Egba background. General reflections on the unwritten laws of West Africa occur in the first two chapters of Robert Smith's *Warfare and Diplomacy in Pre-Colonial West Africa*, 1989, and on the power of the Yoruba oba and his people in chapter 8 of his *Kingdoms*.

a short time to comply with his sentence and if thereafter he is recalcitrant, he
has to maintain in his house two or three poor people until the equivalent of
the full fine imposed upon him has been paid. The law is that the debtor in
such a case is responsible for the lives of the dependants entrusted to him
and this is a heavy responsibility since they are usually old and infirm. If
one of these guests should die, no one can save the master of the house
from being accused of having poisoned him.

Under criminal law, wilful murder, armed assault and sacrilege are
punishable by death. For minor offences culprits are sentenced to two or
three years imprisonment with their feet bound in chains. There is moreover
always a fine of cowries and other things to be paid to the injured party or the
heir. The injured party always has the right to ask that corporal punishment
is changed to a fine fixed by the court and paid to him. If the condemned man
is unable to pay this fine, his relatives are held responsible and if there are
none, then the community has to pay the required amount. One of the
worst offences which, in the opinion of the Africans, merits most severe
punishment is the theft of slaves. Until recently it was punishable by death
but today the culprit has his goods confiscated and is sent to prison for
five or six months. On top of this he is publicly reviled and debarred from
the company of his peers. This punishment which is worse than death is
carried out in the following way. The King, if this happens in the capital,
and the governors or tribal chiefs in the villages, nail their staff of justice
to the door of the condemned man's hut. This is the sign that no one may
trade or have anything to do with him. It is a form of religious excommuni-
cation practised with all the severity of ancient times. The unhappy wretch,
excluded from any form of human companionship, abandoned by wives,
children, relatives and friends, hated and rejected by everyone, tries, if he
is rich, to have the staff of justice removed by making generous gifts to the
King, the chiefs and the priests, or if he is poor, he runs away from the
town and wanders about in distant lands or else, as is frequently the case,
he commits suicide.

Adultery is usually punished by enslavement. If the husband catches the
lovers *in flagrante delicto* he has the right, by law, to kill them or make them
slaves, with the option of selling them, exchanging them or forcing them to
work on his farms. He usually chooses the last alternative as being more
profitable than killing them.

In Lagos, in the reign of Kosoko, adultery was punished more severely.
The woman was shut up in a cask bristling with very sharp nails with their
points towards the inside and thrown into the river. Her lover was also
thrown into the river with arms and legs tightly bound and a weight attached
to his feet. The sentence was usually pronounced by the King. Adultery is
however rather rare among the blacks because of the ease of divorce and

the freedom of polygamy. African women are not shut up in a harem or watched over by eunuchs as in Muslim or Asiatic societies. They are not veiled, in fact they wear almost nothing, sometimes not even the most indispensable garment, the traditional fig leaf. Nevertheless they rarely abuse their freedom and are generally respected by the men. The King's wives are considered as sacred and when an African meets one of them in the street he respectfully retreats. They say that Europeans who have had relations with one of the King's wives have had to wash the stain from the royal bed with many barrels of rum. No African would have been let off so lightly; he would indeed have been put to death for sacrilege.

The Africans still use torture which is practised as follows. If the accused will not confess his crime, he is put in prison, with an iron ring round his neck. From this ring hangs a long chain, the end of which passes through a hole in the wall into the room adjoining the prison. From this room the chain is pulled so that the prisoner cannot bend over or sit down, but has to stand upright all the time. After two or three days of this he either confesses or gives up the struggle and dies. They also stretch their victims with ropes in exactly the same way as the Europeans did before our worthy Beccaria.[11]

As I have said, the Africans are polygamous and have as many wives as they can maintain, as well as innumerable slaves over whom they have all sorts of rights. The number of his wives is a matter of pride and respect for a rich man and it is not unusual for him to have 30, 50 or even 100. Kings and tribal chiefs often have more than a hundred. The poor are obliged to be satisfied with one, or at most two, but as the women have to do all the work in the home and in the fields, a woman will often beg her husband to take another wife to help her in her daily chores. The marriage ceremony is very simple. When a young man wants to marry a girl, he sends someone to ask her relatives who agree or refuse according to circumstances, but on no account do they seek the girl's consent. If they agree, the man has to give them a gift in proportion to his means. Then, on the agreed day, he goes with his relatives and friends to the girl's home where she is handed over to him by her relatives and goes with him to the paternal home accompanied by pipes and drums. The bridegroom's father, or the head of the family, receives the bridal pair and splits the symbolic kola into three parts, giving one to each of them and keeping the third for himself. When the kola has been eaten the matrimonial ceremony is over. Wives live in the compound of the husband's family but each has her own hut. Children of either sex belong to their mothers; and their fathers have nothing to do with their

---

[11] Cesare, Marchese di Beccaria (1738–1794), was an Italian political and philanthropic writer who advocated and helped to bring about reforms of the judicial code at Milan.

upbringing. They are breast fed until they are three years old and during that period the women have no relations with the men. The mothers love their children passionately and their love is equally returned. Often an African will hardly know his father but will always adore his mother. He goes to her for advice, helps her in case of need and gives her the fruits of his labour. He helps her in old age, consoles her in misfortune and swears by her. An oath sworn on the mother's head is one of the most sacred and feared and it is very rare for a son to violate it.

The laws of succession conform to these bonds of affection. Only the sons inherit their mother's property, and the mother the son's property. If the son has uterine brothers, the mother inherits a portion equal to that of each of the brothers. A father's property is inherited by his lateral relatives. If a woman dies without children, her property goes to her husband.

The Africans greatly despise sterility and this affords one of the principal reasons for divorce. Even after ten or twenty years of marriage the husband may send away a wife who is sterile. By a strange contradiction excessive fertility is punished. If a woman gives birth to twins, the babies and the mother are immediately put to death by order of the King. The husband is obliged, on pain of death, to denounce the double birth, but he usually kills one of the twins himself to save the other and the mother. The reason for this abominable custom, in so far as it can be understood, is the natural envy to which such extraordinary fertility gives rise in other families. It is indeed difficult to reconcile this concept of equality with a country where slavery is accepted.[12]

The Africans in all the provinces between Cape Palmas and Fernando Po, from the coast to about 200 miles inland, are generally between 5 and 6 feet tall, well-built, strong and extremely agile in sports, such as fighting with cudgels, riding, swimming, jousting and hunting, The women are about the same height and are slender, delicate and rather attractive in countenance. They have big, lively eyes, very white teeth, wide nostrils, thick lips and

---

[12] This cruel practice seems not to have obtained widely, perhaps not at all in the form described, among the Yoruba, although the birth of twins was regarded by them as an unusual event which called for consultation with a diviner. Often the making of twin figures *ibeji*, of which many examples can still be found, was then prescribed. F. Willett, *African Art, passim*, especially p. 89 and illustration 68. Forde, 1951, 1969, p. 28, writes: 'In Ondo twins were formerly disposed of, and Bascom states that in Ife the less healthy one of a pair of twins was allowed to die; here the twin born first is regarded as the younger'. Johnson, 1921, p. 80, probably basing his information on practices in the Yoruba Kingdom of Oyo, writes of twin births: 'No condition is invested with an air of greater importance, or has a halo of deeper mystery about it. ... Twins in Yorubaland are almost credited with extra-human powers, although among some barbarous tribes they are regarded as monsters to be despatched at once.' On changes and regional variations in the *ibeji* cult, see further T. J. M. Chappel, 'The Yoruba cult of twins in historical perspective', *Man*, 1974.

woolly hair. Since they are accustomed from infancy to riding, swimming and manual work, they acquire strength and vigour and a certain military air which adds to rather than detracts from their appearance. Their deportment is modest but dignified and their movements are graceful. They are hard-working, sober, discreet in company and somewhat indifferent to their husbands, a very natural consequence of polygamy.

Men and women usually go about naked except for a little apron around their haunches which seldom hangs down as far as their knees. The most elegant wear short striped trousers and a wide cloth of silk, cotton or wool reaching half-way down their legs and which can be easily slung over their shoulders to form a cloak; the rest of the body is naked. The differences between the three races of which I have already spoken is mainly noticeable in the women's breasts. Those of southern origin have very long breasts which hang so far down that they can throw them over their shoulders to suckle the infants which they carry on their backs. Women from the North and West have rounder and firmer breasts.

The ornaments which the Africans most value are bracelets and beads, worn, by men and women alike, round the neck, arms and legs. These orna-ments are made of ivory, brass, iron, gold, silver or beads of coloured glass, according to the wealth of the individual. Sometimes they are so big and heavy that the victim of fashion has difficulty in walking. They also wear round their necks and arms a number of amulets and little fetishes to which they are particularly devoted and these are thought to be the best protection against evil and misfortune.

From time immemorial there has existed among all Africans the cruel and barbaric custom of cutting marks on the faces of new-born infants to distin-guish between the different races, nations and tribes. This painful operation is performed by applying a piece of red hot iron to the part of the place which is to be marked. The Yoruba people generally have three horizontal lines on both cheeks and three vertical with a transverse one on the forehead;[13] the Ashanti have four perpendicular lines, others have five and so on. Tattooing, another painful method of disfiguring these poor people, is also held in great esteem. The operation is performed on the face, chest or any other part of the body and the tattoo generally represents a snake, a crocodile, the head of a tiger or some other animal, or a flower, a plant, or some tool used in a trade. Many women who would be beautiful in their natural state are disfigured in this horrible way. Another no less unpleasant custom practised by all the natives is to anoint their bodies with oil, grease or a butter-like substance. This usage may be hygienic and perhaps give protection against excessive heat, but from the point of view of cleanliness and smell it is truly disgusting.

---

[13] The Yoruba facial marks are described and illustrated by Johnson, *History*, pp. 104–109.

African funerals are solemnized with great pomp and ceremony but are festive rather than sorrowful occasions and often ruinous to the family fortunes. The corpse, anointed and perfumed, is laid on a ceremonial bed and exposed for the contemplation of relatives and friends; then it is lowered into a deep grave dug inside the home because, according to popular super-stition, malevolent enemies might disturb the peace of the dead if their graves were situated in an open or public place. As a result of this superstition there are no cemeteries and if anyone is unable to bury his dead in his own house he takes the body out secretly by night and buries it in a remote and distant place, taking every precaution to remove all traces of the burial. If a King or tribal chief dies, many slaves, both men and women, have their veins opened on the tomb so that they can serve their master after death. Likewise the weapons and favourite objects of the dead man, together with a quantity of cowries, food-stuffs, cloth and all sorts of provisions are cast into the grave. For three days sounds of drums and pipes and gun shots are heard round the house of the dead, but the most important part of the ceremony is the funeral banquet to which friends, relatives and many strangers are invited and entertained in an extraordinarily luxurious manner. An incred-ible sum of money is spent on these feasts which always end in scandalous orgies. Some families ruin themselves completely because they believe this to be the way to prove their affection for the dear departed.

Slavery is in full force throughout almost the whole of Africa and can be considered a social institution, protected by laws and sanctified by religion.[14] Slaves are acquired by inheritance, by sale or exchange or by war or slave raids. One or more individuals can take up arms and go in search of slaves on their own account or else troops can be formed in each town or village for the same purpose at certain times of the year. On their return they have to hand over 20% of their catch to the governor of the province and 10% to the chief who organized the raid. But these regulations are easily evaded because the men do not always return together from the raid. As soon as they arrive in enemy territory the invaders use all their strength and ingenuity to capture the maximum number of slaves for themselves, then they disband and, singly or in small groups, they drive their victims in chains before them and find a means, with the co-operation of the slave traders, of disposing of the best part of their booty on the way home.

---

[14] There is general agreement that slaves, whether domestic or predial, were treated with greater humanity in Yorubaland (and in West Africa) than in the New World. See the Birmingham University Ph.D. thesis by E. A. Oroge, 'The Institution of Slavery in Yorubaland with Particu-lar Reference to the Nineteenth Century', 1971, and Smith, *Kingdoms*, p. 96 and *passim*. The taking of captives in war for use as slaves is discussed in Smith, *Warfare and Diplomacy*, pp. 32, 36–37. See also Kristin Mann's chapter on 'Owners, slaves and the struggle for labour . . .' in R. Law (ed.), *From Slave Trade to 'Legitimate' Commerce*, 1995.

Then, with only a few old and infirm captives, they return by night to the town.

The slaves destined to work on the farms have to work ten hours a day during the first three days of the week for their masters; the remaining three days they can work for themselves, and on the seventh day they rest. From their labours they have to provide their means of subsistence which is not difficult because of the fertility of the land; in fact a slave can, in the course of two or three years, make enough cowries to buy his freedom. This however seldom happens because the emancipated slave, far from his tribe and in a strange land, has no one to protect him and prefers therefore to belong to the family and tribe of his master. Personal slaves live an easier life than the agricultural workers but have less chance of acquiring wealth. They are, however, usually humanely treated by their masters.

The laws regulating slavery compared with the slave laws of America appear to be mild and humanitarian. A master may not kill or mutilate a slave; he may punish him but may not shed blood. A master who maltreats a slave will not only be dishonoured by his tribe but may well cause an uprising among his own slaves who will regard the persecution of one of their companions as harmful to them all. Sometimes a persecuted or ill-treated slave will flee from his master and seek safety and protection from someone else. This protection is always granted except in cases of serious offence. The person whose protection has been sought will go to the fugitive's master and promise to return him on condition that he is not punished for his flight and is more humanely treated in future. If the master agrees and then fails to keep his word, the protector will make it a point of honour to save his protégé, either by buying him or helping him to escape to some distant country. In general a master who is so cruel to his slaves that they flee from him loses his reputation and is disliked by everyone.

If a slave fails to fulfil his duty he is judged by his fellow slaves. All the slaves in the household hear his case, consider the evidence and pronounce and execute the sentence. This procedure is a safeguard for the slave and for the master from whom the onus of punishment is removed.

Marriage among slaves is not only allowed but encouraged by their masters, particularly in rural areas where the number of workers constitutes their owner's chief wealth. If a farm is contiguous to uncultivated and unoccupied land, the owner may, if he wishes, take into his own farm this land which belongs by right to the first occupant provided that he cultivates it and pays a tax of 3% of the net product. Therefore it is in the master's interest to encourage his slaves to marry in order to increase their numbers, an interest which would be even greater if the land was not from time to time devastated by war and slave raids.

A strange characteristic of Africans, slaves and freemen alike, is that each individual prepares his own food separately from the others. Everyone has his own pot, his own fire and his own provisions. They never eat together. If there is no domestic economy in this custom, at least everyone can eat according to his own taste and a great deal of dissension and argument is spared.

The African's usual food is, as I have already said, maize, potatoes (yams), manioc [cassava], vegetables, beef or mutton, game, fish, milk, fruit etc. Their methods of cooking are extremely simple.

Maize, which abounds from Cape Three Points to Fernando Po, is ground in a kind of mill made out of two round stones placed one on top of the other with a hole bored through them to hold an iron pivot with a handle at the end of the upper stone to facilitate the movement of the hand. The flour so obtained is certainly not of the finest, but when boiled in water and mixed with honey it makes a nutritive and healthy porridge and usually constitutes the main family meal. Little rolls and buns are also made from this flour and sold at the market for 5 cowries, about two *centesimi* in our money. In the same way, cassava, the root of the plant of the same name, is pounded in a wooden mortar, grated on stones, dried in the sun and made into little cakes. Vegetables are boiled in water and seasoned with salt and oil, or also fried in oil in small earthenware pots in the same way as sea or river fish of which the Africans eat a great many. Beef and game are nearly always roasted but these are rare and considered a luxury. Africans also eat dogs, cats, rats and such other unclean animals. Their meals are less copious but more frequent than those of Europeans. It is not unusual for a native family to eat seven meals in a day.

Their wine is a strong liquor extracted from the palm tree. Towards evening an incision, two or three inches long, is made in the trunk of the palm tree and a receptacle capable of holding about two gallons of liquid is attached to the tree. By the next morning this receptacle is full. This system is gradually falling into disuse in Yorubaland since it was realized that trees which are tapped too often within a short time cease to bear fruit and become dry. Commercial interest prevailed over animal appetite, and benefited the people in two ways, making them both more sober and richer in natural harvests. This type of wine or liquor, which is potent and capable of producing the same drunkenness as does the lamentable misuse of alcoholic drinks in Europe, is becoming rare in Yoruba markets and will, we hope, finally disappear altogether.[15]

The most common fruits in West Africa are oranges from Porto Novo which are harvested twice a year, very sour limes, pineapples, bananas, plums, and nuts called kola which are used in religious ceremonies.

---

[15] Palm wine is still a popular drink among the Yoruba, as elsewhere in West Africa.

The Africans have very few cooking utensils, using only some earthenware pots in which they cook their food. Very wealthy people have iron saucepans from England and copper boilers which they buy from European merchants on the coast and then re-sell at an extremely high price in the markets of Abeokuta and other towns in the interior. Cutlery is even more rare as all Africans from the King down to the lowest slave eat with their fingers. Game and large pieces of meat are cut with hunting knives and then each person uses his hands to help himself. Forks and spoons are completely unknown. Wine and liquor are drunk from gourds which are brought by the guests for this purpose.

The King eats apart seated on a sofa, served by his two favourite women and surrounded by the court dignitaries who are present at the royal feast. He eats with his fingers; any morsels he leaves are offered in turn to the courtiers, who take a tiny piece and chew it reverently. It would be a crime amounting to high treason if a crumb of these remains were left. The same may be said of the royal drinks which must be drunk by the courtiers from the same cup and down to the last drop. After every dish, one of the King's favourites presents him with a small basin with sweet smelling water to wash his hands and a small cloth for drying them. The women do not eat in the King's presence and do not share in what he leaves. These same ceremonies are repeated, with less pomp, at the table of the tribal chiefs and less important people, served by their wives and in the presence of their slaves.

I used to take my meals outside my house in full view of the public so as to give the natives an idea of our way of life. At first they were amazed at the number of the implements the Europeans use for such simple operations as eating and drinking. Nevertheless they are gradually beginning to understand their use from the point of view of cleanliness and to respect what at first appeared to be ridiculous. If they had more frequent examples, I am sure they would adopt our habits themselves and I have always noticed that Africans despise the white man who fails to observe the rules of European decorum and tries to live like the natives.

Household furniture is also very simple. In every hall or room there are, along the walls, sofas made of wood or of baked earth which are wide and low and are used for sitting, sleeping, eating etc. These sofas are covered with cloth of cotton, wool, silk, or velvet, or with matting, according to the wealth of their owner. Sometimes there is a roughly carved wooden table in the middle of the room and some stools also of wood. The floor is simply covered with mats and the walls are bare.

The ceremonial used for official meetings and visits is based on an oriental system. Any subordinate who presents himself to the chief on whom he depends, prostrates himself three times and beats his breast three times without rising until he is authorized to do so. To this greeting the chief replies *occu occu* (God be with you). Chiefs appearing before their sovereign follow the same etiquette and remain prostrate on the ground until the King makes a sign with his stick. Soldiers and junior officers greet their superiors in the same way.

The army of the Yoruba Kingdom[16] is about eight thousand strong in peace time and is increased in war time to twenty or twenty five thousand. One-third is composed of cavalry and two-thirds of infantry. Their uniform, just like the dress of the townspeople, consists of striped trousers and a coloured cotton cloth draped round the waist and falling half-way down the legs and a sword attached by a cord to a shoulder belt. All the rest of the body including the head is entirely bare. The cavalry add a pair of riding-boots to which they attach two enormous spurs. They are armed with small carbines, lances and sabres. They are less than mediocre in the use of the carbine and sabre but very skilful in handling the lances. I often saw the cavalry at exercise, charging across the fields and without stopping sending the lances right through a gourd or even smaller object set up as a distant target. In battle the cavalry carry their dead or wounded on their saddles which are very large with cantles, holsters and stirrups in the Turkish style. The infantry is armed with long thin-barrelled guns like those of the Bedouin.[17] Instead of bayonets they attach with cord or leather a long point of iron to the end of the barrel. They attack impetuously, but they retreat easily and scatter in confusion if they meet serious resistance. They fire their guns without taking aim at the enemy, seldom keep in rank or fight in close formations. Their strategy lies entirely in ambushes and in guerilla warfare in order to surprise and attack the enemy from the flank or the rear. Success in the field owes little to the science of the leaders or the steadfastness of the soldiers. If they die in battle from breast wounds,

---

[16] This brief description of an Egba army can be compared with the report by Captain A. T. Jones of the Second West India Regiment on the Egba (that is, Abeokuta) army which he saw encamped and in action against the Ibadan at Ijaye in May and June 1861: Ajayi and Smith, *Yoruba Warfare*, Appendix I. Although Scala does not claim first-hand knowledge of the army other than seeing the 'cavalry' at exercise, his account tallies in several particulars with the professional account of Captain Jones. However, whereas Scala considers that cavalry made up one-third of the army, Jones writes: 'The [horsemen] appear to be used by the generals chiefly in carrying orders and bringing up stragglers', although 'a very excellent irregular cavalry might be speedily organised' (pp. 134–135).

[17] Firearms did not come into use by Yoruba armies until after 1800 and then only gradually. By Scala's time the primary weapons of the Abeokuta soldiers were these long-barrelled flintlock muskets. They were imported from Denmark and hence called 'Dane guns', and also from Holland and England. Bowen, for example, had also noted that all the defenders of Abeokuta in 1851 had guns (*Adventures and Missionary Labours*, 1857, p. 118). The extent to which the trade in guns depended upon that in slaves — the 'slave-gun cycle' — has been much debated: see the discussion in Smith, *Warfare and Diplomacy*, pp. 31–32. Bowen writes (p. 113): 'once begun for political reasons [the Yoruba wars] have commonly been nourished by the slave trade'.

they are comforted by the idea that they will be happy in the next life. If they die in flight, their death agony is increased by the terror of a new life of darkness and sorrow. These superstitions, learnt from infancy and reinforced by the priests, contribute greatly to their facing dangers with courage and taking little heed for their lives.

Horses are usually small but strong and sturdy like those found on the islands of the Mediterranean.[18] The best ones come from the province of Kanem, east of the River Niger where they cost from 40 to 50 francs. In Abeokuta they are worth 100 francs and in Lagos and all along the coast 200 francs. In general, there are few beasts of burden in these parts of Africa. Camels are found in the provinces east of the Niger and are used for the caravans which go from there to Egypt. Mules are extremely rare; donkeys are more numerous and are of a very good breed. They are generally used to transport supplies for the army in war time.

Declarations of war and peace treaties are made by the King with the consent of the Assembly which is supposed to represent the people.[19] Military leaders are nominated by the various corps or chosen from among those who have proved most astute and valiant in previous combats. They ride bigger horses with saddles stuffed with coral, gold and silver and are privileged to carry umbrellas, a sign of honour. A herald walks before them with an unfurled banner to the staff of which are attached horses' tails blessed by the priests and which have the power to protect them from the enemy. This custom doubtless comes from Turkey where horses' tails are used to distinguish the various ranks of the Pashas. The idea that they are talismans has been added by African fanaticism and superstition.

In the market place of every town and village there is a huge shed, sometimes 250 to 300 ft. long by 50 ft. wide and supported by two parallel lines of posts 20 ft. high, with a roof of thatch or leaves. This is intended for public meetings. It serves as a place for daily discussions, a shelter from rain and sun, a market, a promenade, and an arena where the young men practise the arts of war and actors and dancers stage their pantomimes and lewd dances. It is a public hall where the popular assemblies discuss serious matters affecting the district. On such occasions only men are admitted; even though there are no doors or guards, women and children would be

---

[18] R. Law, *The Horse in West African History*, 1980, makes numerous references to the use of horses in Yorubaland.

[19] Scala's account may be compared with accounts in Ajayi and Smith, *Yoruba Warfare*, and in Smith, *Warfare and Diplomacy*. In the former Ajayi writes (with reference to the Ijaye war) (p. 80): 'The chiefs held meeting after meeting, some public, others private, to discuss the issue of war or peace', then ordered a general mobilization, carried out 'The usual ceremonies and sacrifices... including a human sacrifice', and sent out embassies to other states to effect the diplomatic isolation of their enemy, the Ijaye.

chased away and severely punished if they dared to enter. A tribal chief or some other dignitary acts as chairman on these occasions, explains the situation and proposes the measures to be taken. His proposal is accepted or rejected by acclamation, the only form of voting practised by the natives.

IX

TRADE[1]

My chief objective in writing these memoirs is to interest Europe and particularly our own government in encouraging national trade with such an important part of the world, so that the relations between these two countries may bring civilization to the Africans and benefits to all. For many centuries the coasts of Africa (except those of the North) have remained far removed from events in Europe and almost unknown to our sailors. After the discovery of America, Africa was known only through the slave trade. In the course of time, this gave rise to the various colonies set up on the coast by the Dutch, Portuguese, English and French and was supplemented by trade in ivory, gold dust and some other goods of little importance. A few years ago the whole of these exports did not exceed 50,000 or 60,000 tons. Until my arrival in Lagos who would have dreamt that this island, known only as a slave market, would have so rapidly become a flourishing emporium for legitimate trade and which of the European traders in Lagos would have dreamt of the immense natural wealth to be extracted from Abeokuta only a few miles away.

Although African people do not have gentle and civil habits they are not as fierce and inhospitable as many would claim them to be. They are wild and primitive but as susceptible to civilization as any other human beings. Even among the Dahomians who are reputed to be savages by the Yoruba themselves, I have found virtuous patriarchal families and extremely honest traders. In order to assist the civilizing process there must be more contact between the civilized and the primitive man and the best way of achieving this is to offer reciprocal benefits to both.

The natural products of Africa which are already known find easy markets in Europe, but who can guess what wealth remains hidden and yet to be discovered by European research?

[1] Scala provides neither dates nor sources for the information in this chapter and it is impossible, therefore to assess its accuracy. Figures in Consul Campbell's trading reports of the export from Lagos of palm oil and 'manufactured cotton fabrics' in 1856 and 1857 suggest that the figures here are considerably inflated: see Smith, *Lagos Consulate*, p. 76. The picture of trading conditions along the West Coast would have been useful to others engaged in this trade, but it seems unlikely that the book reached a wide readership outside Italy.

A general picture of the import and export trade of the West coast of Africa (or 'the Slave Coast') from 1852, the year of my first visit to Lagos, until today, will show the great benefits which might be derived from it if this trade were not thwarted by the rights claimed by the various military outposts and by the inspections by the cruisers and if it were more efficiently protected by the governments who are signatories to the abolition treaties.

The coast known geographically as the *Slave Coast* comprises all the area between Cape Three Points [in modern Ghana] N. Lat. 4.4 W. Long. 2.5), Benin (N. Lat. 4.2; E. Long. 5.45), and Cape Formoso [at the southern tip of the Niger delta] to Fernando Po (N. Lat. 4.26 E. Long. 7.10). It forms a continuous bay up to N. Lat. 6.29 E. Long. 3.29, the position of Lagos, and covers 660 miles altogether. The principal ports in this area are:

Dixcove (English Fort) and Comenda (station with a Dutch Fort)

	N. Lat	5.5		W. Long	1.3
Elmina	,, ,,	5.5		,, ,,	1.22
Cape Coast Castle	,, ,,	5.6		,, ,,	1.19
Annamaboc [Anomabu]	N. Lat.	5.10		W. Long	1.7
Cormantin	,, ,,	5.10		,, ,,	1.6
Tantomgneny [Tantum-Kweri]	,, ,,	5.12		,, ,,	0.45
Winneba	,, ,,	5.29		,, ,,	0.35
(in the gulf of the Devil's Hill)					
Accra	,, ,,	5.32		,, ,,	0.14
Ningo	,, ,,	5.45		E. Long	0.3
Quitta (Keta)	,, ,,	5.55		,, ,,	0.54
Little Popo	,, ,,	6.16		,, ,,	1.35
Great Popo	,, ,,	6.16		,, ,,	1.46
(at the mouth of the River Whydah)					
Whydah (near Mt. Palavra)	,, ,,	6.19		W.	2.5
Porto Novo	,, ,,	6.29		,, ,,	2.3
Badagry	,, ,,	6.29		,, ,,	2.52
Lagos	,, ,,	6.29		,, ,,	3.28
Palma (King Kosoko's new port)	,, ,,	6.38		,, ,,	4.-
Benin	,, ,,	6.8		,, ,,	4.5
Reggio (in the Benin river)	,, ,,	5.33		,, ,,	5.11
New Town	,, ,,	4.16		E. Long	5.11
River Nun or Brass	,, ,,	4.16		,, ,,	6.6
(mouth of the Niger)					
New Calabar River	,, ,,	4.38		,, ,,	6.55
Bonny	,, ,,	,,		,, ,,	,,
Old Calabar	,, ,,	,,		,, ,,	,,
Cameroon	,, ,,	,,		,, ,,	,,

The provinces of the interior from where the slaves and the goods are brought are those occupied by the Fulani; the Gold Coast (known also as the 'Savage Country' of Ashanti); the Kingdoms of Dahomey, Yorubaland, the capital of which is Abeokuta,[2] Ibadà [Ibadan], Ijaye, Lagos, Ijebu, Epe (whose only port is Palma), the ancient kingdom of Benin (capital: Benin), and new and old Calabar.

Trade goods imported are: acquavita from Brazil, the United States, and Havana; tobacco from Brazil (rolled and American leaf); cotton goods from Manchester; silk and velvet from France and from the Sardinian states; damask; corals from Tunisia, glass beads from Venice, carbines, pistols, gunpowder, sabres, knives, metal cooking utensils, iron bars, nails and iron hoops, English refined salt, pine and fir planks, macaroni, salt meat, preserves, shells from the East Indies and cheap trinkets of all kinds.

Exports are: various kinds of palm oil, oil from other seeds, vegetable fat, which I discovered in Lagos, best quality ivory, native cloth which is sold in Brazil, grain, cotton, wool for dyeing (indigo not explored), local silk, gold dust, skins of monkeys, deer, giraffe and other animals, ostrich feathers and various gums.

At the time of my arrival in Lagos the major import and export transactions were divided as follows:

Imports	Exports
Dixcove cotton and silk goods, corals, glass beads, rum, American leaf tobacco, planks, flints, guns, gun-power, flour, rice, oil, biscuits and other foodstuffs	Palm oil, gold dust. This area is protected by an English fort which takes a 20% levy on all trade carried out under its jurisdiction, and 16 *colonnati*[3] per ship is paid to the Dutch fort at Commenda for the right of anchorage if this has not already been collected at Elmina.
Elmina Idem: dues of 16 *colonnati* paid to the Dutch fort	Idem

[2] Abeokuta was not the capital of Yorubaland but the federated town of the Egba: see Chapter V, note 1, above. Ibadan was the largest and most powerful town of the original 'Yoruba', having been founded by refugees from the former Oyo kingdom and empire in c. 1828. For the recognition of the port of Palma by the British, see Chapter IV, note 14 above. But 1862, the year of publication of Scala's *Memorie*, also saw Kosoko's withdrawal from his miniature state at Epe and return to Lagos as a pensioner of the new colony, so that his port at Palma lost its importance.

[3] For '*colonnati*', see Chapter IV, note 12 above.

Imports	Exports
Cape Coast Castle. Idem. dues — 2% and £2 for the harbour light to the English fort.	Palm oil, gold dust, Ivory.
Anomaba: Idem. 2% dues is paid to the English. There are no harbour lights.	Idem.
Manfort [Mumford]: Idem. Dutch Possession — no dues.	Idem.
Winneba: Rum, leaf tobacco, very few manufactured goods	Palm oil, gold dust in large quantities and grain.
Accra: Rum, leaf tobacco, carbines, gunpowder, shells, corals and manufactured goods.	Oil, gold dust, gems, skins of monkeys, deer and giraffe.
Quitta: Idem.	Poor quality oil. 2% dues to be paid to the English.
Little Popo: Idem.	Palm oil of mediocre quality.
Whydah: Idem plus tobacco and rum from Brazil and green and red Sardinian velvet — French factories. They are beginning to want, as money, the so-called black or dead (cowrie) shells, from Quitta up to Benin.	Palm oil. A levy of 10 *colonnati* per ship's mast, plus 3% on the goods exported paid to the local government.
Badagry: Idem.	Palm oil — levy of 2% paid in cowrie shells to the local chief.
Lagos: All kinds of imported goods, plus large quantities of salt and shells (levy of 400 shells per 120 gallon cast of oil).	Prime quality palm old, palm nut oil and various grains *denti di cavallo marino* [lit, sea horse teeth].
	Vegetable tallow, ivory and cotton.
Benin	Palm oil.
Brass or Nun	Rum from Giam [Jamaica ?]
New Calabar	Idem
Bonny	Important markets
Old Calabar, Cameroon	whose trade is monopolized by English traders from Liverpool.

Annual Export

Dixcove	Oil tons	4000	Gold ounces	4000
Elmina	,, ,,	5000	,, ,,	5000
Cape Coast	,, ,,	2000	,, ,,	12000
Annamaba	,, ,,	2000	,, ,,	3000
	Ivory, quintals	4000		
Manfort	Oil tons	2000	,, ,,	2000
Ineba [Winneba]	,, ,,	1000	,, ,,	500
	Maize, quintals	15000	'Pistucci' (nuts) mixed	4000
Accra	Oil tons	3000		
	Monkey skins	200000	Gums (Gold ounces)	10000
			Gold total	0.31500

Quita	Oil tons	2000
Porto Siguro	,, ,,	1000
Little Popo	,, ,,	1000
Agné [Agué]	,, ,,	2000
Great Popo	,, ,,	2000
Ajuda [Whydah]	,, ,,	10000
Badagry	,, ,,	3000

Lagos and surroundings, including Palma.

,,	Palm oil	tons	10000
,,	Palm nuts		1000
,,	Ivory, Quint.		1000
,,	Cotton Balls		5000
Lagos	Maize		100
,,	Cloth (locally woven) Bales		15000
,,	Tallow, vegetable		1500
Benin	Oil tons		4000
Brass	,, ,,		4000
New Calabar	,, ,,		2000
'Bonin' [Bonny]	,, ,,		22000
Old Calabar	,, ,,		15000
Cameroon	,, ,,		10000

Total tons 109600

* This trade is monopolized by English ships from Liverpool. There are also ships from Liverpool in N. Lat. 4, belonging to the G. Laird Company, which run a monthly service, carrying from 900 to 12000 a month, calling at Madeira, the Canaries, Sierra Leone, Cape Palmas, Cape Coast, Accra, Lagos, Benin, Brass, Bonny, Old Calabar, Cameroon and Fernando Po on outward and return voyages.

In Bonin [Bonny?] palm oil is very abundant, and is brought there from the interior. Difficulties in loading and unloading hinder a greater export.

Annual Average for Ships Trading Between Cape Three Points and Cameroon

English	No. 120	Tons from	250 to 1000
Hamburg	40	,, ,,	200 to 500
French	30	,, ,,	200 to 500
American	20	,, ,,	200 to 800
Sardinian	20	,, ,,	150 to 250
Portuguese	20	,, ,,	150 to 250
Spanish	30	,, ,,	100 to 200
Dutch	30	,, ,,	150 to 300
Total Number	300		

Articles Imported from the Different Nations

English	£st.
Cotton manufactured goods	720,000
Silk	140,000
Carbines and other arms	250,000
Gunpowder in barrels	100,000
Barrels of Flints	40,000
Iron bars of different kinds, 6 ft. long by $2\frac{1}{4}$ in. thick	250,000
Spirits, wines and foodstuffs	250,000
Salt, tons	10,000
Cowrie shells	40,400
Iron rings	260,000
Crockery	20,000
Total £	2,071,000

French	
Cowries (shells from the Indies)	£st.
3000 tons @ £20 per ton	60,000
Cotton goods manufactured in France	20,000
Cotton goods manufactured in England	100,000
French silk	20,000
Venetian glass and beads	20,000
Italian coral	20,000
Foodstuffs	20,000
Total £	260,000

American		£st.
Rum, 800,000 gallons		100,000
Virginian tobacco 20,000 Quintals		60,000
Pine planks 5,000,000		50,000
Gunpowder in 25 lb. barrels		10,000
Cotton manufactured goods		50,000
	Total £	270,000

Hamburg		£
Cowries 6000 tons		120,000
Hamburg manufactured goods		10,000
English manufactured goods		20,000
Gin, 20,000 cases		10,000
Tobacco and rum from Brazil		20,000
	Total £	180,000

Sardinian		£st.
from Brazil with tobacco and rum		40,000
from England with English manufactured goods		40,000
from Genoa with Macaroni, foodstuffs, silk, velvet and coral		20,000
	Total £	100,000

Portuguese		£st.
from Brazil with rum and tobacco		80,000
from Portugal with foodstuffs and grappling hooks		10,000
	Total £	90,000

Spanish		£st.
Rum from Havana 1000 casks		8,000

Dutch		£st.
Dutch manufactured goods		10,000
Carbines		40,000
Gunpowder in 25 lb barrels, 50,000		50,000
Gin		7,000
	Total £	107,000

Grand Total £st.	3,158,000

Goods are exported in the following way:

The English, Portuguese, Sardinians and Spanish take cargoes for England; the French carry some cargoes to England and some to France; the Americans to America; the Hamburg ships to Hamburg, and the Dutch to Holland.

This trade, although it seems very considerable, is in fact very limited if one considers the extent and immense wealth of the country.

In the last decade it has increased by 50% but it could easily be increased by more than 1,000% if the European governments would take it seriously.

From Cape Three Points and Accra the White traders may not engage in any retail buying or selling; this trade belongs exclusively to the natives. Some Europeans however are secretly engaged in it, using an African as an intermediary, and they derive great profits from it.

From Dixcove to Accra, manufactured cotton and silk are sold in the piece which varies from 16 to 50 yards in length.

Coral is sold in strings and is usually valued in Spanish *colonnati* and exchanged for *acki* of gold (i.e. $\frac{1}{8}$ of an ounce).

Best quality ivory weighs 50 lbs. a piece and is sold for $1\frac{1}{4}$ *colonnati* per il., a piece weighing 20 lbs. to 50 lbs. is sold for one *colonnato*, a small piece from 20 lbs. down to 12 lbs. is sold for $\frac{3}{4}$ *colonnato*, and a piece weighing less than 12 lbs. for $\frac{1}{2}$ *colonnato*.

Gum varies according to demand. On average it is sold at the rate of 12 lb. for 1 colonnato. The Americans have the absolute monopoly of this item.

Rum is sold at 40 to 50 *centesimi di colonnato* per old gallon.

Palm oil measured in old gallons is sold at the rate of $\frac{1}{3}$ *colonnato* per gallon and the captain has to pay a loading charge of 1 *colonnato* for every 120 gallons. Casks: 5 *centesimi di colonnato* per gallon.

American leaf tobacco—from 16 to 20 *colonnati* for each 100 lbs.

English carbines—from $2\frac{1}{2}$ to 5 *colonnati*.

Gunpowder 16 *colonnati* for 112 lbs.

Gold dust 2 *colonnati* per *acko* [*sic*], i.e. a West Coast weight equivalent to $\frac{1}{8}$ of a European ounce. If carefully weighed there is 10% to 12% profit on the comparative weight.

Unless otherwise stipulated, the buyer has the option of paying in Spanish, American or English money according to the following tariff: Spanish gold ounces (coins) 16 colonnati; Mexican gold ounces 15; £ sterling $4\frac{1}{2}$. The buyer can, unless otherwise stated, pay in palm oil, ivory, gold dust or in cash according to the rates already mentioned.

From Cape St Paul to Lagos (Western Gulf of Guinea) the old Portuguese system of weights and measures is still in use.

Cloth of any kind must be of uniform length and width. The principal articles are cottons measuring 30 English yards in length and 28 to 30 inches in width. The types in greatest demand are *cotton* 30 yds. long and

Madapalano 24, 40 and 50 yds. long and 34 ins. wide. *Silks*, silk velvet is in great demand and preference is given to that which comes from Italy. Reds and greens are the most popular colours. It is sold in 16 metre lengths.

Corals are preferred threaded and are sold by the String.

Venetian glass beads sold in bundles by the pound or by 100 lb. boxes.

Leaf tobacco from 16-20 colonnati per 100 lbs.

Brazilian tobacco in rolls from 5–10 colonnati per roll weighing 64 lbs. (Portuguese)

English carbines 3 *colonnati* each.

Gunpowder from 5 to 6 *colonnati* quintal of 112 lbs. (English).

Wines from Spain, Oporto and Bordò [Bordeaux] (in small quantities), price varies according to demand.

Olive oil 6 *colonnati* per case of 12 bottles.

Sugar (small quantity) 2 *colonnati* per loaf or 4 *colonnati* per *rubbo* in powdered form.

Buyers load at their own expense but pay no duty on imports. Native governments collect a duty on exports of 3% in cowries, that is two heads equal to 4,000 cowries, for every 120 gallons of palm oil. There is 1% duty on ivory.

Trade from Benin to the Cameroon is carried on almost on the same scale as that described above, which can be applied to all the West Coast provinces. Gold dust is used as an indication of nominal value, as a substitute for the Spanish royal gold ounce. Four ounces of gold are equivalent to a cask of oil (200 imperial gallons). The imperial gallon is 20% more than the old gallon. Almost all the traders have adopted the very wise measure of having casks and divisions of casks of standard capacity. This makes trading easier and avoids the difficulties which are bound to arise in a country where there is no fixed system of weights and measures. Casks can be used for any merchandise and are often filled with goods other than those they originally contained. All goods sent from the coast to the interior and vice versa are packed in casks.

Ships whatever their tonnage which load and unload in the ports between Benin and the Cameroon have to pay a duty of 10 casks to the native governments. This does not seriously affect large ships but is very hard on ships of 150 to 200 tons.

Cowries,[4] otherwise sea-shells, are used as money by the natives. There are two qualities, the 'live' and the 'dead' thus named according to whether

[4] For the procurement and use of cowry shells as money, see A. G. Hopkins, 'The Currency Revolution', and Hogendorn and Johnson, *Shell Money*. Briefly, cowries were coming into fairly general use in West Africa as money by the late eighteenth century, although there is evidence of their earlier use at Benin and in the West Sudan. The first cowries in such use, known as 'moneta', were shipped from the Maldives by the Indians to Europe and thence brought to the West African coast. In the second half of the 19th century Hamburg merchants were shipping larger cowries, known as annuli, direct from Zanzibar. This was soon copied by others and the growing supply from East Africa resulted in an inflation which persisted until cowries went out of use as a medium of exchange towards the end of the 19th century. See Chapter VI, note 9 above.

the crustacean inside the shell was alive or dead when it was found. The first are the most sought after and cost more because they last longer. Some are white and others black. From Mumford to Accra the black ones are not in circulation, and the white ones, which are preferred also because they are smaller, become more valuable as their weight decreases. The black ones are in circulation from Cape St Paul to Lagos, and are valued according to the tariff mentioned below. From Lagos to the Cameroon there is a demand for cowries as articles of trade to be sold in the inland provinces and on other points along the coast.

These shells which are of such importance in Africa are brought from the East Indies. The Indians catch them in nets as we catch mussels, and stack them in warehouses until the crustacean rots away, then they wash them out, dry them in the sun and wash them again. They are sold to the English and Hamburg firms which bring them directly to Africa. Their cost price there is 2 or $2\frac{1}{2}$ *colonnati* per quintal (112 lbs.) and they are sold for 6 colonnati, thus, black shells sell according to size and white shells, alive or small, cost double. Since they have no other means of representing the value of goods, particularly in the retail trade, the Africans have given these shells a nominal value on the following scale:

> One Toke or the equivalent of 40 shells $= 0.05$ L.It.
>
> One 'gallina' equal to 200 shells $= 0.25$
>
> One Head 2,000 shells $= 2.50$
>
> One bag of ten heads, 20,000 shells $= 25.-$

This money is, however, little used by the Europeans from Benin to the Cameroon. When a White man buys goods at the retail price from the natives he pays with leaves of tobacco, clay pipes, metal spoons, mirrors, scissors, and other such cheap trinkets.

This system based, as we can see, on prices relative to demand and not according to the intrinsic value of the goods, is open to serious abuse of which the Africans are always the victims.

X

NAVIGATION

From Cape Palmas 4.24' Lat. North, 7.45' Long. West, as far as the great river Cameroon 3.50' Lat. North 9.34' Long East.[1]

Cape Palmas is a landmark for ships trading along the coast of the Gulf of Guinea. They usually come in here from W.S.W. and lie 4 or 5 miles out to wait for the Crumani [Krumen], the labourers from Palmas who handle all the cargoes. These strong, tireless men carry out their task with great energy and intelligence and at the hottest times of the day they take on all the work of the crew. They are paid at the rate of 4 *colonnati* per man per month, plus 5 *colonnati* to their headmen, paid in manufacturing goods, gunpowder, guns etc. according to the local exchange rate. The captain has to send them back to Cape Palmas at his expense or bring them back on his own ship on the return voyage.

Cape Palmas has a lighthouse 40 metres high which was erected last year (1858). About three miles off-shore there are various reefs at the same level as the water, visible and easy to avoid in the day-time but extremely dangerous at night. I would advise all sailors to observe extreme caution at night and not to go too near the land because of the currents which become stronger and can easily draw the ship into the narrows. Beyond these reefs the coast, steep and rugged near the shore, goes N.E. to the Grand Bassam River, then bends S.E. as far as Cape Apollonia about 30 miles from Cape Three Points. Cape Apollonia is easy to recognize from the sea because of a high steep mountain which stands out on the horizon like a half-ruined column or a great tree alone in a desert of sand.

Grand Bassam was for ten years an important trading post on the coast. The French had set up a factory there protected by two small warships and a

---

[1] In this chapter Scala is describing the navigation of sailing vessels to and from what were still known as the Grain, Ivory, Gold and Slave Coasts of West Africa, and the coast beyond as far as the Cameroon river. Cape Palma (or Palmas) is at the south-eastern extremity of the then scattered settlement already known as Liberia. At this time steam power was only gradually displacing sail at sea. Professor Law points out that much of this chapter reads as though it had been taken from a navigational guide such as the *African Pilot*.

little fort occupied by a garrison of 20 soldiers and one officer. Frequent hostilities between the French workers and the natives, fever and other difficulties obliged the Government to abandon the fort and the factory.

Along the coast from Cape Palmas to Cape Three Points the seaman would be wise not to land. The inhabitants of these shores have the reputation of being rapacious and inhuman. Traders usually trade from their ships on this coast. As soon as a ship is sighted the natives rush out to it in their tiny canoes offering to exchange gold dust for European goods and begging the captain to drop anchor and come ashore. If he rashly agrees he runs the risk of becoming a victim of their cupidity. Eight or nine years ago a French ship in these waters was approached by a number of canoes manned by natives who courteously invited the captain to come ashore to see the land and trade profitably with them. The captain weakly accepted their invitation, but as soon as he landed he was arrested and held hostage until an exorbitant sum was paid for his release. The crew after trying every possible means of conciliation, set off in search of a cruiser. Fortunately they soon met a French warship which was obliged to bombard the area so as to obtain the captain's release.

The chief trade of this part of the coast is in palm oil, sold in small jars, and gold dust which the natives bring in little bags hanging from their necks. The gold is sold by the ounce weighed on scales made out of skins of fruit and with grains the size of peas for weights. It is wonderful to see the dexterity with which the Africans weigh the gold in these skins and how accurate their weights are when checked on European scales. The articles for which gold is exchanged are striped cotton cloth, brightly coloured scarves, guns, gunpowder, mirrors, flour, biscuits, salted meat, rum, tobacco, coral and trinkets.

The first point on this coast at which the captain can land with safety is Axim, a Dutch possession to the west of Cape Three Points, but this is not a very important station for ships coming from the Mediterranean. This Cape is subject to very strong currents of two to three miles velocity flowing eastwards. When there are strong East winds the currents suddenly change direction and for a few days flow from East to West. This happens about twice a month in the lunar phase when there are strong E.S.E. winds. Most sailing charts show a dangerous bar above Cape Three Points. I have sailed several times around this Cape and examined the whole area very carefully. I have noticed a change in the colour of the water two miles south of Cape Three Points over all the area indicated on the charts as 'Bar'. After carefully sounding it, I found a depth of 60 fathoms throughout. So the bar does not exist. A particular stretch of the sea floor producing a change of color has given rise to this error.

A ship sailing towards Dixcove which has not found an anchorage before dark should drop anchor. If it heaves to, as some have done, it may be carried from fifteen to ten and from ten to five miles to leeward where even if it avoids the bars which prevent access to the coast three, four, or five miles out, it may then lose eight, ten or more days before it gets back on course. This is due to the strong currents which prevent it from regaining the wind. Ten miles from Dixcove are other bars visible by day but extremely dangerous by night. In any case, one should as far as possible bear to the South keeping clear of the shore. In general one can anchor at twelve or even 10 fathoms; it is wise however to take soundings throughout the night so as not to find oneself in less deep water. East of Cape Coast the lighthouse is visible from a distance of five miles.

Cape St Paul is formed by a long sandbank which marks its circumference. To the west is the River Volta which is extremely fast flowing and tidal near the sea. Ships passing the Cape at night should take care to keep to a depth of fifteen or at least twelve fathoms so as to avoid being blown by the wind or drawn by the currents into the mouth of the river. Several ships have been completely wrecked in this way. Cape St Paul can be recognized from the sea by two huge coconut trees which dominate the end of the promontory and by a thick forest four miles to the North called Acce. Following the line of the forest for fifteen miles from the Cape one reaches Keta which used to be a Danish possession. From Keta to Port Siguro [Porto Seguro] the coast is recognizable from the sea by the lights of many fires, but they are misleading because the natives often light these fires five or ten miles inland and endanger the ships which take their bearings from them.

In 1850 the Danes sold Keta to the English who fortified it by sea and land, placed a garrison there and imposed, as they always do, a duty of 2% on all import transactions. This annoyed the natives who refused to pay the duty and tried to chase the new invaders away. The small English Garrison, surrounded by large numbers of the enemy would have been put to flight had they not sought the aid of a passing French warship. On hearing what the trouble was the French without further ado bombarded Keta on behalf of the English and reduced it to ashes. The inhabitants abandoned their town, some retreating a little way inland and others transferring their trade to various points along the coast. Three days later, the same French ship came back past the ruins at night time and deceived by the above-mentioned fires came too near the shore and ran aground. The crew managed to escape by swimming or on rafts, but the ship was lost and the natives saw this catastrophe as the just punishment for an act of cold-blooded savagery.

The settlement of the refugees from Keta soon grew and became a town called Gerocafe (which means Divine Justice) probably as a result of the wreck of the French ship; nevertheless despite the allegorical name the 2% duty was not only maintained on all goods loaded or unloaded in Keta from ships of all nations but is still collected today even in Gerocafe which did not take long to fall into the hands of the English.[2] Moreover these arbitrary impositions upset the natives and deterred them from trading with the Europeans. Even in Cape Coast and Accra where the English have two forts, they wanted to impose a poll-tax of one shilling a year. Because of this the black traders gradually moved away from these shores and a 5% decrease in trade has been calculated since that time.

From Cape St Paul one can follow the coast N.E. to Porto Seguro keeping three miles away from the shore and anchoring in not less than ten fathoms of water. Porto Seguro is about 40 miles away and can easily be recognized by the same line of big trees rising from the shore. Thirty miles further East, keeping one mile out, at a depth of ten fathoms one reaches Little Popo. From this point as far as Lagos, the coast runs due East with a regular depth. Ships can keep at ten fathoms. On reaching Lagos, in order to take up a position facing the mouth of the river, the ship must bear South to keep clear of the ring of sandbanks blocking the river mouth, until the Eastern headland N.W. of the river is sighted and then bear North to a depth of six fathoms before anchoring. The Eastern headland can be recognized from far out at sea by a huge tree which dominates the point.

Palma, otherwise called Port Kosoko,[3] created by the English Consul in 1855, is 30 miles East of Lagos. Sixty miles further is Benin, which can be distinguished, from the sea, by two mouths of the river which are quite different in appearance. The Eastern mouth is in the midst of a high, dense forest and the Western one forms a low bay in the shore.

Ships anchor five miles from the shore facing the river mouths at a depth of five fathoms. They unload half their cargo into canoes and take on the pilot to enter the river up which they sail for three miles with a draught of ten or twelve English feet. When they leave they take on half their cargo in the river and the other half out at sea. The mouths of the river face S.E.[4] There is no real difficulty in entering or going out because of the W.S.W. winds which prevail almost the whole year round. There are no charges while the ship stays in the

---

[2] The affray described by Scala seems to be a recollection of an episode which took place in 1844 when a Danish sergeant released a party of slaves taken by a 'Portuguese' trader. This led to a rising by the people of Keta town and the other local Anlo during which the Danish garrison of Keta fort suffered a long siege. The garrison was relieved by the arrival of a French warship, the *Abeille*, and a Franco-Danish 'punitive expedition' was mounted. During these operations Keta town was destroyed and only rebuilt after 1850. Keta was among the five forts sold by the Danes to the British in 1850 for £10,000; it had been 'a notorious den of slavers'. W. E. F. Ward, *A History of Ghana*, 1965 ed., pp. 224–7; A. van Dantzig, *Forts and Castles of Ghana*, 1980, p. 72.

[3] Palma, east from Lagos, presumably so-called by the Portuguese, can now be recognized under its Yoruba name of Orimedu. For its recognition as Kosoko's 'port of trade' in 1854 (not 1855), see Chapter IV above and note 14, also Appendix 2.

[4] The estuary of the Benin river faces west-south-west.

roads, but on entering the river one pays 500 *colonnati* for the right to trade and 50 for the pilot, that is about one *colonnato* for each ton registered.

A ship going to points further along the coast such as Brass, New Calabar, Bonny and Cameroon has to take on a pilot to enter these rivers. Just beyond Cape Formoso there are several shallows which merit attention by day and must be sounded during the night. The mouth of the Brass River[5] can be recognized by the Western point which is high and looks like an island. The Eastern point however is five miles away and very low. Ships have to anchor to the East before going up the river.

On leaving Brass for New Calabar and Bonny it is advisable to steer directly to the South-East to avoid the shallows lying along the coast, eight or ten miles out. The West bank of the great river of New Calabar is one mile East of E. Long. $7°$ and N. Lat. $4,25'$ $30''$. The Western point belonging to the Bonny River is E. Long 7.8 and on the same latitude as the opposite headland. If, in dull weather or fog, a captain making for this point cannot observe his longitude with great accuracy he should anchor at ten fathoms and send a launch to the shore to pick up a pilot or else identify his position on the chart. The centre of the river mouth is blocked by a sand-bank two miles in circumference, covered with three feet of water at low tide and thirteen feet at high tide. A captain who proposes to enter the mouth either to reach New Calabar or the Eastern bank or to trade in the town of Bonny, must make sure of his precise longitude on the chronometer. If the weather is dull and stormy he must heave to or drop anchor in not less than ten fathoms, about 15 miles from the East bank. If the weather is fine he can risk entering the river, sailing to the West of the bank which he cannot fail to recognize by the colour and continuous bubbling of the water at high tide and keeping as far as possible in mid-channel, thus avoiding the dangerous shoals on both side. The Eastern channel, called commonly the 'smugglers' channel', is the easiest way to leave the river. In any case it is necessary to take soundings up to $4\frac{1}{2}$ or five fathoms. A captain making his first voyage to Old Calabar and Cameroon must take on a pilot to sail in these waters.

Fernando Po[6] appears to the navigator as a peak, quite high above the level of the water with a slight declivity on both sides, giving it a regular

---

[5] The Brass river forms a part of the estuary of the Niger, flowing south through the wide delta of that river.

[6] Fernando Po was 'discovered' in the late fifteenth century by a Portuguese navigator, ceded to Spain in 1778, and occupied by Britain with Spanish consent between 1827 and 1844, after which the Spanish resumed control of the island. A Roman Catholic mission had been established there in 1740 but did not succeed. An energetic Spanish chaplain, Jeronimo de Usera, who was working there from 1851, re-established the mission and brought other Catholic priests to the island. Between 1843 and 1858 there was also a Protestant mission there, run by English Baptists.

conical shape. There is a very good port on the Eastern side, frequented by
American and Spanish ships in particular. This island is not very fertile
but its geographical position is such that it seems destined to become for
West Africa, what Sira [Siros] in the Cyclades is for Greece and Turkey, a
central depository for all exports from the rivers of the coast and for imports
from America and Europe. The inhabitants are less amenable to European
civilization than those of the rest of the continent because no one has yet
made them aware of its advantages. The Catholic missionaries sent by the
Spaniards, instead of appeasing them, have increased their natural difference
and contributed in no small way to making them hate the very name of the
white man. Catholic or even Protestant missions are certainly good institutions and necessary among primitive peoples to complete the work of
civilization begun by the traders. These, at first pioneers of civilization,
bring material advantages, gentle manners and civil and political emanci-
pation; on the other hand the missionary brings moral advantages important
in a very different way: divine truth, Christian morals, charity and emancipa-
tion of the spirit. The obstacles which the missionary has to overcome are far
greater than those which beset the trader in unknown lands and the cruiser
along the coast; there are inveterate errors to dispel and infamous customs
(like polygamy) to eradicate. Woe to the missionary who sins by an excess
of zeal! His work is wasted. Instead of reaping love and virtue, he reaps
hatred and aversion as was the case with the fiery Spanish priest.[7]

The conversion of the heathen demands time, patience and indefatigable
love.

The Spanish government have built a fortress in Fernando Po where they
have a garrison of 400 or 500 men. They have also stationed there some small
warships which cruise along the Old Calabar. Many people from the island
of Principe emigrate and settle in Fernando Po and others come from the
continent. There is a population of about 10,000, some living in the so-
called coastal towns, the others on the steep crests of their mountain which
are the most fertile parts of the island. These mountain dwellers rarely
leave the heights and refuse to have any contact with the white men or
with the people of their own race who live on the plain. They are rough,
wild and fanatical. In the town there are some factories and commercial
houses. We do not know whether, in the course of time, the Spanish will
succeed in civilizing these people. The methods of force and terror which
they have chosen do not seem to be the best.

---

[7] The early Christian missions in the area of the Niger estuary have been studied by A. F. C.
Ryder: see his articles, 'The Benin Missions' and 'Missionary Activities' in *JHSN*, 1960, 1961.
Also see R. Law, 'Religion, Trade and Politics' in the *Journal of Religion in Africa*, 1991.

XI

RETURN VOYAGE TO EUROPE

A ship leaving the coast of Africa from any point East of Cape St Paul[1] must head South at least as far as the Equator keeping as far West as possible of Principe. By sailing East of the island, especially from September and October until May, one runs the risk of falling to leeward on being becalmed for ten, twelve or more days without moving at all. If a contrary wind, or one's own first direction, does not allow one to sail immediately West of the island, rather then decide to go East it would be better to keep two or three degrees North of the latitude of the island, in order to be in position to go West of it. If the wind is blowing to Westward, it is certainly wise to sail in that direction until it backs at least to half strength. If then you tack at least forty miles South of Cape Three Points, even if the wind does not allow you to go West it is better to tack West-North-East, since before reaching Cape Palmas and the longitude of Great Bassam the wind changes to West-South-West. Then you have to continue one hundred miles West of Cape Palmas and then bear West-North-West. From May to October, you should keep further North, but from October to April you have to keep further South because of the heavy rains which fall on the coasts of Sierra Leone and Senegambia and break the uniformity of the winds. It is always wise to keep well out from the coast in this season, on both outward and return voyages. From May to October, you can easily continue to tack even with the wind to the leeward between Cape Verde and the islands, because as you go on you will run into the constant North East winds. By altering course you will come into the region of variable winds which in a very short time will lead you into difficulties.

I said at the beginning that to arrive at the total abolition of the Slave Trade, cruisers alone are not enough and legitimate trade in these regions must be developed and increased as a substitute for the Slave Trade. The present system of vigilance established by various governments who have possessions and naval and military stations along the coasts, far from

---

[1] Cape St Paul (Scala's Capo S. Paolo) lies immediately to the east of the Volta estuary.

protecting and encouraging the free development of European trade, is a
burden and a hindrance to it. It drives ships from these shores and thwarts
their trade.

There are along the Coast of Cape Palmas to Fernando Po some small
English, French and Dutch military bases which under the pretext of
preventing the Slave Trade impose crippling duties on the natives and on
the ships. While these bases are most often incapable of preventing the
embarkation of the slaves, they drive out of range the African people who
would otherwise have wished to trade their products with the Europeans;
moreover, many European ships whose own interests would lead them to
trade at these places, go elsewhere since in addition to the hardships of a
long and dangerous voyage, the unhealthy climate and many other disadvantages, there are enormous customs duties, great expenses and vexations of
every kind which nullify the profits of the enterprise.

The Sardinian Government gave its sanction to the treaties drawn up
between France and England to abolish the Slave Trade. We bless this act
of political morality and thank the Government for it; only we should
have liked a more careful examination of the separate clauses of these treaties, an examination which would certainly have advised the suppression of
some of these clauses as being useless to the aims of the contracting parties
and very harmful to trade. I will quote only one example: among the many
rules and regulations which are in force and to which the agents and captains
who trade on the African coast are subjected, there is one customs regulation
which demands a guarantee for every ship sent to these parts. This measure
would seem to be a sufficient guarantee against any unlikely wish on the
agents' part to become involved in the wicked slave traffic. However, to
this precaution is added that of the Naval Customs Decree, by which every
ship which leaves from one of the ports of this state with a definite number
of puncheons stated in its clearance manifest cannot alter that number without getting a new manifest in a place where the Customs Decree is in force,
subject to the levy of a fine on the vessel. This measure, although apparently
very simple, is the cause of much harm, which a long experience enables me to
describe thus:

(1) Ships which leave Genoa for Africa, usually carrying foodstuffs,
cannot take on a sufficient number of puncheons for the return cargo.
When they have reached Africa and unloaded their goods at various
places they cannot take on the puncheons they need to complete their
cargo without first going to the place where they are to receive it. If they
do otherwise, the number of puncheons on board will exceed the number
shown on their manifest and their ships will be liable to be confiscated.
Then it often happens that not enough puncheons have been returned to

the port where the cargo is to be picked up and as the ships may not go elsewhere to look for empty ones they are forced by this measure to take on only half or a third of their cargo. This regulation applies to all ships wherever they have come from.

(2) A ship which finds itself by accident on the coast hoping to pick up palm oil and is offered a cargo from a port not shown on its manifest cannot go there and is obliged to leave this cargo to the English and French who can go wherever they like. Another ship belongs to an agent who owns two firms in Africa, one in Lagos and one in Accra. This ship comes to Lagos to take on a cargo of oil. The cargo is ready provided that the ship goes immediately to Accra or elsewhere to receive the requisite number of puncheons. But that it cannot do because of the previously mentioned customs regulations. Finally two vessels belonging to the same firm meet on the coast of Africa. One wants to hand over to the other its puncheons to enable it to accept a cargo which it has been offered; this it cannot do without contravening the regulations and exposing itself to the risk of being caught by the cruisers of the various nations.

These cases, of which I often complained officially while I was Consul, are increasing every year and causing the gravest inconvenience to our shipping and trade in these parts. It can be argued that the same regulations are in force for the ships of other nations. This is very true, but I have observed that the presence of English and French cruisers on these shores absolves their own merchant ships from the aforementioned formalities and thus enables them to monopolize at least two-thirds of the trade for their exclusive profit.

In order to obviate this difficulty our government too should send a small ship to cruise on the African coast, to represent our flag and protect our national interest. I sent an official report to this effect to our Minister of Foreign Affairs, the late Count di Cavour, but the political circumstances and restricted finances of our State did not then allow this measure although it was considered very suitable by our government. I also sent to the same Honourable Minister another official report submitting to him a project for the exploration of the Brass River as far as the Niger Confluence. This exploration has already been attempted by the British Government some years ago and had failed because of the low water level.[2] Having sailed up the river by canoe I was personally convinced that the low water level referred to was due to the blockage caused by many aquatic plant parasites,

---

[2] The British expeditions of 1832 and 1841 to explore the Niger and also to prospect the river Benue from its confluence with the Niger were thwarted in part by the death toll from malaria among the participants. The next expedition, that of 1854, pioneered the use of quinine as a prophylactic against the disease and achieved considerable success thereby.

tree trunks, and earth swept away by storms and deposited in various creeks
of the river. At the confluence of the Brass with the Niger there is also a reef
at water level on which an English ship was wrecked three years ago.[3] It
seems to me that it would be easy to clear a passage and penetrate further,
with a ship of not more than a six foot draught, into hitherto unexplored
regions. The object of this enterprise was to open a safe and inexpensive
route into the interior from Lagos, Abeokuta etc. How great the advantage
to European trade in Africa would be if all the people of the interior,
including the immense area bordered by Kanem to the East, Timbuktu to
the North and Senegambia to the West, instead of trading their products
with Egypt, Tunis and Morocco by caravan could take the much shorter
route via Lagos and Abeokuta! What an inexhaustible source of wealth in
trade and industry with peoples whose number is incalculable and whose
products are so rich and varied and not yet all known! What better means
than this of stemming the inhuman slave trade at its very source! Finally
what glory for our nation to have been the first to explore an unknown
region, to draw it out from a state of inertia and savagery and to bring it
into the bosom of modern civilisation! The same political and financial
circumstances did not allow our government to listen to my request and I
was obliged to abandon my project.

Another difficulty causing grave expense and loss of time to the ships of
all nations which come to Lagos is the topography of the river in which this
island lies. All goods for import or export are deposited on the nearest beach
to be transported in open canoes from the island to the ship and vice versa at
great expense and often loss of men and goods.

The commercial firms are situated three miles from the sea shore on the
bank of a river. All the goods loaded at Lagos must first be brought by
canoe from the island to the mouth of the river, then carried from there by
hand across the beach to the loading point. Here they are loaded on lighters
to be transported to the ships which are anchored two or three miles from the
beach. The same process takes place for goods sent from the ships to the
island. The resultant disadvantages are, on the one hand, the frequent
thefts committed while the goods are being taken along the river or across
the beach; the considerable deterioration of goods due to breakage, cracking
of casks and contact with the salt water which comes into the lighters, and, on
the other hand, the loss of life and property when the canoes or lighters cap-
size in rough weather. To this must be added the delay on the beach while the

---

[3] Scala apparently refers here to the wreck of the steamer *Dayspring* in 1858 on the Juju Rock on
the Niger during the expedition of 1857 led by Dr. Baikie. The Rock, however, is over 300 miles
above the confluence of the river Brass with the main Niger stream and it cannot properly be
described as a 'reef'.

goods are waiting to be loaded and the expense of warehouses, employees etc. The losses on imports are calculated as follows:

on puncheons 5%
on boats capsizing 5%
on deterioration caused by salt water 10%
on employment of assistants and bearers 10%
TOTAL 30%

This expense could be spared by using tugs to bring the ships up to the town of Lagos and in bad weather to transport the goods from the town to the ships and vice versa. These difficulties and damages greatly affect the export of such articles as grain, groundnuts, oil seeds etc., and are very detrimental to cottons; they also make many merchants hesitate to undertake commercial ventures at Lagos and thus keep away capital which would be useful to European trade and in civilizing the country. The present cost of shipping palm oil is nine shillings per puncheon. The last official report stated that 4091 tons had been shipped in the course of the previous year. That, at 130 gallons per puncheon, gives a total of 10700 puncheons which, at a cost of nine shillings each, makes £4,815 for loading this article alone from the beach to the ship. If you add to this, two shillings and three pence per puncheon, the tariff for carrying them by canoe from the factories to the river mouth, the cost rises to £1,203 and the overall total is £6,018. The cost of loading and unloading other articles like raw and manufactured cotton, ivory, etc. are proportionate, at a rate of six shilling and nine pence per crate. Altogether on exports and imports there is a total charge of not less than £13,000 per year.[4]

It has been observed that the loading and unloading operations could easily be undertaken by two small steam boats with a draught of five or six feet, assisted if necessary by two big iron sloops. These boats could unload and receive cargoes at a general depot on the island, which would only cost a small amount to build; they could go right up to the ships in the roads, pulling the sloops and then bring them back up the river, to Lagos. In this way, the thefts, deterioration of goods, loss of life and of time, and the exorbitant charges would be avoided.

I would advise our government to undertake this enterprise with small boats belonging to the state, which could on occasion serve even more useful purposes exploring the Lagos River to East and West from Cape

---

[4] British consular figures, cited in chapter IV, note 6, and chapter VI, note 10, above, showed a decline in the amount of palm oil exported in 1858 to 4612 tons. Difficulties in shipping mail and cargo into and out of Lagos persisted until the construction, begun in 1907, of the breakwater.

Palmas to Badagry and going on up the Abeokuta River. Otherwise a company could be floated with a capital of £10,000 made up of 400 shares at £25 each used as follows: £8,000 for two small paddle-steamers of 150 tons and 60 h.p.; £2,000 to cover the cost of two sloops and a warehouse-depot which would serve as an off-loading point, in Lagos.

Such a fortunate enterprise would soon lead to the promotion of others, which could navigate all the rivers and open up trade routes between the coast and the interior. An enormously advantageous development of European trade and of African civilisation and the total abolition of the Slave Trade would be logical and direct results of the plan I have suggested.

What European merchant in Africa or ship's captain who frequents these shores does not suffer from the difficulties I have described and would not be grateful for the advantages to trade in general if these difficulties were to disappear? What European Government would not gain from such an enterprise? Why has it not yet been done?

We hope that we shall not have to wait too long for the answers to these questions.

XII

NOTES ON CLIMATE

The climate of the West African Coast is temperate. In summer the temperature rises to 40°–42° (Réaumur); in winter it drops to 10° or 15° above zero but both maximum and minimum temperatures are always felt shortly before or after a storm. The rains are intermittent from March to May but from May to July they are frequent and very heavy. They are one month later for every 2° farther from the Equator. Fevers and dysentery prevail at this time and usually occur in March. Fevers can hardly ever be completely cured but their intensity is reduced by taking five grains of quinine three times a day, being careful however to have cleared one's stomach by mean of gentle purgatives.[1]

The best season for living in Africa is from October to March. The most appropriate rules of hygiene for the prevention of fevers are: moderation in liquor and meat; mild physical exercise; avoiding as far as possible going out in the open air before and after sunset.

Dysentery usually results from:

(1) a violent fever;
(2) sun-stroke;
(3) indigestion;
(4) humidity;

---

[1] The high mortality of Europeans and others, including (although to a lesser extent) the indigenous population, on the West Coast of Africa, was due mainly to two ailments, fever and dysentery. These were caused not so much by the climate as by physical conditions, those prevailing at Lagos being especially dangerous. The island with its numerous swamps, stagnant inlets from the lagoon, and flooded holes resulting from building work, was a breeding place for mosquitoes (not yet recognised as carriers of malaria), while the water-table lay so near the surface as to cause serious pollution to the wells. Advances had already been made in the avoidance and treatment of malaria by the prophylactic use of quinine, but less was known about 'the fluxes' which were still treated in the same way as fevers in temperate climates. Meanwhile intending visitors were advised to 'Beware and take heed of the Bight of Benin, where few come out while many go in'. See Smith, *Lagos Consulate*, pp. 75, 91, 96, and 166 note 2. P. D. Curtin examines the problem in *The Image of Africa — British Ideas and Action, 1780–1850*, 1964, especially in chapters 7 and 14; see also P. Allison, *Life in the White Man's Grave*, 1988.

(5) sudden change of temperature;
(6) mental or physical exhaustion.

If you have an attack of dysentery, you should first take castor oil, then starve for two days if possible, and on the third day take only rice-water. After this treatment you should, if your conditions allow, try to live in dry houses, take regular meals and drink very little wine. These observations do not apply to ships sailing in these waters. The unhealthiness of the climate being the effect of exceptional deposits in the ground does not extend beyond the shore. The health measures adopted on board some ships and to some degree included in the regulations are all but superfluous.[2]

---

[2] Scala does not mention the traditional treatment of illness among the Yoruba, despite the existence of many professional herbalists in the community and of a wide range of treatments based on medicines which were usually concocted from such natural substances as leaves and bark. See Anthony D. Buckley, *Yoruba Medicine*, 1985.

XIII

CONCLUSION

After the defeat of the Dahomians, the Yoruba Kingdom returned to its ancient calm and was secure, at least for a long time, from the attacks of its dreaded neighbours. It could enjoy long days of peace and go back, without fear, to its agricultural and commercial activities. Tinubu, who was suspected of having started the whole stormy affair, deemed it prudent to keep away, in the bosom of her tribe, apparently occupied solely in the Slave Trade, but still in the shadows intently weaving her seductive web which could lead her to power. The King Abbuké[1] feared her and kept watch on her, but did not dare to take any active measures against her for fear of starting civil war in Abeokuta.

Lagos, governed by the feeble Dosunmu, also enjoyed years of uninterrupted peace under the protection of the English cannon which had put an end to Kosoko's incessant raids. The latter, confined to his deserted and not very flourishing Kingdom of Palma,[2] wandered like a caged lion about his harem and cast an angry glance every now and then at Lagos where the ashes of his forefathers lay and to which he could not renounce his claims. In spite of his solemn agreement to the treaties against the Slave Trade he had not given up his habits as a slave merchant either, and more than one slave ship, unnoticed by the cruisers, slid away from Palma bearing a human cargo. The missionary Gollmer, more skilled in political intrigue than in spreading the Faith, had been recalled to England to the great satisfaction of everyone. I did not notice any trace of Christianity left in Lagos by this fine worker in Our Lord's vineyard, in spite of his long stay on the island.[3] The Hon. Mr. Campbell, a man of true integrity and good

---

[1] This was presumably Alake Okukenu. Cf. Chapters V, note 9, and VI, note 4, above.

[2] The capital of Kosoko's miniature and short-lived state was at Epe on the mainland rather than at Palma (Orimedu) his port. See map 3 above, and G. O. Oguntomisin, 'New Forms', Ibadan Ph.D. 1979.

[3] An odd remark, since there were flourishing congregations at three CMS churches by 1859 — though comprising mainly immigrants from Sierra Leone rather than converts made actually in Lagos.

intentions, had gradually softened his prejudices against the Yoruba, and now he sent news officially to Europe about the establishment of a white merchant in Abeokuta, a town of some importance in the interior of Africa, not yet explored and not in fact 'savage'. With the remarkable intelligence characteristic of the diplomats of his nation in everything which extends and favours trade, Mr. Campbell, when he saw the happy outcome of my enterprise, persuaded his compatriots in Lagos to follow my example and set up their business in Abeokuta. To give greater prestige to this venture he undertook to accompany them himself to that city and to present them officially to the King.[4]

I had now been in Africa for eight years, three of them in Abeokuta, and was already beginning to gather the fruits of my labours and to see the realisation of the plan which I had cherished for so long. In spite of past vicissitudes and persecutions my business prospered wonderfully, as was quite natural in a district where I held the sole monopoly of local trade with Europe.

The people of Abeokuta, once initiated into the new life of legitimate trade, reaped more and more benefits from it every day, gave up their former idle ways and eagerly farmed their land. The traffic in slaves, although not entirely destroyed, was notably diminished and slave raids became rare through lack of markets. The people were not unaware of all I had done and showed their gratitude in every possible way, in public and in private. I was worshipped by everyone (if I may say so without vanity) and called father and benefactor of the people. My influence at the Court and with the tribal chiefs was unlimited. No decision of any importance was taken by the Government without my first being consulted, so that when the English Consul asked permission for his compatriots to settle in Abeokuta, the King replied that he could not agree until he had heard what I had to say about it. I need not say that I advised him to grant the request and to favour white settlement in the Kingdom in every way because from it would be derived very great advantages for his subjects and the regeneration of his country.

Everything was going according to my wishes and I was hoping for a brighter future when I was struck by an enemy more terrible than religious fanaticism, the slave traders, the women of Aro and even Tinubu herself, and I was forced to leave, at least temporarily, a country of which I was very fond, my factories, my Consulate and my dearest hopes. For some

---

[4] Consul Campbell visited Abeokuta in November 1855 and May 1858. On the latter occasion he persuaded the Alake and other chiefs to sign a commercial agreement allowing the settlement of foreign traders in the town. Campbell's successor, Henry Foote (consul, 1860-1861), proposed the appointment of a British vice-consul to Abeokuta but the Foreign Office took no action on the recommendation.

time I suffered from the recurrent fevers and dysentery which often attack one in the rainy season and are so fatal to Europeans. In vain I had adopted all the remedies suggested by the art of medicine to fight this illness. My recovery was becoming more than problematical and a radical cure was considered necessary. Dr. Baikie of the Niger expedition had advised me some time before to leave Africa and return to Europe to breathe my native air. I delayed following this advice for as long as I could but, feeling the illness getting worse every day, I decided in the end to act upon it.

As soon as the news of my departure spread around Abeokuta, a large number of people of all conditions and ages came one after another to visit me and to ask why I was leaving, assuring me that had it not been for reasons of health they would not let me go. They all entreated me to return to Abeokuta as soon as I was better. The King and the tribal chiefs advised me to leave early in the morning to avoid the throngs of people who might hinder my departure. I accepted this advice, and I decided to go to Lagos by land. The King had presented me with two magnificent horses and given me an escort of eight men, bearing the usual staff of command; these slept for a few days in my house to make sure that I was not prevented from departing. I had also taken on eight more very strong men to carry my hammock when the road would not allow me to go on horseback, and to look after the baggage animals.

At 3 o'clock in the morning of 15th June 1859, having taken leave of the King and tribal chiefs the previous evening, I set out accompanied by my guards and servants for Aro where the King's canoes were waiting to take me across to the West bank of the river along which lay the route I was to follow.

On arriving at Aro I found myself in the midst of a thick crowd coming out of the town and trying, like me, to cross over to the West side of the river. I asked the reason for this early morning exodus of so many people; there must have been four or five thousand of them. I was told that they were Yoruba farmers living on the Dahomey border who, for the fear of nocturnal raids from their neighbours, retreated behind the walls of Abeokuta or Aro every evening and returned each morning to their farms. It is sad to think of the difficult and precarious existence of these poor people, forced to go so many miles every day to farm their own lands, under the continual threat of losing in one night the fruits of their labours and seeing destroyed the most fertile and best cultivated lands of the Kingdom from which the capital and chief towns draw their food supplies.

When I reached the West bank of the river I mounted my horse and rode Northwards[5] across a vast plain planted for the most part with yams, grain,

[5] Scala's ride to Lagos via Ota took him nearly due *south* from Abeokuta so that his reference to setting out *northwards* seems to be an error.

beans, cassava and grasses especially grown for thatch. There were also, at rare intervals here and there, palms and banana trees. The grasses which covered most of the fields made the way difficult and unhealthy because it was high enough to grow above the horse and up to the rider's waist, and also because it was impregnated with dew which after a short time literally drenched both men and horses. This continuous soaking is dangerous to one's health, particularly in this climate.

Nothing remarkable happened on the way, only that the people I met knelt down on the ground according to African custom and cried out: *Akabo Baba Scala* (Welcome, Father Scala). I replied *Ocu* (greetings).

At 4 p.m. we reached a place called Ode where there is no settled population but only a few huts to shelter travellers coming into the neighbourhood from Abeokuta. In the rainy season or in war time this place is much more frequented and becomes a common refuge for people escaping from floods or enemy invasions.

The traveller, overcome with weariness or unexpectedly caught by the rain and unable to reach his destination that evening, stops here and prepares to spend the night. His preparations for a comfortable night are very simple. He usually takes a bath in the river which flows nearby, then eats his food, if he has any, or goes to look for fruit or roots in the forest. Finally he chooses a place to sleep, makes a bed out of palm leaves with a tree trunk for a pillow, lights a big fire near his head to keep away the insects, lies down and goes to sleep. He rarely sleeps in the huts unless forced to do so by bad weather and prefers the open air to the unpleasant insects which infest the huts.

About two or three hundred people are thought to spend the occasional night here. I had my hammock slung between two trees with my men around me. Each had his own fire so that I was surrounded and suffocated by the smoke, but I preferred this to the much worse torments of the insects.

At 5 in the morning we set off so as to be able to reach a village called Bado by nightfall. Along the track we saw enormous trees and some watercourses more than 100 metres wide and deep enough for the water to come higher than a man's waist, so that the two very tall youths who were carrying my hammock, although they had put the poles to which it was attached on their heads, could not keep me above the water and two more men had to hold up the hammock itself on their shoulders. These channels are full of uprooted trees and plants which make the water overflow the banks and, because of the low-lying land, cause a veritable flood.

At 5 in the afternoon we reached Bado, a small village of about five or six hundred people who only live there, however, in the rainy season. When I arrived the village chief, accompanied by the local dignitaries, came to visit me and made me a present of four boiled corn cobs, some honey and a half calabash full of palm-wine. I showed my gratitude by giving them biscuits, acquavita and sugar which they devoured immediately with great satisfaction.

In my honour they set fire to all the gunpowder they possessed and put on one of their usual dances which lasted all night and prevented me from sleeping. Human kindness has its disadvantages even in Africa.

Bado is situated in the midst of a thicket of trees which look like umbrellas, and in which thousands of birds make their nests and fill the air with various gay songs. A little way off the vegetation is thicker and more impressive and there, in abundance, are the great trees used for the construction of canoes,[6] the chief industry of these people. There are also many fruit trees. About a miles from the town a fine wide road begins, bordered on both sides by tall, leafy trees planted in a straight line and offering the traveller cool, uninterrupted shade.[7] This road leads to the East Gate of Ota.

On entering the town, the first thing I did was to go to the house of my old friend, a Protestant missionary of African origin, the Rev. Mr White.[8] He gave me the warmest and most friendly welcome one can imagine. He made me his guest and introduced me to the town chiefs who came to visit me a little later on. I spent a delightful night talking to my friend, enjoying all the comforts that one can hope for in these towns.

Ota was formally an impressive town and is said to have had fifty thousand inhabitants.[9] Although surrounded by powerful kingdoms this town has been able for some time to keep its independence of which it was extremely jealous and was declared neutral by all the neighbouring nations who were jealous of one another. But independence without the strength to make it respected is only a chimera. On the pretext that it favoured one of the rival nations more than the other, and did not keep strict neutrality, its neighbours made frequent raids into its territory and took away the awkward inhabitants. Powerless to resist the armies of numerous enemies in open battle, the people of Ota hid in the forests, lay in wait for them as they passed and were always the victors, putting their invaders to flight. The town of Ota

---

[6] These were probably silk cotton trees (*Ceiba pentandra*) which are commonly used in canoe building in parts of West Africa; one of the softer woods, they can be easily carved.

[7] The making of earth roads to replace the bush paths through the forests in Yorubaland developed only with the growth of the palm oil trade, and Abeokuta was until then normally approached from the south by canoe up the Ogun and through its channels. Scala does not mention the 'cask roads', constructed for rolling the casks containing the palm products; these were well-known on the Gold Coast and probably a feature in parts of southern Nigeria. See Philip Allison, *Life in the White Man's Grave*, 1988, pp. 88–89.

[8] The Rev James White, a former catechist of Gollmer's, had been born of Yoruba parents in Sierra Leone, and as a catechist he conducted the first Christian services in Lagos. Scala renders his name as 'Waith'. See references in Smith, *Lagos Consulate*, pp. 38, 53, 66, 132.

[9] The natives of Ota belong, like the original Lagosians, to the Awori section of the Yoruba. Their town had been made virtually subject to Abeokuta in 1842.

was never taken nor occupied by enemy armies, but the repeated victories of
the citizens were themselves to bring about their ruin in the end. After each
victory, the number of inhabitants decreased considerably, the country,
devastated by war, was abandoned, trade languished, man-power was
scarce, and today the vast, heavily populated town of the past has only a
few thousand inhabitants.

Ota, which is centrally placed for the chief markets of the area, is thirty
miles from the West bank of the River Lagos, forty miles from Porto
Novo to the North East, thirty miles from Aboyi, a town at the source of
the Abeokuta River where formally the general market for the interior
regions was situated, and four miles from Ikorodu to the East which has
today become the general market in place of Aboyi.

At 6 o'clock on the following day, I took leave of my host and friend the
Rev. Mr. White, and left Ota for Lagos. The way became extremely easy and
pleasant, along the wide paths made by nature through shady woods of thick
trees and past streams of clear water. Half-way between Ota and Lagos there
is a great stone statue, roughly carved and seated on a stool, its arms spread
out as if to divide the land. This statue marks the border between the two
states. The lands on the Ota side are wild and uncultivated, while on the
Lagos side they are pleasant and very well cultivated. They belong to the
important chiefs of the island who have rented them to Spanish and Brazilian
tenants. The usual crops of vegetables and grain however are cultivated here
and I did not see any plants imported from Europe at all.[10]

Along the road from Abeokuta to Lagos, my mind was constantly occupied with the idea of establishing a railway between these two places.
Although I am not a competent judge of such matters, such an enterprise
does not seem difficult. The land does not seem to present many difficulties
as it is fairly flat with no mountains or large rivers to cross. At some
places the ground is swampy but as there is abundant wood of every size
and quality it should be easy to remedy this by putting down piles etc. The
advantages would be incalculable.[11] In five years these vast areas, so naturally fertile, could be planted with cotton and other products for two to
three hundred square miles. From Abeokuta one could communicate with
the Niger by steamship and that city would become the centre of the whole
legitimate trade of the interior, replacing that in slaves.[12] The western side

---

[10] No trace seems to remain of this remarkable statue; nor is it referred to in any of the many
accounts of journeys between Lagos and Abeokuta in the CMS missionary records. The 'Spanish' and 'Brazilian' tenants referred to as cultivating the land on the Lagos side were repatriated
slaves from whom many of the wealthier families of Lagos descend.

[11] This railway project was realized by the colonial government some forty years later. The wide
bends taken by the track recall the earlier paths in their circuit around swamps and fallen trees.

[12] The river Ogun which flows through Abeokuta connects not with the Niger but with the
lagoon north of Lagos and would be impracticable for steamships.

of Africa where the slave trade is carried on comprises the area which lies between the Senegambia river on the West and Old Calabar a short distance from the nearer foothills of the so-called Mountains of the Moon, and the river Formoso of the Brass on the east. It is a general belief held by the blacks that by ascending the Old Calabar or Benin rivers it is possible to reach the Niger and thence the Senegambia.[13] Accepting this hypothesis for the moment, Europe would thus easily be able to trade with all the peoples who live between the Great Desert [the Sahara] and the coast on the two shores. The whole Sudan, upper and lower, would accept with joy the opportunity to exchange gold dust, skins, ivory, and gums, beside many other minerals which occur in abundance but are for the most part unexplored, with the manufactures and general goods of Europe brought to the very fertile banks of the Niger. When one takes into consideration that twice every year there leave from the Sudan very numerous caravans to carry such products from Timbuktu to Tunis, crossing the Great Desert from Mandara, Musfeia, Konka to Darfur[14] and to penetrate into Nubia and Egypt; when one considers that these take twelve whole months on the outward and return journeys, it is easy to realize the advantages which would accrue from transport by light-weight steam boats which in ten or fifteen days would bring Europe's commerce to these peoples. The absolute impossibility of transporting a great quantity of merchandise by caravan across the desert gives rise to a sense of hopelessness among the inhabitants, leading to aggressiveness, wars. man-hunts. Ease of communications would enable the land to realize its true value, a man's worth would be judged according to whatever the cultivation of his land produced; industry, commerce, and along with these the refinement of manners, the adoption of equalizing and protective laws, and all that is understood by civilizing influences will come to pass very quickly as the direct result of this one same cause. The exploration of the Brass river and of the Senegambia would require one or two expeditions. The advantages which would accrue from these would in one year multiply an hundred-fold the present returns from the import and export trades.

About 4 in the evening I arrived in Lagos where I was welcomed by my old friends and acquaintances, who all thanked me for having opened a new highway for European commerce and for having made known to the world an important city in the interior.

---

[13] Scala seems here to conflate the Senegal and Gambia rivers into one, *il fiume Senegambia*. The term 'Senegambia' correctly denotes the 500 mile coastline between the estuaries of the two rivers and the hinterland. The Brass river is adjacent to Cape Formoso, the southern tip of the Niger delta.

[14] Mandara and Musfeia both lie south of Lake Chad. 'Konka' is unidentified but presumably lies to their east.

On 22 June I embarked in Lagos on the *Erminian*, an English mail-boat which served these shores. Thus I visited in turn the whole west coast as far as Benin, Bonny, and Old Calabar. On 16 July we set out towards England where I arrived on 10 August [1859], and on 1 October I greeted with joy and gratitude the noble queen of Liguria, my country.

Finding myself again in the bosom of my dear relations and friends on the eastern side of the Ligurian Sea, I revisited in my mind past events, and it occurred to me that by re-counting these it would be possible to contribute towards the commercial and shipping interests of my country, and to kindle in others the desire to undertake similar projects on a greater scale. I thought that by the truthful description of a pitiful state of affairs and by showing what would be the best ways of improving matters, it would be possible to persuade the governments of Europe to pay greater attention to that most interesting part of our world, and by prompt and effective measures to extend civilization. Convinced likewise that it would be a worthy object to recount again experiences already recounted by others so as to hasten on the good work, I wrote the present memoirs with all the rough candour of a seaman, although one favoured by fortune in the hope that they would earn the approval of the kindly reader.

Appendix I

A CHRONOLOGY

1815		Sardinian kingdoms constituted: Piedmont amalgamated with the former Ligurian Republic.
1817	20 August	Birth of Giambattista Scala at Chiavari near Genoa.
1825		Scala begins his seafaring life, joining his father's ship at Genoa.
1845	July	Kosoko replaces Akitoye as Oba (king) of Lagos. Akitoye escapes to Abeokuta.
1846	March	Akitoye removes to Badagry and looks to the Egba at Abeokuta and to the British for help in re-establishing himself at Lagos.
1851	20 February	Palmerston (British Foreign Secretary) authorizes Consul Beecroft to conclude a treaty with the ruler of Lagos to end the slave trade there.
	3 March	Dahomians attack Abeokuta, repulsed by the Egba (battle of Aro).
	25 November	First British attack on Lagos repulsed.
	24–28 December	Second British attack on Lagos. Oba Kosoko flees to Epe. Oba Akitoye reinstated.
	31 December	Akitoye signs anti-slaving treaty with British.
1852	1 January	British treaty with Akitoye signed in confirmation.
	January ?	Akitoye joined in Lagos by Madame Tinubu (his niece ?)
	10 February	Scala reaches Lagos and begins trading.
	28 February	Akitoye and his chiefs sign a commercial agreement with group of European merchants in Lagos (Scala not a signatory).
	November	Consul Beecroft presents Vice-Consul Frazer to Oba Akitoye.
	December	Frazer opens British Consulate in Lagos.
1853	?	Scala meets Benjamin Campbell in Freetown.
	June	Akitoye orders arrest of slavers; the 'Amadie affair'.
	21 July	Benjamin Campbell replaces Frazer as British Consul and is presented to Oba Akitoye.

1853	5–6, 11–13 August	Kosoko attacks Lagos.
	2 September	Death of Oba Akitoye
	? September	Dosunmu chosen as Oba of Lagos.
	September–October	Two abortive joint British–Lagosian attacks on Kosoko's position at Epe.
1854	January	Consul Campbell opens negotiations with Kosoko at Epe.
		Negotiations continued on the Palaver Islands in the lagoon.
		Scala a participant or observer.
	March	Commercial agreement signed between Oba Dosunmu and merchants; Scala a signatory.
	September	Campbell renews negotiations with Kosoko at Epe.
	28 September	Treaty of Epe signed between Kosoko and Consul Campbell with Royal Navy representatives: Scala a witness.
	June	Niger-Benue expedition (in the *Pleiad*) calls at Lagos and is joined by Rev. Samuel Crowther.
1855	January/February	Local plots against the life of Campbell; Madame Tinubu implicated.
	November	Scala appointed Consul for Sardinia in Lagos.
1856	February	Campbell presents Scala as consul to Oba Dosunmu.
	May	Dosunmu accepts Scala's offer to farm the royal customs: the other merchants complain.
1857	January	Saro (Sierra Leonian) merchants in Lagos try to arraign Scala before the mercantile court set up by Campbell, who then rules this matter to be beyond the court's competence.
	c. June	Oba Dosunmu complains about Scala's proposal to use tiles on new warehouse, and accuses Campbell of undue partiality to Scala.
	June	Second Niger-Benue expedition leaves Fernando Po for the Delta (in *Dayspring*); leader Baikie (*vice* Beecroft), Glover and Crowther members.
	13 September/ 29 October	Scala visits Abeokuta.
	4 November	Scala returns to Lagos.
1858	February	Scala returns to Abeokuta and sets up his business there.
	April/May	Scala's canoes robbed by pirates on lagoon. Burning of Scala's premises in Aro adjacent to Abeokuta. Dahomian attack? A false alarm.
	7 October	Wreck of *Dayspring* at Jebba. Niger expedition sets up camp, then proceeds by land.

	24 October	Favourable report to Turin on Scala by captain of Sardinian vessel *Colombo*.
1859	February	Oba Dosunmu makes new agreement with Lagos merchants (signed by Paggi on behalf of Scala). Concessions includes rescinding of ban on use of tiles by commoners.
	February or March	Favourable account of Scala by Rev. Samuel Crowther at Abeokuta.
	c. March	Possible Dahomian attack on Abeokuta defeated by flooding of enemy camp by Egba, as related to Scala.
	March/May	Attack by 'Lagosians' on Baikie's party and seizure of Glover's 'loads' near Abeokuta.
	15 June	Scala leaves Abeokuta for Lagos.
	16 July	Scala leaves Lagos for Italy via England.
	1 October	Scala reaches Italy, and home in Liguria.
1861	January	Italy united, except for Rome and the Papal States.
	6 August	'Port and island' of Lagos ceded to British Crown by Oba Dosunmu.
1862		Scala's *Memorie*, 'corrected' by Federico Campanella, published at Sampierdarena.
1863		Scala awarded medal by King Victor Emmanuel II.
1865–71		Florence replaces Turin as capital of Italy, until move of capital to Rome.
1865		Presumed closure of Italian consulate in Lagos on death of Vincenzo Paggi, vice-consul.
1876	3 December	Scala dies at Lavagna, aged 59. Buried at Chiavari.

Appendix II

THE TREATY OF EPE,
28 SEPTEMBER 1854

Agreement entered into this 28th day of September 1854 between Kosoko his Caboceers and Chiefs, and Benjamin Campbell Esquire Her Britannic Majesty's Consul for the Bight of Benin, and Thomas Miller Esquire Commander H.M. Sloop *Crane*, Senior Officer in the Bights of Benin and Biafra.

1st. Kosoko his Caboceers and Chiefs solemnly pledge themselves to make no attempt to regain possession of Lagos either by threats, hostilities or stratagem.

2nd. Kosoko his Caboceers and Chiefs claim Palma, as their port of trade, and Benjamin Campbell Esquire Her Britannic Majesty's Consul, and Thomas Miller Esquire Commander and Senior Naval Officer in the Bights, engage to recognise Palma, as the port of Kosoko and his Caboceers and Chiefs, for all purposes of legitimate trade.

3rd. Kosoko his Caboceers and Chiefs do most solemnly pledge themselves to abandon the slave trade, that is the export of slaves from Africa, also not to allow any slave trader to reside at their port or any other place within their jurisdiction and influence.

4th. Kosoko and his Caboceers and Chiefs solemnly bind themselves to give every protection and assistance to such merchants and traders as may wish to reside among them for the purpose of carrying on legitimate trade — also to assist Her Britannic Majesty's Consul to reopen the markets on the Jaboo shore viz. Agienu, Ecorodu, and Aboyee, and in maintaining order and security at those markets.

5th. There shall be levied at the Port of Palma, an export duty of one head of cowries for every Puncheon of Palm Oil of the average size of one hundred and twenty gallons and two strings of cowries per lb. on all Ivory exported from the above Port for the benefit of Kosoko.

6th. Benjamin Campbell Esquire Her Britannic Majesty's Consul engages on behalf of Her Majesty's Government that for the due and faithful performance of this engagement on the part of Kosoko his Caboceers and Chiefs there shall be paid to Kosoko by Her Majesty's Government an annual allowance for his life of Two thousand heads of cowries or one thousand dollars at his option.

7th. This engagement to have full force and effect from this day until annulled by Her Britannic Majesty's Government.

Signed up the Lagoon at Appe this 28th day of September 1854

Kosoko X
Oloosema X   Bagaloo X
Oloto X   Apsee X
Pelleu X   Oleesau X
Tapa X   Ettee X
Agenia X   Lomosa X
Bosoopo X   Otcheodee X
Agagoo X
Obatchi X
Whydobah X

B. Campbell (Her Britannic Majesty's Consul for the Bight of Benin)

Thos. Miller (Commander H.M.S. *Crane* and Senior Officer of the Bights of Benin and Biafra) in the presence of

Herbert L. Ryves, Lieut. Commander of *Minx*
A. P. Braund, Master H.M.S. *Crane*
Francis Wm Davis, Assistant Surgeon, *Minx*
Geo. Batta. Scala, merchant of Lagos
A. R. Hansen, merchant of Lagos
Jose Pedro da Cousta Roy, merchant of Lagos
A. B. Williams, merchant of Lagos and interpreter.

Appendix III

BRITISH CONSULS AND ACTING CONSULS AT LAGOS

Bights of Benin and Biafra
Louis Frazer, Vice-Consul . . . . November 1852–July 1853

Bight of Benin
Benjamin Campbell[1] . . . . July 1853–April 1859

(Absent on leave, 6 June 1858–23 January 1859)

Lieut. E. F. Lodder, R.N., Acting Consul . . . . June 1858–January 1859
. . . . April 1859–November 1859

George Brand[2] . . . . November 1859–June 1860

Lieut-Commander Henry Hand, R.N., Acting Consul . . June 1860–December 1860
Henry Grant Foote[3] . . . . December 1860–May 1861

William Grant McCoskry, Acting Consul . . . . May 1861–August 1861
and Acting Governor. . . . . August 1861–January 1862

[1] Died at Lagos 17 April 1859.
[2] Died at sea 16 June 1860 (buried at Badagry).
[3] Died at Lagos 17 May 1861.

BIBLIOGRAPHY

Note: The intention of this bibliography is, first, to give details of the works quoted or cited summarily in the notes to the Editorial Introduction and to Scala's text. Secondly, it lists works, most of which have been cited in the notes, which provide general information about Lagos and Abeokuta and the Yoruba, their history and peoples.

Abbreviations

HA	*History in Africa*
JAH	*Journal of African History*
JHSN	*Journal of the Historical Society of Nigeria*
JICH	*Journal of Imperial and Commonwealth History*

I. PRIMARY SOURCES

(a) English

1. *Public Record Office, London (PRO)*
FO2 series: Consular correspondence
FO84 series: Slave Trade, general correspondence
ADM 123 series: Admiralty correspondence

2. *British State Papers*
PP 1852 LIV (221), *Papers Relative to the Reduction of Lagos*
PP 1862 (2982) (3003), *Papers Relating to the Occupation of Lagos*

3. *Missionary Records*
Church Missionary Society (CMS), files (CA) and journals
Methodist Missionary Society, files and journals

(b) Italian

Despatches and correspondence from and to the Sardinian/Italian Consulate at Lagos are in the keeping of:

(i) Archivio Storico del Ministro degli Affari Esteri, Rome
(ii) Archivio di Stato, Sezione Prima, Piazza del Castello 205, Turin.

Note: These archives are briefly described by R. Gray and D. Chambers, in *Materials for West African History in Italian Archives*, London 1965, pp. 112–113, 147–149.

(c) French

(i) Société des Missions Africaines: *Journal de Francesco Borghero, premier missionaire du Dahomey (1861–1865)*. Editions Karthala, Paris 1997.

II. SECONDARY SOURCES

(a) *Printed Sources: Books*

Adefuye, A., Agiri, B. A., and Osuntokun, J. *History of the Peoples of Lagos State*, Lagos 1987.
Ajayi, J. F. A., *Christian Missions in Nigeria, 1814–1891*, London 1965.
Ajayi, J. F. A., and Smith, Robert S., *Yoruba Warfare in the Nineteenth Century*, Cambridge 1964, 2nd. ed. 1971.
Ajisafe, A. K. *The Laws and Customs of the Yoruba People*, London 1924.
—— *A History of Abeokuta*, Abeokuta 1924, 2nd. ed. 1964.
Akinjogbin, I. A. *Dahomey and its Neighbours, 1708–1818*, Cambridge 1961.
Allison, P. *Life in the White Man's Grave*, London 1988.
Anon, *The Destruction of Lagos*, London n.d. ?1852.
Argyle, W. J. *The Fon of Dahomey*, Oxford 1966.
Avoseh, T. O. *A Short History of Epe*, Epe 1960.
Ayandele, E. A. *The Missionary Impact on Modern Nigeria*, London 1966.
Barnes, S. T. *Patrons and Power*, Manchester 1986.
—— (ed.) *Africa's Ogun*, Indiana 1989.
Biobaku, S. O. *The Egba and their Neighbours, 1842–1872*, Oxford 1957.
—— (ed.) *The Sources of Yoruba History*, Oxford 1973.
Bowen, T. J. *Adventures and Missionary Labours in Several Countries in the Interior of Africa from 1849 to 1856*, Charleston 1857.
Brignardello, G. B. *Giambattista Scala, Capitano Marittimo*, Florence 1892.
Buckley, A. *Yoruba Medicine*, Oxford 1985.
Burton, Sir R. F. *Abeokuta and the Camaroons Mountain*, London 1863a.
—— *Wanderings in West Africa*, London 1863b.
—— *A Mission to Gelele King of Dahome*, London 1864, new ed. 1966.
Clarke, W. H., (ed.) Atanda, J. A. *Travels and Explorations in Yorubaland 1854–1858*, Ibadan 1972.
Cole, P. D. *Modern and Traditional Elites in the Politics of Lagos*, Cambridge 1974.
Crowther, S. A. *A Grammar and Vocabulary of the Yoruba Language*, London 1843, 1852.
Crowther, S. A. and Taylor, J. C. *The Gospel on the Banks of the Niger. Journals and Notices of the Natives accompanying the Niger Expedition of 1857–1859*, London 1859.
Curtin, P. D. *The Image of Africa — British Ideas and Action, 1780–1850*, Wisconsin 1964.
Dainelli, G. *Gli Esploratori italiani in Africa*, 2 vols., Turin 1960.
Dantzig, A. van *Forts and Castles of Ghana*, Accra 1980
Dike, K. O. *Trade and Politics in the Niger Delta*, Oxford 1956.
Elias, T. O. *The Nature of African Customary Law*, Manchester 1956.
Euba, A. *Yoruba Drumming: the Dùndún Tradition*, Bayreuth 1990.

Fadipe, N. A., (ed.) Okediji, F. O. and O. O., *The Sociology of the Yoruba*, Ibadan 1970.

Falola, T. (ed.) *Pioneer, Patriot and Patriarch, Samuel Johnson and the Yoruba People*, Wisconsin 1993.

Foote, Mrs. *Recollections of Central America and the West Coast of Africa*, London 1869.

Forde, D. *The Yoruba-speaking Peoples of South-Western Nigeria*, London 1951, 1969.

Gbadamosi, T. G. O. *The Growth of Islam among the Yoruba 1860–1908*, London 1978.

Gollmer, C. H. V. *Charles Andrew Gollmer, His Life and Missionary Labours*, London 2nd. ed. 1889.

Hargreaves, J. D. *Prelude to the Partition of West Africa*, London 1963.

Hastings, A. C. G. *The Voyage of the Dayspring*, London 1926.

Hogendorn, J. and Johnson, M. *The Shell Money of the Slave Trade*, Cambridge 1966.

Hopkins, A. C. *An Economic History of West Africa*, London 1973.

Idowu, E. B. *Oludumare — God in Yoruba Belief*, London 1962.

—— *African Traditional Religion: a Definition*, London 1973.

Isichei, E. *A History of Nigeria*, London 1983.

Johnson, Rev. S. *The History of the Yorubas*, London 1921.

Jones, A. M. *Studies in African Music*, 2 vols., London 1959.

Kopytoff, J. H. *A Preface to Modern Nigeria: the 'Sierra Leonians' in Yoruba, 1830–1890*, Wisconsin 1965.

Law, R. *The Horse in West African History*, London 1980.

—— (ed.) *From Slave Trade to 'Legitimate' Commerce*, Cambridge 1995.

Lewis, I. M. (ed.) *History and Social Anthropology*, London 1968.

Lloyd, C. *The Navy and the Slave Trade*, London 1949.

Lloyd, P. C. *Yoruba Land Law*, London 1962.

—— *The Political Developments of Yoruba Kingdoms in the Eighteenth and Nineteenth Centuries*, London 1971.

Losi, J. B. *History of Lagos*, Lagos 1914, 1967.

—— *History of Abeokuta*, Lagos 1924.

Lucas, J. O. *The Religion of the Yorubas*, Lagos 1948.

Mann, K. 'Owners, slaves and the struggle for labour in the commercial transition at Lagos': see Law (ed.) 1995 above.

Mbaeyi, P. M. *British Military and Naval Forces in West African History, 1807–1874*, New York 1978.

Murray, J. (ed.) *Cultural Atlas of Africa*, Phaidon, Oxford 1981.

Newbury, C. W. *The Western Slave Coast and its Rulers*, Oxford 1961.

Ojo, G. J. A. *Yoruba Culture*, London 1966.

Parrinder, G. *African Traditional Religion*, London 1974.

Payne, J. A. O. *Table of Principal Events in Yoruba History*, Lagos 1893.

Peel, J. D. Y. *Ijeshas and Nigerians*, Cambridge 1983.

Robertson, G. A. *Notes on Africa*, London 1819.

Robinson, R. and Gallagher, J. *Africa and the Victorians*, London 1961.

Room, A. *Dictionary of Coin Names*, London 1987.

Schnapper, R. *La Politique et le commerce français dans le Golfe de Guinée de 1838 à 1871*, Paris 1961.

Smith, R. S. *Kingdoms of the Yoruba*, London and Wisconsin 1969, 1988.

—— *Warfare and Diplomacy in Pre-Colonial West Africa*, London and Wisconsin 1976, 1989.

—— *The Lagos Consulate*, London and Berkeley 1978.

Snelgrave, Captain W. *A New Account of Some Parts of Guinea and the Slave Trade*, London 1734.

Stock, E. *A History of the Church Missionary Society*, 4 vols., London 1916.

Townsend, G. *Memoir of Henry Townsend*, Exeter 1887.

Ward, W. E. F. *A History of Ghana*, London 1965

—— *The Royal Navy and the Slavers*, London 1969

Willett, F. *African Art*, London 1971.

Wood, Rev. J. Buckley *Historical Notes of Lagos*, Lagos 1878.

Yemitan, O. *Madame Tinubu, Merchant and Kingmaker*, Ibadan 1987.

(b) *Printed Sources: Articles*

Ajayi, J. F. A. 'Henry Venn and the Policy of Development', *JHSN* I, 4, 1959.

—— 'The British Occupation of Lagos, 1851–1861', *Nigeria Magazine* 69, 1961.

Austen, R. A. 'The Abolition of Overseas Slave Trade: a Distorted Theme in West African History', *JHSN* V, 2, 1970.

Chappel, T. J. M. 'The Yoruba Cult of Twins in Historical Perspective', *Man*, 44 (1974).

Davidson, A. McL. 'The Early History of Lagos', *Nigerian Field*, xix, 2, 1961.

Gavin, R. J. 'Nigeria and Lord Palmerston', *Ibadan* 12, 1961.

Hopkins, A. G. 'The Currency Revolution in South-West Nigeria in the Late Nineteenth Century', *JHSN* III, 3, 1966.

—— 'Property Rights and Empire Building: Britain's Annexation of Lagos, 1861', *Journal of Economic History* XL, 4, 1980.

Horton, R. 'The High God. A Comment on Father O'Connell's Paper', *Man*, LXIII, 1962.

—— 'Conference: the High God in West Africa', *Odu* NS, 11, 2, 1966.

Law, R. 'The Dynastic Chronology of Lagos', *Lagos Notes and Records* II, 2, 1968.

—— 'Trade and Politics on the "Slave Coast": the Lagoon Traffic and the Rise of Lagos, 1500–1800', *JAH* 24, 1983.

—— 'Religion, Trade and Politics on the "Slave Coast": Roman Catholic Missions in Allada and Whydah in the Seventeenth Century', *Journal of Religion in Africa* XXI, 1991.

—— 'The "Amazons"', *Paideuma* 39, 1993.

—— '"Here is No Resisting the Country": the Realities of Power in Afro-European Relations on the West African "Slave Coast"', *Itinerario* 18/2, 1994.

—— 'The Politics of Commercial Transition: Factional Conflict in Dahomey in the Context of the Ending of the Atlantic Slave Trade', *JAH* 38, 2, 1997.

—— 'Ethnicity and the Slave Trade: "Lucumi" and "Nago" as Ethnonyms in West Africa', *History in Africa* 24, 1997.

Lynn, M. 'Consul and Kings: British Policy, "The Man on the Spot", and the Seizure of Lagos, 1851', *JICH* X, 2, 1982.

Miller, N. S. 'Aspects of the Development of Lagos', *Nigerian Field* XXVIII, 4, 1963.

—— 'Ile Ajele, the First British Consulate in Lagos', *Nigerian Field* XXXVII, 4, 1972.

Newbury, C. W. 'Credit in Early Nineteenth Century West African Trade', *JAH* XIII, 1, 1965.

Ross, D. A. 'The Career of Domingo Martinez in the Bight of Benin, 1833–64', *JAH* VI, 1, 1965.

Smith, R. S. 'The Canoe in West African History', *JAH* XI, 4, 1970.

—— 'Giambattista Scala: Adventurer, Trader and First Italian Representative in Nigeria', *JHSN* VII, 4, 1973.

Verger, P. 'Notes on Some Documents in which Lagos is referred to by the Name "Onim"...' *JHSN*, I, 4, 1959.

—— 'The Yoruba High God', *Odu* NS 2, 2, 1966.

(c) *Unpublished Works*

Aderigbigbe, A. B. 'The expansion of the Lagos Protectorate', Ph.D. thesis, University of London, 1959.

Brown, H. B. 'A History of the People of Lagos, 1852–1894', Ph.D. thesis, Northwestern University, U.S.A., 1964.

Mabogunje, A. 'Lagos, a Study in Urban Geography', Ph.D. thesis, University of London, 1962.

Ogunremi, G. O. 'Pre-Colonial Transport in Nigeria', Ph.D. thesis, University of Birmingham, 1973.

Oguntomisin, G. O. 'New Forms of Political Organisation in Yorubaland in the Mid-Nineteenth Century: A Comparative Study of Kurunmi's Ijaye and Kosoko's Epe', Ph.D. thesis, University of Ibadan, 1979.

Oroge, E. A. 'The Institution of Slavery in Yorubaland with Particular Reference to the Nineteenth Century', Ph.D. thesis, University of Birmingham, 1971.

Phillips, E. H. 'The Church Missionary Society, the Imperial Factor and Yoruba Politics, 1842–1873', Ph.D. thesis, University of South California, 1966.

Scotter, W. H. 'International Rivalry in the Bights of Benin and Biafra, 1815–1855', Ph.D. thesis, University of London, 1933.

INDEX

Most of the general entries refer to the Yoruba people; in many instances they apply also to the other West Africans observed by Scala.

A selection of information in the footnotes has been included in the index.

tribute 14, 15
Tripoli (North Africa) 3
Turin, archives at xiv, xxi
Turkey 105

Ulsheimer, Josua 14

Venice, compared to Aboyi 54
Victor Emmanuel II, King of Italy xvii
Volta river 17, 119

wage rates 70
warfare 104–5
　African wars as slave raids xx, 7–8,
　　100–101, 104
　prisoners 7–8, 28, 30–33
　war and peace, declarations of 105

see also 'slave-gun cycle', adaptation, crisis
　of
Waterwitch, HMS 36
'white' (European) settlement, Scala
　advocates 75
White [Waith], Rev. James, CMS 135–6
Whydah [Ouidah, etc] xii, 17, 27
Wilmot [Willmouth], Commander R.N.
　22–3

Yoruba, Yorubaland [Yarriba, Orobù
　etc] xiii, xvii, 26, 53, 55
　general situation in xix–xx, 64
　population 69

Zabarah 56
　see also Aburah